Systematic searching

Systematic searching

Practical ideas for improving results

Edited by

Paul Levay and Jenny Craven

facet
publishing

Published by Facet Publishing,
7 Ridgmount Street, London WC1E 7AE
www.facetpublishing.co.uk

Facet Publishing is wholly owned by CILIP: the Library and
Information Association.

British Library Cataloguing in Publication Data
A catalogue record for this book is available from the British Library.

ISBN 978-1-78330-373-1 (paperback)
ISBN 978-1-78330-374-8 (hardback)
ISBN 978-1-78330-375-5 (e-book)

First published 2019

Text printed on FSC accredited material.

Typeset from editors' files by Flagholme Publishing Services in 11/14pt
Palatino and OpenSans
Printed and bound by CPI Group (UK) Ltd, Croydon, CR0 4YY

Contents

Figures, tables and case studies

Figures

Tables

Case studies

Contributors

Alison Bethel has been working as an Information Specialist with the Evidence Synthesis Team at the University of Exeter Medical School in the UK since 2011. She has been the information specialist in over 20 published systematic reviews; these include Cochrane reviews, quantitative reviews and mixed methods reviews. Alison has developed an interest in teaching other information professionals about systematic reviews (through the workshop 'Searching and Beyond'), as well as search methods research in the health and the environment and human health fields. She has over 20 years' experience as an information professional, ranging from managing small government libraries to working in the tourism sector as a knowledge manager.

Andrew Booth is a qualified Information Specialist with almost 25 years' experience as a systematic review methodologist at the School of Health and Related Research (ScHARR) at the University of Sheffield in the UK where he is Reader in Evidence-Based Information Practice. He is a Co-Convenor of the Cochrane Qualitative and Implementation Methods Group. He is Co-Director of one of the three National Institute for Health Research Evidence Synthesis Centres for the Health Services and Delivery Research Programme. He is a former Associate Editor for *Systematic Reviews* and current Associate Editor for *Research Synthesis Methods,* and he is the lead author of *Systematic Approaches to a Successful Literature Review* (2nd edn, SAGE Publishing, 2016). Andrew has co-authored over 120 systematic review outputs including, as lead author, the Department of Health review on Minimum Alcohol Pricing, which continues to influence UK policy.

Alison Brettle is a Professor in Health Information and Evidence-Based Practice at the University of Salford in the UK. Her teaching and research interests include evidence-based practice, the effectiveness and impact of library services, systematic reviews and systematic review methodology. Alison is widely published in the information and health and social care fields and has had a number of editorial roles within the *Evidence Based Library and Information Practice* journal. She is passionate about involving librarians within the whole of the systematic review process. Alison is currently Chair of the CILIP Library and Information Research Group, International Programme Chair for the EBLIP10 Conference and is an academic expert on the Knowledge for Health Quality and Impact Group.

Jenny Craven is an Information Specialist at the National Institute for Health and Care Excellence (NICE) in the UK. Her role at NICE involves supporting the information needs for a variety of programmes across the organization. She also works on projects to improve service delivery, to evaluate information skills training and to explore methods for the effective retrieval of information. Previously, Jenny worked at the Centre for Research in Library and Information Management (CERLIM) at Manchester Metropolitan University; she worked on practical information-related projects, with a particular focus on improving access to information for people with visual impairments. During this time, she was on the standing committee of the International Federation of Library Associations and Institutions (IFLA) Libraries Serving Persons with Print Disabilities group and, for the FORCE Foundation charity, ran a series of workshops in developing countries on providing accessible library and information services.

Pip Divall is Clinical Librarian Service Manager at University Hospitals of Leicester (UHL) NHS Trust in the UK. She has managed the team of Clinical Librarians in Leicester since 2010 and has been a Clinical Librarian since 2004, working firstly to establish a Clinical Librarian Service at George Eliot Hospital before joining the Leicester team later that same year. Pip has worked in NHS libraries since graduating from Loughborough University with a master's degree in Information and Library Studies in 2002. Her interests are in faculty development, leading sessions on the improvement of teaching within

UHL NHS Trust and information literacy. Pip is the Health Representative on the CILIP Information Literacy Group Committee.

Richard Epstein is a Research Fellow at Chapin Hall Center for Children at the University of Chicago in the USA. He oversees efforts to improve child welfare programmes, support strategic planning and shepherd implementation of evidence-based practices for vulnerable youth in care. Richard is a clinical psychologist and epidemiologist, with more than ten years' experience with research methods and policy recommendations. Through his academic training, research experience and collaborative engagement with policymakers and stakeholders, Richard leverages knowledge management concepts to assess feasibility and fidelity of complex interventions for vulnerable children and families in the real-world setting. His methodological expertise and research strengths include conducting systematic and comparative effectiveness reviews, using administrative medical claims data and administrative child welfare data, and adapting clinical best practice and methodologic quality standards for policy-related evaluation research, with the goal of improving care for vulnerable children and families by promoting research evidence use by practitioners and policymakers.

Julie Glanville is a qualified librarian who has been working in the field of systematic reviews for more than 20 years. Since 2008 she has co-ordinated information and review services at York Health Economics Consortium (YHEC) in the UK for customers who require literature searches and reviews of all types. Julie manages reviews ranging from rapid reviews to systematic reviews, conducts research into information retrieval issues and is an active trainer. Before joining YHEC, Julie was Associate Director and Information Service Manager at the Centre for Reviews and Dissemination (CRD) at the University of York for 14 years. Julie managed information support for systematic reviews and technology assessments within CRD and to external customers, and managed CRD's NHS Economic Evaluation Database. Julie is a Co-Convenor of the Cochrane Information Retrieval Methods Group, co-author of a chapter on searching for evidence in the *Cochrane Handbook for Systematic Reviews of Interventions* and has contributed to the development of systematic review guidance for several organizations, including the Centre for Reviews and Dissemination and the European Food Safety Authority. Julie is an Associate Editor for the journal *Research Synthesis Methods*.

Su Golder is a qualified Information Specialist with over 20 years' experience. She has worked in many different settings and has a wide breadth of experience in supporting systematic reviews of healthcare interventions. She has specialist expertise in systematic review methodology and systematic reviews of adverse effects, and has taught in this field. Her PhD on optimising the retrieval of adverse effects data was funded by the Medical Research Council (MRC) and has made an important contribution to the retrieval of information on adverse effects both nationally and internationally. Her current research is on the use of unpublished data, text mining and social media to maximise the efficiency and effectiveness of the retrieval of adverse effects data and has been funded by the National Institute for Health Research (NIHR) in the UK.

Elke Hausner is a trained nurse with a bachelor's degree in Nursing Sciences and a master's degree in Public Health. She has worked in the field of information retrieval since 2006 and is currently working as a Senior Information Specialist at the German health technology assessment (HTA) agency, the Institute for Quality and Efficiency in Health Care (IQWiG), in Cologne. She has a special interest in information retrieval methods and has published articles on objective approaches for developing search strategies and on validating study filters for non-randomised studies. She is also a co-author of the EUnetHTA guideline on information retrieval.

Shannon Kugley obtained professional experience as a Health Sciences Librarian at the Eskind Biomedical Library in Nashville, Tennessee, in the USA. She served as a Protocol Analyst for a regulatory research board prior to joining the Evidence-based Practice Center at Vanderbilt University to conduct literature searches, appraise evidence and manage the production of complex comparative effectiveness reviews consistent with the methodologic standards of the Effective Healthcare Program at the Agency for Healthcare Research and Quality. Shannon is currently a Researcher at Chapin

Hall at the University of Chicago, providing targeted knowledge management support for project development, implementation and evaluation of services for vulnerable youth. Shannon continues to leverage her information science training and knowledge management experience to explore the application of traditional systematic review methods for evidence synthesis in time- and resource-limited settings.

Carol Lefebvre is an independent Information Consultant with more than 25 years' experience in the field of systematic reviews and searching. Until 2012, she was the Senior Information Specialist at the UK Cochrane Centre, where she was a founder member of Cochrane in 1992. Prior to joining Cochrane, she had worked, since 1986, as the Deputy Librarian responsible for information services at the Cairns Library, serving the University of Oxford teaching hospital. Carol is the founding Co-Convenor of the Cochrane Information Retrieval Methods Group, serves on the Cochrane Methods Executive and is lead author on the searching chapter of the *Cochrane Handbook for Systematic Reviews of Interventions*. She was awarded an MSc in Library and Information Science from the University of Loughborough in 1985 and an Honorary Fellowship of CILIP: the Library and Information Association in 2007. Carol now focuses on teaching and consultancy in information retrieval for evidence synthesis, such as systematic reviews, health technology assessment and guideline development.

Paul Levay is an Information Specialist at the National Institute for Health and Care Excellence (NICE) in the UK. Paul's role focuses on supporting technology appraisals of pharmaceutical products and providing expert searches for guidelines on public health topics. His research interests include assessing the databases and search techniques that can make systematic reviews more effective and efficient. He has previously worked in libraries providing criminal justice information to a government body and environmental evidence to the Greater London Authority. Paul has been a Chartered Member of CILIP since 2003.

Steve McDonald is Co-Director of Cochrane Australia based at Monash University in Melbourne. He has been an Information Specialist with Cochrane for over 20 years and provides searching expertise to support Cochrane Australia's evidence synthesis work. He also leads the learning and education programme of Cochrane Australia and regularly contributes to training courses on research synthesis and meta-analysis. He is currently enrolled in a PhD that is evaluating new approaches to identifying studies and evidence surveillance that make use of machine learning. His research interests include methods for overviews of reviews, search strategy design and automating the identification and retrieval of studies for systematic reviews and guidelines. He is part of Cochrane 'Project Transform' which is developing and evaluating new technologies to facilitate the move towards living evidence systems.

Michelle Maden is a Post-doctoral Research Associate in Evidence Synthesis at the University of Liverpool in the UK. Her main research interest is in developing and testing methodologies for incorporating health inequality considerations in systematic reviews. Michelle is also an Associate Tutor at Edge Hill University where she delivers seminars on systematic reviews and undertakes supervision of masters students working on systematic reviews. She has authored and co-authored different types of published reviews, including systematic reviews, critical interpretive synthesis, realist reviews, mixed-methods reviews and scoping reviews. Prior to undertaking her PhD, Michelle worked as a Clinical Information Specialist supporting the research needs of staff at Edge Hill University and at University Hospital Aintree in Liverpool. She is also the co-developer of the LIHNN 'Introduction to Literature Searching' MOOC and the Health Education England 'How to search the literature effectively' e-learning modules.

Chris Mavergames has a background in information science, information architecture and knowledge management with an emphasis on web and application development, database and metadata management and information retrieval. Most recently, his focus has been on semantic web and linked data technologies in the area of evidence-based health care. Currently, he is Head of Informatics and Technology (IT) Services and Chief Information Officer for Cochrane, a large, global health research organization working in the synthesis of health evidence for decision-making. His role is to lead Cochrane's technology and knowledge management infrastructure and to provide vision and leadership for Cochrane's technology strategy. Previously, Chris worked at the British Library in London on a Sound Archive digitisation project and previous to that at the New York City College of Technology as the Director of the Multimedia Resources Centre. He has research interests in semantic technologies and a real passion for metadata! Chris is also interested in the intersection of people, process and technology and how these elements contribute to more effective and efficient teams and organizations.

Andy Mitchell is currently the Associate Director for Information Architecture, Search and Business Analysis at the National Institute for Health and Care Excellence (NICE) in the UK. Andy has a degree in electronics and information systems and worked as a Research Associate at the University of York developing digital Artificial Neural Networks. Andy has worked across the commercial and public sectors within the field of data and information processing for over 15 years. Andy is working to introduce linked data principles into the way that NICE guidelines are developed and published. Andy also co-founded the Manchester Linked Data group to help share best practice and is a member of the W3C Semantic Web in Healthcare and Life Sciences community group.

Anna Noel-Storr has worked for Cochrane since 2008 as an Information Specialist for the Cochrane Dementia and Cognitive Improvement Group based at the University of Oxford in the UK. During that time she has played a leading role in the development and implementation of crowdsourcing in health evidence production. This began with the 'Trial Blazers' study for which she won the Thomas C Chalmers Award in 2013. Since then, she has led a number of initiatives exploring the role of crowdsourcing and citizen science in systematic review production and evidence synthesis. She currently leads Cochrane Crowd, a component of Cochrane 'Project Transform'. This work involves the development of a crowd platform offering willing contributors a range of micro-tasks to dive into, all of which are designed to enhance Cochrane's content and speed up the review production process without any compromise on the exceptionally high quality expected of Cochrane systematic reviews.

Morwenna Rogers is an Information Specialist with the Evidence Synthesis Team at the University of Exeter Medical School in the UK. She has worked in the information field since qualifying with an MSc in Information Management from the University of Sheffield in 1998, initially in the pharmaceutical industry as a Medical Information Officer and then as Library and Information Manager at the Royal College of Psychiatrists. She has worked in her current role since 2011, developing and running searches for systematic reviews, carrying out search methods research and running occasional workshops on search techniques.

Margaret Sampson is the Medical Librarian at Children's Hospital of Eastern Ontario, Ottawa, Canada, managing the medical and family resource libraries. Her specialty is information retrieval for systematic reviews where her research has focused on improving search quality. Margaret graduated from the University of Western Ontario with her Master of Library and Information Science degree in 1997, and in 2009 she completed her PhD through the University of Wales. She has over 100 peer reviewed publications and in 2010 was awarded 'Hospital Librarian of the Year' by the Canadian Health Library Association. With Jessie McGowan, Margaret was a lead on the original version of PRESS and the 2015 update. In her spare time, Margaret enjoys motorcycling, photography and music.

Claire Stansfield is a Senior Research Associate at the EPPI-Centre, UCL Institute of Education, London in the UK and is involved in developing and applying research methods for systematic literature searching across a range of public policy areas in health promotion, public health, social care and international development. She supports research groups internationally to learn and use literature searching methods for systematic reviews, particularly within the international development field.

James Thomas is Professor of Social Research and Policy at the EPPI-Centre, UCL Institute of Education, London in the UK. His research is centred on improving policy and decision-making through the use of research. He has written extensively on research synthesis, including meta-analysis and methods for combining qualitative and quantitative research in mixed method reviews. He also designed EPPI-Reviewer, software which manages data through all stages of a systematic review, which incorporates machine learning. He is principal investigator of the Evidence Reviews Facility for the Department of Health and Social Care, England, a large programme of policy-relevant systematic reviews with accompanying methodological development. James is co-lead of Cochrane 'Project Transform' which is implementing new technologies and processes to improve the efficiency of systematic reviews. He is also co-investigator on a major Collaborative Award from the Wellcome Trust, led by Susan Michie (UCL), to develop novel technologies to organise, synthesise and present the behavioural science literature.

Siw Waffenschmidt trained as a sports scientist and worked at the German Sports University Cologne before moving to Germany's health technology assessment agency, the Institute for Quality and Efficiency in Health Care (IQWiG). She initially started working in IQWiG's Information Management Group and has headed the newly established Information Management Unit since 2011. Her main responsibilities are developing comprehensive search strategies and the peer review of literature searches. Siw's research focus is on the further development of information retrieval methods for systematic reviews. She is the chair of the Health Technology Assessment International (HTAi) Information Retrieval Interest Group and the spokesperson of the newly established Information Management Working Group in the German Network for Evidence-based Medicine.

Gil Young has worked in the academic, health and public library sectors. She is currently employed as the NHS LKS Development Manager North West for the Health Care Libraries Unit North in the UK. Gil is a Fellow of CILIP and an associate member of the Chartered Institute of Personnel and Development (CIPD). She is a CILIP mentor and was the first winner of the CILIP Mentor of the Year award. Gil is the co-author of *Practical Tips for Developing Your Staff* (Facet Publishing, 2016). She was also part of the team leading a project to develop a MOOC to deliver literature search training for health librarians. Her main professional interest is the importance of continuing professional development for all levels of library and knowledge services staff and looking at innovative ways of delivering this.

Acknowledgements

Paul and Jenny would like to thank all of the authors who have contributed chapters and case studies for inclusion in this book. Their time, experience and knowledge have been invaluable. Paul and Jenny are grateful to Damian Mitchell and Lin Franklin at Facet Publishing for coaxing this book through its production.

Paul and Jenny would also like to thank all of their colleagues at the National Institute for Health and Care Excellence (NICE), particularly Janette Boynton. We are grateful to Mike Raynor and Tom Hudson for their comments. The chapters here capture some of the discussions we have had at the NICE Joint Information Day and at the meetings of the Information Specialist Subgroup of InterTASC.

The introduction draws on the many discussions that Paul has had with Suzy Paisley and work that they have done jointly with Mike Kelly and Sophia Ananiadou.

Paul would like to acknowledge all of those people, in addition to the contributors to this book, with whom he has discussed public health searching, including Chris Cooper, Alison Weightman and Fiona Morgan.

Paul is grateful for the role played by Sue King and the Bramshill team, Cliff Davies and Jane Garnett, John Rudge, Suzanne Mahadea and Emma George.

Disclaimer

The views expressed in this publication are those of the authors and not necessarily those of the National Institute for Health and Care Excellence (NICE).

Abbreviations

AAHSL	Association of Academic Health Sciences Libraries (USA)
AHRQ	Agency for Healthcare Research and Quality (USA)
AMED	Allied and Complementary Medicine Database
API	Application Programming Interface
ASFA	Aquatic Sciences and Fisheries Abstracts
BASE	Bielefeld Academic Search Engine
BNI	British Nursing Index
CADTH	Canadian Agency for Drugs and Technologies in Health
CENTRAL	Cochrane Central Database of Controlled Trials
CILIP	CILIP: the Library and Information Association (UK)
CINAHL	Cumulative Index to Nursing and Allied Health Literature
CNKI	China National Knowledge Infrastructure database
CONSORT	Consolidated Standards of Reporting Trials
CREBP	Centre for Research in Evidence-Based Practice, Bond University, Australia
CRS	Cochrane Register of Studies
CSV	Comma-separated Values
DOI	Digital Object Identifier
EAHIL	European Association for Health Information and Libraries
EBM	Evidence-based Medicine
EBP	Evidence-based Practice
EMA	European Medicines Agency
ERIC	Education Resources Information Center database
EudraCT	European Clinical Trials database
EUnetHTA	European Network for Health Technology Assessment
FaBiO	FRBR-aligned Bibliographic Ontology

FDA	Food and Drug Administration (USA)
HMIC	Health Management Information Consortium database
HTA	Health Technology Assessment
HTAi	Health Technology Assessment international
ICMJE	International Committee of Medical Journal Editors
ICTRP	International Clinical Trials Registry Platform
InterTASC	'Inter' conveys collaboration. TASC stands for Technology Appraisal Support Collaboration
IOM	Institute of Medicine (USA)
IQWiG	Institut für Qualität und Wirtschaftlichkeit im Gesundheitswesen (Institute for Quality and Efficiency in Health Care, Germany)
ISSG	Information Specialist Subgroup of InterTASC (UK)
LIHNN	Library and Information Health Network Northwest (UK)
LILACS	Latin American and Caribbean Health Sciences Literature
LIS	Library and Information Science
LSR	Living Systematic Review
MeSH	Medical Subject Headings
MLA	Medical Library Association (USA)
MOOC	Massive Open Online Course
NaCTeM	National Centre for Text Mining (UK)
NICE	National Institute for Health and Care Excellence (since 2013). Previously National Institute for Clinical Excellence (1998-2006) and National Institute for Health and Clinical Excellence (2006-2013) (UK)
NLP	Natural Language Processing
ORCID	Open Researcher and Contributor ID
OSF	Open Science Framework
OVHLA	Ottawa Valley Health Libraries Association (Canada)
OWL	Web Ontology Language
PEDro	Physiotherapy Evidence Database
PICO	Population, Intervention, Comparison, Outcome
PRESS	Peer Review of Electronic Search Strategies
PRISMA	Preferred Reporting Items for Systematic Reviews and Meta-analyses

PROSPERO	Prospective Register of Systematic Reviews
RCT	Randomised Controlled Trial
RDF	Resource Description Framework
ROBIS	Risk of Bias in Systematic Reviews
SCIE	Social Care Institute for Excellence (UK)
SOP	Standard Operating Procedure
SPP	Social Policy and Practice database
SQL	Structured Query Language
SRDR	Systematic Review Data Repository
SuRe Info	Summarised Research in Information Retrieval for HTA
SWIFT	Sciome Workbench for Interactive computer-Facilitated Text-mining
TRoPHI	Trials Register of Promoting Health Interventions
URI	Uniform Resource Identifiers
W3C	World Wide Web Consortium
XML	Extensible Markup Language

Foreword

Carol Lefebvre

Paul Levay and Jenny Craven have amassed, as editors of this book, an impressive, international array of information specialists and librarians together with other information retrieval experts and methodologists from academia, evidence synthesis organizations, libraries and elsewhere with considerable but diverse experience and expertise in systematic searching. In the early days of evidence-based practice, the role of the information specialist or librarian tended to be to help practitioners and researchers to identify systematic reviews and other evidence-based syntheses in the published literature, through searches of bibliographic databases and other related resources. Nowadays, information specialists and librarians serve as expert searchers in efficiently identifying not only systematic reviews but also relevant studies for inclusion in systematic reviews and other evidence syntheses across a wide spectrum of disciplines. The focus on searching for published studies identified solely from bibliographic databases has been replaced with a recognition of the importance of considering unpublished studies and those published in grey literature and the need to use a much wider range of sources, including trials registers, regulatory agency sources and other diverse sources of data. In order to do this, they employ an increasingly diverse and complex range of skills and techniques in both identifying a wider range of resources and exploiting these resources to their full potential, to meet the ever-changing needs of the evidence synthesis community.

Systematic searching is essential for 'traditional' systematic reviews within highly-focused research topics and for broader-based topics such as public health, for mixed methods reviews, rapid reviews, realist syntheses, scoping reviews and surveillance, to name but a few. There is a growing recognition of the need for timeliness in evidence syntheses, not only with respect to the amount of time taken to identify the studies and assess their eligibility for inclusion but also with respect to how out-of-date the searches might be at the time of publication of the evidence synthesis. The concept of living systematic reviews and guidelines has been developed to address this, where surveillance techniques are employed to identify studies as soon as their results are made available (either in published or unpublished sources) and the results of the studies are incorporated as quickly as possible into the reviews or guidelines. Newer technologies such as machine learning, text mining and other aspects of automation have developed rapidly over recent years, permitting more sophisticated design of search strategies and ranking of search results, to allow for more efficient assessment of eligibility. Increasing opportunities associated with linked data allow for information retrieval to be conceptualised in novel ways.

All these developments in data sources, search techniques and technology require a highly-skilled, well-educated and well-trained workforce. There is a need for appropriate education, training and continuing professional development to ensure that we have access to a workforce with the knowledge, skills and attributes to contribute meaningfully to and flourish in this fast-moving world. Systematic searchers need to embrace new technology and think about the evidence synthesis process in different ways. They must adapt to and adopt these new ways, while being instrumental in forging them. They have valuable contributions to make at many stages of the research process, including search strategy design and conduct as well as protocol development, study selection, authoring and peer review. They need to identify evidence-based practice in other disciplines for their clients and learn to be reflective practitioners in their own right. This will involve appraising and basing their professional practice on evidence from within the field of information retrieval and contributing to this field where appropriate. This presents an opportunity to showcase the skills of systematic searchers as expert searchers and methodologists in their own right.

The recognition of the importance and value of systematic searching and the role and value of the expert searcher have placed the information specialist or librarian centre stage, especially in the field of evidence synthesis. Evidence-based practice across all disciplines requires a team approach, involving stakeholders such as consumers of services and their advocates; funders; information specialists and librarians; policymakers; practitioners such as clinicians, educators and social workers; and researchers.

Embracing the various challenges and opportunities should enable information professionals to remain centre stage as these developments continue. All the above issues and many more are covered in detail in the following chapters of this book.

1

Introduction: where are we now?

Paul Levay and Jenny Craven

What is systematic searching?

Systematic searching is one of the fundamental building blocks to using evidence in a rigorous way to make decisions on policy and practice. The search is a key component of a systematic review. A review cannot be systematic if it is based on evidence that has been identified through a partial, unsound or incomplete search. We must first discuss what a systematic review is and why the search is so important. This book covers searching for a wide range of topics in the social sciences, however systematic reviewing grew out of the evidence-based medicine movement so let us start there for a definition:

> A review of a clearly formulated question that uses systematic and explicit methods to identify, select, and critically appraise relevant research, and to collect and analyse data from the studies that are included in the review. Statistical methods may or may not be used to analyse and summarise the results of the included studies.
>
> (Cochrane, 2018)

Evidence-based medicine has been recognised since Archie Cochrane's book *Effectiveness and Efficiency: random reflections of health services*. Cochrane warned 'how dangerous it is to assume that well-established therapies which have not been tested are always effective' (Cochrane,

1972, 29). By the 1990s, the movement was well established in terms of methods, organizations and education (Sackett et al., 1996). Evidence-based medicine meant that decisions would not depend on a doctor trying to read every single study that might be published, they would not be limited to the evidence that a pharmaceutical company or prominent clinician were keen to promote, and they would take into account the often competing or contradictory conclusions from different studies.

The purpose was to develop a set of methods that would provide unbiased ways of comparing one medical treatment to another. It was important to gather evidence on treatments in a systematic fashion so that patients would have the most appropriate care and would not be harmed by the decisions affecting them. A complex set of methods has subsequently been developed to account for sources of bias and to return trustworthy results that show the findings from synthesising the results of multiple studies. As the Cochrane definition shows, this process has to be systematic and explicit.

It is clear that before we can assess the evidence and synthesise it, we must first identify it. A summary of evidence on, say, the effectiveness of a drug at treating lung cancer would have little value if it had only analysed the clinical trials where the drug had a positive effect and ignored those where the drug had a negative effect. It is perhaps unlikely that we would find a review with such blatant publication bias as this, but how can we be sure that all the evidence has been identified before the selection, appraisal and synthesis of studies began? That is the role of the systematic search. Let us turn again to Cochrane for a fuller definition of what constitutes a systematic search:

> Systematic reviews of interventions require a thorough, objective and reproducible search of a range of sources to identify as many relevant studies as possible (within resource limits). This is a major factor in distinguishing systematic reviews from traditional narrative reviews and helps to minimize bias and therefore assist in achieving reliable estimates of effects.
>
> (Lefebvre, Manheimer and Glanville, 2011, 6.1.1.2)

The methods for conducting searches to support systematic reviews have been developed to ensure that they are thorough, objective and reproducible. There are handbooks covering all the stages in the systematic search process (Kugley et al., 2017; Lefebvre, Manheimer and Glanville, 2011). There is guidance on the sources to search (for example, Bramer et al., 2017), ways to minimise publication bias (Ioannidis et al., 2014) and language bias (for example, Morrison et al., 2012), and on the best ways to record and report a search to enable other people to reproduce it (for example, Rader et al., 2013). Publication bias is the tendency that means 'studies with statistically significant or clinically favourable results are more likely to be published than studies with non-significant or unfavourable results' (Ahmed, Sutton and Riley, 2012, 1).

This book is not an attempt to provide a step-by-step guide to doing a systematic search because they already exist (for example, Booth, Sutton and Papaioannou, 2016). The purpose of this book is to explore the themes that are emerging from the current work on systematic searching and to see how they are being applied in new directions. The book explores the challenges in transferring and applying methods originally developed in evidence-based medicine to the social sciences, education and other behavioural topics, showing how we need to adapt our practices. It is an opportunity to take stock and to plan for the future.

The contributions cover new developments in search methodology (Chapters 2 to 5) and then explore how new technologies are being deployed to identify evidence (Chapters 6 to 9). There remains an essential question: who carries out a systematic search? Chapters 10 to 13 cover the people involved, the skills they need and the knowledge they have – the key to everything being systematic is an expert searcher.

What are we trying to find?

The immediate answer might seem obvious: we should be trying to find everything relevant to our systematic review. Looking again at the Cochrane definition of a systematic search, we can see that there is an important qualification because the purpose is to find 'as many relevant studies as possible' (rather than *all* studies) and this must be done within resource limits. We are aiming to *minimise* bias, which means we must acknowledge that we are unlikely to *eliminate* it completely. The *Cochrane Handbook* chapter on searching goes on to say:

> Time and budget restraints require the review author to balance the thoroughness of the search with efficiency in use of time and funds and the best way of achieving this balance is to be aware of, and try to minimize, the biases such as publication bias and language bias that can result from restricting searches in different ways.
>
> (Lefebvre, Manheimer and Glanville, 2011, 6.1.1.2)

The constraints on the search are a major theme of this book. How can we get the most out of our searches with the methods, technology and people we have available? We must remember that the purpose is usually to support decision-making, rather than to satisfy academic curiosity, and so a late or over budget systematic review would be problematic. The real risks of trying to meet an impractical expectation and thus delivering a late, or worse, partial review, are to the people affected by the decisions the review is meant to support. The people affected could be individual patients requiring treatment or they could be whole populations who will be influenced by government policies.

One clue to how a search might proceed is in the methods guide that the National Institute for Health and Care Excellence (NICE) has published on how it will identify evidence for the guidelines it produces in the UK:

> NICE encourages the use of search methods that balance recall and precision. The aim is to identify the best available evidence to address a particular question without producing an unmanageable volume of results.
>
> (NICE, 2014, 81)

Here, again, there is an acknowledgement that we are looking for the best available evidence and that it must be located within the limits of the project. It is this theme of being as systematic as possible within the practical constraints that underlines each of the following chapters.

What is a typical systematic search?

A typical systematic review on a medical topic might attempt to compare two treatments for a condition. The question might ask whether the drug gefitinib is more clinically effective than erlotinib for treating adults with locally advanced or metastatic non-small-cell lung cancer that has progressed after chemotherapy (NICE, 2015). This is why the Population, Intervention, Comparison and Outcomes (PICO) framework is often used to write systematic review questions and to plan the searches. There is a clear PICO to the question, as shown in Table 1.1.

Table 1.1 *PICO framework for a systematic review on a medical question*

Population	Adults with locally advanced or metastatic non-small-cell lung cancer that has progressed after chemotherapy
Intervention	Gefitinib
Comparison	Erlotinib
Outcomes	Clinical effectiveness, measured in terms of: • Overall survival • Progression-free survival • Adverse effects of treatment • Health-related quality of life

We can reasonably expect that there have only been a limited number of clinical trials that have tested these two drugs in this specific population of adults. The systematic search could aim to retrieve a comprehensive set of these clinical trials.

There are well developed methods for conducting this type of search (Lefebvre et al., 2013), including discussions on the sources to use (Booth, 2010) and the most effective search strategies (Wong, Paisley and Carroll, 2013). The searching is not necessarily straightforward and it must take into account how often trials are published in peer-reviewed journals (Zwierzyna et al., 2018) and how to access the data from the unpublished trials (Isojarvi et al., 2018). (Chapter 5 provides suggested resources for identifying unpublished data.) The consequences of these factors in systematic reviewing can be profound. Take for example the Cochrane review of neuraminidase inhibitors for influenza and its conclusion that 'policy-makers should urgently revise current recommendations for use of the neuraminidase inhibitors for individuals with influenza' (Jefferson et al., 2014). An estimated $20 billion had been spent on stockpiling drugs around the world (Abbasi, 2014) and so this systematic review raised serious questions about whether governments had made cost-effective decisions on dealing with flu epidemics.

We are still dealing here with definable conditions, with specific interventions and measurable outcomes. The evidence might be difficult to find and need careful detective work to uncover and synthesise it but we still know what gefitinib and erlotinib are called, there are standardised diagnostic criteria for non-small-cell lung cancer, and there are sets of core outcomes that a clinical trial in this area should measure.

We have focused so far on the origins of systematic reviewing in evidence-based medicine. There have been many developments outside the medical sphere and this has opened up some fundamental questions for systematic searching. What if we do not know who the population is, how to define the intervention of interest or which outcomes to select? A systematic review about encouraging 'vulnerable people' to attend testing for tuberculosis does not have an easily definable population. Reviewing the evidence on which lifestyle services can most effectively manage weight in children with obesity issues at least has a definable population but it does not have a list of interventions (therefore all comparators will be relevant too). A review on community engagement to reduce health inequalities must first decide how we can measure and then detect a reduction in such a concept. Systematic reviews exist on all of these topics (Cooper et al., 2014; NICE, 2013; O'Mara-Eves et al., 2014) and so it is feasible to search systematically for them. We must ensure we have the right toolkit of methods and technology, implemented by experts, to do the searching well.

The underlying reasons for these issues go well beyond systematic searching and into the realm of philosophy (Kelly and Moore, 2012). Evidence-based medicine has famously been defined as the 'conscientious, explicit, and judicious use of current best evidence in making decisions about the care of individual patients' (Sackett et al., 1996). The systematic reviews we have discussed in this section are concerned with communities or populations, rather than individuals, and this makes it difficult to apply the same set of methods (Kelly et al., 2010). This means that different methods, drawing on different models of information retrieval, have been developed in other domains, such as public health (Alpi, 2005) and social care (Stansfield and Liabo, 2017). The reviews we encounter do not just differ in terms of methods, they can also reflect different theoretical understandings of knowledge, in which we can compare rationalist and empirical thought (Kelly, 2018). This is pursued further in Chapter 2. Reviews that collect empirical data according to well-defined criteria have a different theoretical and methodological basis to those that are 'trying to interpret and understand the world' and 'arranging (configuring) information' (Gough, Thomas and Oliver, 2012, 3). We need to explore the appropriate models of information retrieval for these different types of review.

How do we find evidence?

Information retrieval models are important because methods in one domain may not necessarily be transferable to another. It is worth exploring the theoretical basis of what we are doing when we want to move beyond medicine to tackling questions that occur in the social sciences, such as vulnerable populations and health inequalities.

Single query, single output

Let us turn back to our lung cancer example in Table 1.1 and examine how we conceptualise the search when we use PICO or a similar question framework. We are essentially creating a single query and expecting a single search output in return (Bates, 1989). We convert our research question into search terms and run these on the database of interest. The database is a collection of entries that represent documents by indexing them in specific fields. Our search strategy is an attempt to match how we have represented our review question with the way that the database has represented the articles. We should be able to obtain a relatively accurate match: when we represent our intervention gefitinib with the index heading 'gefitinib' we can be confident that we are understanding the concept in the same way. The search may well still need to undergo several versions (for example, 'should we search for non-small-cell lung cancer or lung cancer?'; 'is this an appropriate search filter for clinical trials?') but it is still essentially trying to find a single match between question and query. The implication is that there is a definitive set of evidence waiting to be discovered: we know there must be a finite number of clinical trials that have ever tested gefitinib in a relevant population. This means that there are tests we can use to measure the completeness of our search. Recall is a measure of how good the search is at finding the available, relevant material and precision is a measure of how efficient the search is in avoiding irrelevant results.

Bit-at-a-time searching

The examples we discussed above (a vulnerable population; lifestyle interventions for obesity; outcomes relating to health inequalities) cannot be captured in a single query. The concepts are not precisely defined before the search starts, in the way that gefitinib, lung cancer or overall survival are. The concepts are not easily defined and so we could not capture the evidence through a single query with a single output.

Take the example of a systematic review that is investigating a whole-systems approach to preventing obesity (Garside et al., 2010; NICE, 2012). We need to know what this concept of a 'whole system' means, both in terms of the underlying theory and its practical application. The purpose of our search will be to make sense of the concepts involved. Little work may have been done on this concept in the field of obesity prevention, but we could try to understand how it has been applied in another arena. The whole-system approach to smoking cessation could be a useful avenue to explore and if that gives us a clearer understanding of the concept, we might be able to find case studies showing its impact (Levay, Raynor and Tuvey, 2015). We might be interested in evidence of both quantitative outcomes (such as teenagers smoking a reduced number of cigarettes) and more qualitative outcomes (such as whether the participants' attitudes to smoking changed).

This evidence may seem to be a departure from preventing obesity, but we are helping to develop our understanding of a whole-system approach. The search strategy is not presuming there is a definitive set of evidence waiting to be discovered. We are doing the search a bit-at-a-time: reviewing one area of evidence, moving on to another and building up a picture of the field through a series of iterations. Later in the book, Chapter 3 explores the overall approach and Chapter 4 considers the relevant sources in more detail.

Looking back at the quotation from the NICE manual above, searchers are advised to find a balance between recall and precision. The search should find the best evidence but, at the same time, it should not overwhelm the review team with an unmanageable number of references. There is no guidance on what an 'adequate' balance would look like and it will be a matter for each review team to decide. We can deal with this dilemma by remembering that Cochrane tell us to find 'as many relevant studies as possible' and NICE tell us to find 'the best available evidence'. This means it may not be appropriate to aim for completeness. The purpose of a systematic search can be to retrieve a representation of the evidence and this will be judged on how well the sample has been constructed rather than by how many publications it has retrieved.

Models of information retrieval

The single query with a single output that underpins PICO-based searches is usually characterised as the classic model of information retrieval (see Bates, 1989). There are several alternative models that can help us to think about systematic searches in a dynamic way, enabling a review team to follow a process of sense-making as new directions emerge from the evidence and help them to understand the concepts of interest more fully.

The berrypicking model is based on an 'evolving search' in that 'the query itself (as well as the search terms used) is continually shifting, in part or whole' (Bates, 1989, 410). The model illustrates that useful information can be identified at each stage in the search so that it draws on 'a series of selections of individual references and bits of information at each stage of the ever-modifying search' (Bates, 1989, 410). The evidence is, therefore, not comprised of a single, final search (that may have been refined several times) but by 'a bit-at-a-time retrieval' (Bates, 1989, 410). One of the important features, as Bates noted, is that the search should not become a series of 'mini-matches', where a sensitive search is used at each point in the process, as this would not account for the way the query itself is continually evolving (Savolainen, 2018).

A related model is found in information foraging theory, which suggests that when browsing or searching we might 'choose to continue these activities in the same region or choose to identify a new region in which to look' for evidence (see Savolainen, 2018, 585). The search then proceeds in terms of identifying 'patches' that can be 'foraged' for information before deciding that it offers nothing new and that it would be better to move onto a new area. In our case, the new area might be a website, a database in a different subject or a set of journals in a related discipline.

It is worth noting the influence of the Information Search Process (Kuhlthau, 1993), which has six evolving stages to which emotions or feelings can be attached. The stages and likely emotions are made up of:

- Initiation   Apprehension; Uncertainty
- Selection   Optimism
- Exploration   Confusion; Doubt
- Formulation   Clarity
- Collection   Sense of direction; Confidence
- Presentation   Satisfaction (or Disappointment).

The initial stages will begin with uncertainty and this can lead to anxiety as the search will seem vague and ambiguous. The actions taken as the search progresses should help to focus our thoughts as the areas of interest become clearer, and we may gain in confidence as a sense of direction begins to emerge. We may be apprehensive when we start to look at the smoking cessation literature when our topic is obesity prevention, but this could lead to clarity in our understanding of a whole-systems approach, which in turn should build our confidence in the definitions we are using.

Conducting a systematic search is not easy and it can lead to apprehension, confusion and doubt. On the other hand, persevering with a difficult search could lead to a better product, with more meaningful conclusions, because we have chosen a representative sample of evidence carefully. This should be preferable to constructing an apparently sensitive search that portrays a sense of completeness that may not actually have been achieved (for example, smoking-cessation terms would probably seem irrelevant in a search strategy for preventing obesity).

We must not unfairly characterise reviews as simple, old fashioned or static if they have adopted an approach, such as PICO, that is suitable to the aims and objectives of the research question. The methods underpinning systematic searching have always been innovative and responsive to trends in the scientific community (Lefebvre et al., 2013). It is equally plausible for, say, a public health topic to utilise the PICO model as it is for a medical question to require something more complex. A review on a topic relating to public health, for example, might ask 'is varenicline more effective than bupropion for sustained abstinence from tobacco in adults wanting to quit smoking?' and draw its evidence from randomised controlled trials (RCTs) (Cahill et al., 2016). The key is to always select the model and methods appropriate to the review, the subject area and the type of evidence required.

Where should we search?

The berrypicking and information foraging models both suggest that the process will involve exploratory browsing and focused searching (Savolainen, 2018). This means that the searcher has two tasks to consider:

1 Exploiting the current patch effectively.
2 Searching for the next patch of information.

We could start from a scoping search on a database, which might lead to a journal article. In the article's references there could be a useful report, which leads to the website of a related organization. The searcher has to both identify a website where the literature is likely to be found and then search it appropriately for relevant reports. The sensitive database strategy is not the only component of a systematic search, even if it will remain an important part.

For this reason, we are advised to develop a 'literature search toolbox' that incorporates a range of techniques for identifying evidence (Booth, 2008). Chapters 3 and 4 cover this in detail. The Campbell Collaboration provides guidance on systematic searching in social science, behavioural and educational topics and not only states that we must 'go beyond the main subject database' but suggests that relying on database searches is 'considered inadequate' and that we need to 'incorporate alternative strategies' (Kugley et al., 2017, 10). These ideas can lead in interesting directions, for example, NICE has identified that a core list of databases might not be appropriate (Levay, Raynor and Tuvey, 2015) and then tested whether a review can be based on forwards citation searching if it finds the best evidence without an unmanageable volume of results (Levay et al., 2016).

Five techniques (contacting authors, citation searching, handsearching, using trials registers and web searching) are relatively well studied and there are case studies demonstrating how they have identified additional evidence for reviews (Cooper et al., 2017a). Newer techniques that take advantage of text mining and other technology are now being deployed to support systematic reviewing (Shemilt et al., 2013), as Chapters 7, 8 and 9 explore. It is important to judge these techniques in their own right according to the value that they bring to a review, rather than perceiving them as somehow supplementary to database searching.

The value of a search technique lies in the contribution that the includable studies it retrieves make to the evidence synthesis (Cooper et al., 2017b). We can assess the impact of each publication on the review, considering for example whether it adds to the weight of a conclusion that would have been made anyway or whether it has moved the conclusions in a different direction or changed the recommendations. We might also judge the value of a study more highly if it is well-conducted and reliable or if it is conducted in a setting relevant to the context that we are studying (such as developed or developing countries). We should also consider if the study is unique to that source and not retrieved from any other database or technique.

We are judging the search on its contribution to the synthesis and not on the number of results it retrieves. The search is still using 'systematic and explicit methods' but these could be derived from berrypicking, information foraging or another model of information retrieval. Using a range of search techniques enables us to follow the clues in the evidence that might not have been apparent at the beginning of the process. These steps can be recorded and reported so that the review remains transparent. We are no longer confined to constructing a database search that must achieve the difficult balance between recalling all the relevant results without creating an unmanageable number for screening. The database search does still have a role, of course, where it is appropriate for the characteristics of the review. A search that is built from a different model of information retrieval and identifies evidence with a range of search techniques could add value to the process and lead to a better systematic review.

What is an expert searcher?

Systematic reviews need systematic searches and systematic searches need systematic searchers (McGowan and Sampson, 2005). One way to think about who should do the search is to examine the requirements of a well-conducted systematic review. Risk of Bias in Systematic Reviews (ROBIS) is a tool for appraising reviews and it asks four questions about the search elements:

- Did the search include an appropriate range of sources for published and unpublished reports?
- Were methods additional to database searching used to identify relevant reports?
- Were the terms and structure of the search strategy likely to retrieve as many eligible studies as possible?
- Were restrictions on date, publication format, or language appropriate?

(Whiting et al., 2016, 229)

ROBIS does not state that it is mandatory to use an expert searcher, instead suggesting that 'ideally, this search is carried out by or with guidance from a trained information specialist' (Whiting et al., 2016, 230). However, it is unlikely that anyone would be able to fulfil those four criteria unless they are actually an expert searcher given the level of knowledge required. Chapter 10 investigates the challenges involved in getting the right people trained to carry out this role.

The evidence suggests that reviews that fail to engage the services of an expert searcher can indeed be of varying quality. One study of 630 systematic reviews found that 45 listed an expert searcher as an author and 147 acknowledged their involvement, leaving 438 (70%) without an information professional being mentioned (Rethlefsen et al., 2015). The study found that the reviews with an expert searcher 'had significantly higher odds' of meeting search standards (Rethlefsen et al., 2015, 621) and were 'correlated strongly with using more methods of reducing bias' (622), with both the search itself and the way in which it was reported being of 'higher quality' (623).

There are at least 18 distinct roles relating to information retrieval in systematic reviewing, including planning, searching, peer reviewing, reporting and teaching (Spencer and Eldredge, 2018). It can require a substantial investment in time, and therefore resources, to execute the information-retrieval tasks with the required expertise (Bullers et al., 2018). This is not a trivial requirement for review teams. Chapter 11 considers how the information professional collaborates with the review team and Chapter 12 reflects on the requisite communication skills in more detail.

This book is more concerned with ensuring that the right people are involved in systematic searching at the right time than with the job titles that they might have. Table 1.2 is compiled from a brief, informal survey of the editors' colleagues and the attendees at a conference that their department at NICE organised in February 2018. It shows the range of job titles held by the searchers involved in systematic

Table 1.2 *Job titles of people involved in systematic searching*

Clinical effectiveness librarian	Information scientist
Clinical evidence specialist	Information services manager
Clinical librarian	Information specialist
Evidence and information scientist	Information worker
Evidence specialist	Informationist
Evidence synthesis co-ordinator	Knowledge and evidence specialist
Expert searcher	Knowledge transfer manager
Health information scientist	Knowledge services lead
Information analyst	Librarian
Information and search lead	Library and knowledge manager
Information assistant	Literature searcher
Information consultant	Medical librarian
Information management lead	Researcher
Information manager	Senior information manager
Information professional	Systematic reviewer
Information research associate	Systematic searcher
Information resources co-ordinator	Trials search co-ordinator

reviewing, many of which involve various combinations of evidence, information or knowledge with specialist, manager or professional. The job titles do reflect differences: the information specialist at NICE embedded in systematic review teams (Raynor, 2012) does not perform the same role as, say, a medical librarian in a hospital who participates in systematic reviews less frequently.

This book is aimed at all library and information professionals who take on systematic searching roles. We have used 'information pro-fessional' as an umbrella term to mean the whole array of people who might be involved in systematic searching, as illustrated by Table 1.2. We have tended to use 'information specialist' when we are referring to someone more frequently involved in systematic reviewing, with a good understanding of the methods, technologies and sources required. The term 'expert searcher' is also used throughout to describe the role that can be played in a systematic search, whether it is approached from a librarian's or an information specialist's perspective.

Who should read this book?

This book is an attempt to survey the current trends in systematic search-ing and to suggest ways of harnessing new methods and technologies to ensure information professionals continue to play a strong role in evidence-based policy and practice. It demonstrates the practicalities involved in systematic searching and advises information professionals on the decisions that they are frequently called upon to make.

The existing guidance (for example, Kugley et al., 2017; Lefebvre, Manheimer and Glanville, 2011) provides useful instructions on plan-ning and conducting systematic searches. This book aims to provide an insight into the reality of the processes to give information professionals ideas to test and hopefully incorporate into their own practice. The contributors are experienced in their field and they illustrate the chapters with case studies and practical examples showing how the theory has been applied to improve results.

Systematic searching might have emerged out of evidence-based medicine but it has certainly not stayed there. This book makes frequent references to searching for medical or other health-related evidence, as the methods are well-established. The book should also be of interest to a much wider audience, including those conducting reviews in social care, education, criminal justice or other behavioural subjects. The methods and techniques described here are widely applicable and they have partly been developed in response to the needs of systematic reviews beyond the domain of medicine.

The book does not set out the tasks required at each stage in a systematic search and assumes that readers will have some familiarity with the relevant guidance (for example, Kugley et al., 2017; Lefebvre, Manheimer and Glanville, 2011). Experienced searchers who are looking for advice and ideas to enhance their current practice will find numerous suggestions in the book. It will also appeal to new professionals and anyone seeking to move into systematic searching, as it provides an in-depth look at the reality of being an expert searcher and the requirements of the role.

What does this book cover?

The book is broadly arranged into three parts. The first part (Chapters 2 to 5) is concerned with the methods and techniques underlying systematic searching. In the second part, Chapters 6 to 9 focus on new technologies and how these are leading to new directions in evidence gathering and analysis. There would be little value in developing methods and technologies without the right people to implement them appropriately and effectively; in the third part, Chapters 10 to 13 therefore consider the people involved to ensure that systematic searching benefits from having expert searchers.

Andrew Booth in Chapter 2 explores different approaches to evidence synthesis and the implications that these have for the search process. He explains the purpose of a mixed methods review and realist synthesis before going on to consider how the relevant evidence might be captured through a search. The chapter presents a number of search question formats that help to conceptualise searches that do not fit the PICO formulation.

In Chapter 3, Claire Stansfield shows how these approaches have been applied in broad-based topics that span subject areas and make it difficult to perform sensitive database searches. The chapter considers how a search can be planned to capture an appropriate sample from a diverse and fragmented evidence base, stressing the importance of choosing which sources to search and searching them appropriately. These decisions are made according to the research question, the type of review and the resources available.

Chapter 4 provides an in-depth account of choosing the right sources. Alison Bethel and Morwenna Rogers discuss the factors that need to be taken into account when choosing the right databases for a review. They consider the other search techniques available and when they might be usefully deployed to identify a sample of evidence. They end with an appeal for the sources contributing to a systematic review to be recorded more consistently.

Shannon Kugley and Richard Epstein in Chapter 5 tackle the issue of identifying and analysing evidence from grey literature and unpublished data. They discuss the value of this evidence to systematic reviewing and the challenges associated with using it. The chapter provides an overview of the current tools and strategies available for locating grey literature and unpublished data.

In Chapter 6, Su Golder takes the issue of unpublished data further and examines whether social media can enhance the evidence available in a systematic review. She discusses how social media has been used in a research context and identifies the ways in which social media can be useful to systematic reviewers. Su provides a round-up of the tools and sites that enable systematic searchers to make the most of social media.

In Chapter 7, Julie Glanville explores the potential benefits of text mining tools for information professionals. These tools analyse the frequency and relationship of words in texts, which means that they can assist with developing strategies for broad-based topics, managing large volumes of results and identifying relevant studies. The chapter provides an extremely valuable table of selected text mining tools.

In Chapter 8, Andy Mitchell and Chris Mavergames introduce the concept of linked data. This is an exciting area of development that has the potential to revolutionise how evidence is identified and synthesised. The chapter sets out how thinking about the granularity of evidence moves us away from always seeing systematic reviews as complete documents. It goes on to consider the importance of capturing the provenance of this data. The chapter then highlights the value of semantic search technologies for bringing together a better understanding of the information being searched with an awareness of the searcher's intentions.

In Chapter 9, James Thomas, Anna Noel-Storr and Steve McDonald explain the concept of the living systematic review and how it is being utilised to deal with the problem of 'data deluge'. They provide a detailed insight into the value of automation technologies in evidence surveillance so that new research is identified and incorporated into existing systematic reviews as quickly as possible. They describe how introducing an up-front surveillance process transforms searching and makes surveillance a powerful and dynamic tool.

It is crucial that information professionals stay up to date with new methods and technologies if they are to retain their role at the heart of systematic reviewing. In Chapter 10, Michelle Maden and Gil Young explore the challenges in training a new generation of information specialists to be expert searchers. The chapter summarises the knowledge and skills required and considers how these might be acquired. It highlights the importance of gaining confidence and understanding context, which makes context-led training, observation and the support of peers essential components of the learning environment. The chapter also describes a successful Massive Open Online Course (MOOC) on systematic searching.

The information professional must work as part of a systematic review team and in Chapter 11 Siw Waffenschmidt and Elke Hausner examine the benefits of effective collaboration. They explore the key areas in which the information professional needs to collaborate with the review team to produce a successful search. They discuss the value of information professionals collaborating with one another on day-to-day, local, national and international matters.

Good communication skills are the foundation of collaborative working and in Chapter 12 Margaret Sampson investigates this vital competency. She considers how effective communication within the team enables the information professional to understand the review and deliver the right kind of systematic search. She then explores communication in its wider sense, as a means of establishing professional practice through peer review, supporting evidence-based practice and promoting open science.

Alison Brettle ties together our themes of methods, technology and people in Chapter 13 on the role of the expert searcher. Alison traces how the role has changed over the last few years and highlights the complexity of the tasks involved in expert searching. The chapter reviews the evidence on the impact of expert searchers. It identifies the potential to establish new and expanded roles for information professionals in the systematic review team.

Library and information professionals have the potential to learn innovative methods, apply new technologies and develop fresh roles in systematic searching and this book will hopefully be a good starting point in achieving those aims.

References

Abbasi, K. (2014) The Missing Data that Cost $20bn, *BMJ*, **348**, g2695.

Ahmed, I., Sutton, A. J. and Riley, R. D. (2012) Assessment of Publication Bias, Selection Bias, and Unavailable Data in Meta-analyses Using Individual Participant Data: a database survey, *BMJ*, **344**, d7762.

Alpi, K. M. (2005) Expert Searching in Public Health, *Journal of the Medical Library Association*, **93** (1), 97-103.

Bates, M. J. (1989) The Design of Browsing and Berrypicking Techniques for the Online Search Interface, *Online Information Review*, **13** (5), 407-424.

Booth, A. (2008) Unpacking Your Literature Search Toolbox: on search styles and tactics, *Health Information and Libraries Journal*, **25** (4), 313-317.

Booth, A. (2010) How Much Searching is Enough? Comprehensive Versus Optimal Retrieval for Technology Assessments, *International Journal of Technology Assessment in Health Care*, **26** (4), 431-435.

Booth, A., Sutton, A. and Papaioannou, D. (2016) *Systematic Approaches to a Successful Literature Review*, 2nd edn, SAGE Publishing.

Bramer, W. M., Rethlefsen, M. L., Kleijnen, J. and Franco, O. H. (2017) Optimal Database Combinations for Literature Searches in Systematic Reviews: a prospective exploratory study, *Systematic Reviews*, **6** (1), 245.

Bullers, K., Howard, A. M., Hanson A., Kearns, W. D., Orriola, J. J., Polo, R. L. and Sakmar, K. A. (2018) It Takes Longer Than You Think: librarian time spent on systematic review tasks, *Journal of the Medical Library Association*, **106** (2), 198-207.

Cahill, K., Lindson-Hawley, N., Thomas, K. H., Fanshawe, T. R. and Lancaster, T. (2016) Nicotine Receptor Partial Agonists for Smoking Cessation, *Cochrane Database of Systematic Reviews*, **5**, CD006103.

Cochrane, A. L. (1972) *Effectiveness and Efficiency: random reflections of health services*, Nuffield Trust.

Cochrane (2018) *Glossary*. www.community.cochrane.org/glossary

Cooper, C., Booth, A., Britten, N. and Garside, R. (2017a) A Comparison of Results of Empirical Studies of Supplementary Search Techniques and Recommendations in Review Methodology Handbooks: a methodological review, *Systematic Reviews*, **6**, 234.

Cooper, C., Levay, P., Lorenc, T. and Craig, G. M. (2014) A Population Search Filter for Hard-to-reach Populations Increased Search Efficiency for a Systematic Review, *Journal of Clinical Epidemiology*, **67** (5), 554-559.

Cooper, C., Lovell, R., Husk, K., Booth, A. and Garside, R. (2017b) Supplementary Search Methods Were More Effective and Offered Better Value than Bibliographic Database Searching: a case study from public health and environmental enhancement, *Research Synthesis Methods*, **9** (2), 195-223.

Garside, R., Pearson, M., Hunt, H., Moxham, T. and Anderson, R. (2010) *Identifying the Key Elements and Interactions of a Whole System Approach to Obesity Prevention*, University of Exeter Peninsula Technology Assessment Group. www.nice.org.uk/guidance/ph42/resources/review-1-identifying-the-key-elements-and-interactions-of-a-whole-system-approach-to-obesity-prevention2

Gough, D., Thomas, J. and Oliver, S. (2012) Clarifying Differences Between Review Designs and Methods, *Systematic Reviews*, **1**, 28.

Ioannidis, J. P. A., Munafo, M. R., Fusar-Poli, P., Nosek, B. A. and David, S. P. (2014) Publication and Other Reporting Biases in Cognitive Sciences: detection, prevalence and prevention, *Trends in Cognitive Sciences*, **18** (5), 235-241.

Isojarvi, J., Wood, H., Lefebvre, C. and Glanville, J. (2018) Challenges of Identifying Unpublished Data from Clinical Trials: getting the best out of clinical trials registers and other novel sources, *Research Synthesis Methods*, **9** (4), 561-578.

Jefferson, T., Jones, M. A., Doshi, P., Del Mar, C. B., Hama, R., Thompson, M. J., Spencer, E. A., Onakpoya, I., Mahtani, K. R., Nunan, D., Howick, J. and Heneghan, C. J. (2014) Neuraminidase Inhibitors for Preventing and Treating Influenza in Healthy Adults and Children, *Cochrane Database of Systematic Reviews*, **10** (4), CD008965.

Kelly, M. P. (2018) The Need for a Rationalist Turn in Evidence-based Medicine, *Journal of Evaluation in Clinical Practice*, **24** (5), 1158-1165.

Kelly, M. P. and Moore, T. A. (2012) The Judgement Process in Evidence-based Medicine and Health Technology Assessment, *Social Theory and Health*, **10** (1), 1-19.

Kelly, M., Morgan, A., Ellis, S., Younger, T., Huntley, J. and Swann, C. (2010) Evidence Based Public Health: a review of the experience of the National Institute for Health and Clinical Excellence (NICE) of developing public health guidance in England, *Social Science and Medicine*, **71** (6), 1056-1062.

Kugley, S., Wade, A., Thomas, J., Mahood, Q., Jørgensen, A-M. K., Hammerstrøm, K. T. and Sathe, N. (2017) *Searching for Studies: a guide to information retrieval for Campbell Systematic Reviews - Campbell Methods Series Guide 1*, The Campbell Collaboration. www.campbellcollaboration.org/library/searching-for-studies-information-retrieval-guide-campbell-reviews.html

Kuhlthau, C. (1993) *Searching Meaning: a process approach to library and information services*, Ablex Publishing.

Lefebvre, C., Glanville, J., Wieland, L. S., Coles, B. and Weightman, A. L. (2013) Methodological Developments in Searching for Studies for Systematic Reviews: past, present and future?, *Systematic Reviews*, **2**, 78.

Lefebvre, C., Manheimer, E. and Glanville, J. (2011) Searching for Studies. In Higgins, J. P. T. and Green, S. (eds), *Cochrane Handbook for Systematic Reviews of Interventions (version 5.1.0)*, The Cochrane Collaboration. http://handbook-5-1.cochrane.org/

Levay, P., Ainsworth, N., Kettle, R. and Morgan, A. (2016) Identifying Evidence for Public Health Guidance: a comparison of citation searching with Web of Science and Google Scholar, *Research Synthesis Methods*, **7** (1), 34-45.

Levay, P., Raynor, M. and Tuvey, D. (2015) The Contributions of MEDLINE, Other Bibliographic Databases and Various Search Techniques to NICE Public Health Guidance, *Evidence Based Library and Information Practice*, **10** (1), 50-68.

McGowan, J. and Sampson, M. (2005) Systematic Reviews Need Systematic Searchers, *Journal of the Medical Library Association*, **93** (1), 74-80.

Morrison, A., Polisena, J., Husereau, D., Moulton, K., Clark, M., Fiander, M., Mierzwinski-Urban, M., Clifford, T., Hutton, B. and Rabb, D. (2012) The Effect of English-language Restriction on Systematic Review-based Meta-analyses: a systematic review of empirical studies, *International Journal of Technology Assessment in Health Care*, **28** (2), 138-144.

National Institute for Health and Care Excellence (2012) *Obesity: working with local communities (PH42)*. www.nice.org.uk/guidance/ph42

National Institute for Health and Care Excellence (2013) *Weight*

Management: lifestyle services for overweight or obese children and young people (PH47). www.nice.org.uk/guidance/ph47

National Institute for Health and Care Excellence (2014) *Developing NICE Guidelines: the manual. NICE Process and Methods Guidance 20.* www.nice.org.uk/process/pmg20/chapter/introduction-and-overview

National Institute for Health and Care Excellence (2015) *Erlotinib and Gefitinib for Treating Non-small-cell Lung Cancer that has Progressed after Prior Chemotherapy (TA374).* www.nice.org.uk/guidance/ta374

O'Mara-Eves, A., Brunton, G., McDaid, D., Kavanagh, J., Oliver, S. and Thomas, J. (2014) Techniques for Identifying Cross-disciplinary and 'Hard-to-detect' Evidence for Systematic Review, *Research Synthesis Methods,* **5** (1), 50-59.

Rader, T., Mann, M., Stansfield, C., Cooper, C. and Sampson, M. (2013) Methods for Documenting Systematic Review Searches: a discussion of common issues, *Research Synthesis Methods,* **5** (2), 98-115.

Raynor, M. (2012) Case study 7.4 Information Specialist. In Brettle, A. and Urquhart, C. (eds), *Changing Roles and Contexts for Health Library and Information Professionals,* Facet Publishing.

Rethlefsen, M., Farrell, A. M., Osterhaus Trzasko, L. C. and Brigham, T. J. (2015) Librarian Co-authors Correlated with Higher Quality Reported Search Strategies in General Internal Medicine Systematic Reviews, *Journal of Clinical Epidemiology,* **68** (6), 617-626.

Sackett, D. L., Rosenberg, W. M. C., Gray, J. A. M., Haynes, R. B. and Richardson, W. S. (1996) Evidence Based Medicine: what it is and what it isn't, *BMJ,* **312** (7023), 71-72.

Savolainen, R. (2018) Berrypicking and Information Foraging: comparison of two theoretical frameworks for studying exploratory search, *Journal of Information Science,* **44** (5), 580-593.

Shemilt, I., Simon, A., Hollands, G. J., Marteau, T. M., Ogilvie, D., O'Mara-Eves, A., Kelly, M. P. and Thomas, J. (2013) Pinpointing Needles in Giant Haystacks: use of text mining to reduce impractical screening workload in extremely large scoping reviews, *Research Synthesis Methods,* **5** (1), 31-49.

Spencer, A. J. and Eldredge, J. D. (2018) Roles for Librarians in Systematic Reviews: a scoping review, *Journal of the Medical Library Association,* **106** (1), 46-56.

Stansfield, C. and Liabo, K. (2017) Identifying Social Care Research Literature: case studies from guideline development, *Evidence Based*

Library and Information Practice, **12** (3), 114-131.

Whiting, P., Savovic, J., Higgins, J. P., Caldwell, D. M., Reeves, B. C., Shea, B., Davies, P., Kleijnen, J., Churchill, R. and ROBIS Group (2016) ROBIS: a new tool to assess risk of bias in systematic reviews was developed. *Journal of Clinical Epidemiology*, **69**, 225-234.

Wong, R., Paisley, S. and Carroll, C. (2013) Assessing Searches in NICE Single Technology Appraisals: practice and checklist, *International Journal of Technology Assessment in Health Care*, **29** (3), 315-322.

Zwierzyna, M., Davies, M., Hingorani, A. D. and Hunter, J. (2018) Clinical Trial Design and Dissemination: comprehensive analysis of clinicaltrials.gov and PubMed data since 2005, *BMJ*, **361**, k2130.

2

Innovative approaches to systematic reviewing

Andrew Booth

Introduction

This chapter examines developments in systematic reviewing and what they mean for the search process. It introduces recent methods of synthesis, including mixed methods reviews and realist syntheses. It goes on to consider how innovative review types affect how we plan and execute search strategies. The chapter explores the value of other question formats and why you should choose a method appropriate to your review question. It starts by examining acknowledged limitations of the conventional systematic review model, both within health and multiple disciplines in which systematic reviews are gaining traction.

Challenging the conventional systematic review model

Since the mid-1990s, the conventional systematic review model, which assumes a closely focused question, a comprehensive search and a focus on synthesising 'stronger' rather than 'weaker' evidence, has proved remarkably flexible and resilient (Petticrew, 2015). The model has survived transfer to other emerging domains for systematic reviews, such as education, management and environmental science. However, this model faces renewed challenges as decision-makers seek to address ever more complex questions and to explore complex socially-mediated interventions, requiring diverse data and approaches to synthesis, and consequent changes to how studies are identified and selected.

Petticrew characterises the current era as moving from 'What works' to 'What happens' (Petticrew, 2015). Specifically, new forms of knowledge synthesis are required to explore people's perceptions of their situation, to identify underlying theories to explain how an intervention, policy or programme works, or to understand what makes an intervention, policy or programme more or less likely to be implemented (Tricco et al., 2016a). This, in turn, requires 'other types of search approaches (e.g. snowballing of articles, focusing on identification of key theories)' (Tricco et al., 2016b, 20) as well as others covered in this chapter.

The time and cost associated with producing systematic reviews offer a further challenge to their use in supporting decision-making (Tricco et al., 2017). Technical aspects of the search process are challenged by the rapid review movement which has reinterpreted 'How far should you go?' (Ogilvie et al., 2005) as 'How little searching is enough?' (Booth, 2010). One inevitable result is that three assumptions of the 'systematic review catechism' – the question, the comprehensive search and the privileging of rigour – are all receiving critical scrutiny.

Differences between conventional and innovative reviews

Conventional systematic reviews are founded upon pre-defining a clearly formulated question. 'Fuzzy questions tend to lead to fuzzy answers' (Oxman and Guyatt, 1988, 699) was an early mantra of the systematic review movement and persists in current evidence synthesis. Exploring initial questions leads you to identify further questions; the process of formulating a review question is iterative. Numerous question formulation variants seek to accommodate ever more diverse review types (Davies, 2011). The distinction, from evidence-based medicine, between precisely articulated foreground questions (with all four elements of a Patient-Intervention-Comparison-Outcome (PICO) formulation present) and more exploratory background questions (with one or more elements missing) (Richardson and Wilson, 1997) helped to distinguish between a viable and a non-viable systematic review (Counsell, 1997).

Increasingly, the scoping review (which seeks to determine boundaries for a specific PICO) (Tricco et al., 2016a) and the mapping review (which seeks to chart a broader territory) (Miake-Lye et al.,

2016) use the PICO in new and original ways. Innovative types of review either draw on PICO variants or propose completely different question structures (Munn et al., 2018). Clearly, the PICO question no longer holds a monopoly within the wider review family and information specialists must become adept with a wider variety of question types (Roth, 2017).

Qualitative evidence synthesis has challenged the appropriateness of the comprehensive sample as a default for all literature reviews (Hannes et al., 2013). The conventional systematic review considers the comprehensive literature search as a fundamental strategy to minimise bias. Searching across multiple databases and diverse sources counters accusations of 'cherry-picking' and tackles recognised biases in academic peer review (Briner and Denyer, 2012). However, even the *Cochrane Handbook,* the guidance document that underpins the methods of Cochrane reviews and which informs systematic review practice more generally, recognises that the time a review team has to identify studies is limited by time and money (Lefebvre, Manheimer and Glanville, 2011). Information specialists must become more knowledgeable about what different sampling strategies mean in practice and become skilled in constructing appropriate sampling frames.

The number of different types of evidence that inform a particular 'wicked' problem has been greatly expanded (Petticrew and Roberts, 2003; Shepherd, 2013). As well as considering Effectiveness and Cost Effectiveness, we must explore other elements, such as Feasibility, Appropriateness and Meaningfulness (see Table 2.1) (Pearson et al., 2007). Searchers must become aware of sources of alternate types of evidence, acquire a knowledge of an increasingly large array of methodological filters and recognise a diversity of study types. Interest in complex interventions (Petticrew et al., 2015), and in analytical approaches such as realist synthesis, has led to a quest to identify multiple-associated reports ('sibling reports') (Noyes et al., 2016) from the same study in order to add important contextual detail, theoretical legacies and intervention detail to help translate research findings into practice. Often this will require more thorough utilisation of non-English reports, unpublished studies and dissertations (Hartling et al., 2016; Paez, 2017).

What determines choice of innovative approaches?

Decision makers seek to answer an increasing number of questions. The review question influences the review method chosen, which, in turn, determines the search methods used. This relationship is illustrated in Table 2.1.

Table 2.1 *Framework for addressing review questions*

	Feasibility	Appropriateness	Meaningfulness	Effectiveness/ Cost Effectiveness
Domain Definition	Extent to which an activity is practical and practicable	Extent to which an intervention or activity fits with or is apt in a situation	Extent to which recipients experience an intervention or activity positively	Extent to which an intervention, when used appropriately, achieves the intended effect/for affordable cost
Type of Question	What makes the intervention more or less likely to work?	Is the intervention appropriate for this context?	Did the intervention work as planned?	Is the intervention effective? Is the intervention cost effective?
Review Methods	Logistics review Meta-regression Realist synthesis	Qualitative synthesis – Providers Qualitative synthesis - Recipients Realist synthesis	Qualitative synthesis - Recipients Realist synthesis	Meta-analysis Review of Cost Studies/ Economic Evaluations
Types of Material	Process evaluations Reports Correspondence Commentaries	Qualitative syntheses Qualitative studies Surveys	Qualitative syntheses Qualitative studies Surveys	RCTs Cost studies Economic evaluations
Search Methods	Websites Follow up of references Equipment manufacturer Training providers	Use of study filters	Use of study filters CLUSTER searching Search for sibling studies	Use of study filters Trial registers Study linkage

We can further characterise approaches to searching according to the types of knowledge that may be targeted when addressing a particular question (see Table 2.2 opposite).

As seen from Table 2.2, the types of questions to be addressed by a conventional database search are becoming proportionately smaller, opening up the prospect of more extensive use of 'complementary searches' (Cooper et al., 2017a; Cooper et al., 2017b), such as citation

Table 2.2 *SCIE domains of knowledge* (Pawson et al., 2003)

	Organizational knowledge	Practitioner knowledge	User knowledge	Research knowledge	Policy community knowledge
Sources	Standards, regulatory and aspirational Examples of good practice; published audits	Professional publications Colleges Associations Surveys Qualitative research	Surveys Qualitative research	Quantitative research Qualitative research Systematic reviews and Meta-analyses	Government policy documents
Search Methods	Google searches limited by domain (e.g. .org) General databases	Named websites General databases	General databases	Evidence databases General databases	Google searches limited by domain (e.g. .gov)

searching (Belter, 2016). The availability of web search engines (Briscoe, 2017) further extends searching beyond bibliographic databases (Bates et al., 2017). When evaluating the respective yield of conventional database approaches and complementary approaches we must not only consider coverage but also efficiency and potential impact on the final review. A further challenge lies in how to document search results (Stansfield, Dickson and Bangpan, 2016).

How does a review team decide which review method is appropriate for a review question? The EU-funded INTEGRATE-HTA project identified seven considerations when choosing a synthesis method, encapsulated in the RETREAT mnemonic (Booth et al., 2016), initially for qualitative syntheses but equally useful for a broader range of review types:

- Research question
- Epistemology
- Time
- Resources
- Expertise
- Audience and purpose
- Type of data.

Most of the RETREAT criteria are familiar to information specialists. However, the second criterion, Epistemology, requires explanation.

Essentially, epistemology relates to the nature of knowledge and what underpins such conceptions; so, for example, some literature reviews assume that there is a single measurable absolute 'truth' (for example, a meta-analysis) whereas others present the view that 'truth' is relative and in the eye of the beholder (for example, an interpretive review such as a meta-ethnography).

Literature reviews can contribute an understanding in one or more of six ways (Schryen, Wagner and Benlian, 2015):

1 Synthesis.
2 Adopting a new perspective.
3 Theory building.
4 Testing of theories.
5 Identification of research gaps.
6 Providing a research agenda.

Each contribution impacts upon the literature searching process. **Synthesis** approaches require the searcher to identify a relatively similar set of literature within defined limits. In contrast, **adopting a new perspective** requires searches that extend across geographical boundaries, that cross disciplines or that identify unevaluated innovative practice. **Theory building** may require a systematic search to identify wider theory or explanations from the literature (Booth and Carroll, 2015).

Subsequent **testing of theories** requires a search for studies that contain data, usually found in different types of literature from those that highlight conceptual thinking within the same topic area. In essence, a searcher must choose between conducting a single 'big bang' search of a topic area and then leaving the review team to screen into conceptual and empirical papers or, alternatively, conducting separate searches for these two distinct bodies of literature.

The final two contributions – **identification of research gaps** and **providing a research agenda** – require mapping searches across as wide a range of databases as possible using broad topic descriptors. The searcher may need to identify frameworks, taxonomies or classifications to help the review team to make sense of the literature. So, for example, emergency planning is typically conceived as a 'cycle', starting with mitigation and ending with recovery. Labels such as 'mitigation' and 'recovery' from this model can be used to code articles within a map of the emergency planning literature and, thus, to present findings in a way that is meaningful for end users of the review (Challen et al., 2012).

With variation across seven RETREAT criteria, and with over 50 types of review to choose from, how can an information specialist keep up to date with associated search techniques? Almost half of the identified review types relate to syntheses of qualitative research and these are largely covered by generic search guidance (Booth, 2016a). Other types of review adopt the systematic review search method-ology or, in the case of rapid reviews, start from systematic searching before implementing negotiated shortcuts. Further types of review are discipline specific; for example, the integrative review in nursing (Whittemore and Knafl, 2005) and the qualitative interpretive meta-synthesis in social work (Aguirre and Bolton, 2014).

Few individual review methods possess their own guidance for searching and it is not uncommon, as within realist synthesis (Wong et al., 2013) and meta-ethnography (France et al., 2015) for example, for reporting standards to be published well in advance of any guidance on search methods. For most review types the search starts from a generic toolbox of search methods, chosen carefully according to what the review is intended to achieve. Increasingly, this toolbox extends beyond bibliographic database searching to supplementary search methods, such as citation searching (Cooper et al., 2017b), making it more appropriate to label them 'complementary' rather than 'supplementary'.

Realist reviews

Some review types do require specialist search techniques. The realist synthesis, and other theory-informed methods such as framework synthesis, require a search for theory. Review teams seek 'programme theory' (how an intervention is believed to work) or 'mid-range theory' (theory that explains common behaviours or effects across different topic areas, for example smoking cessation and weight management) (Davidoff et al., 2015). Realist synthesis, and many reviews for complex interventions, require a review team to understand the context for a study; information not typically contained in a single study report. So, for example, our original search may have identified a case study where an intervention to help teenage mothers to give up smoking has worked particularly well and another case study where it has not worked at all. Using the retrieved reference for each project (the index paper) we may seek to identify all available published and unpublished papers for each study ('sibling' papers). We can use these sibling papers to build up a picture of the context for each of the case studies. This may help us to explain the success in one instance and/or the lack of success in the other.

Complementary search techniques, as used in the CLUSTER procedure (Booth et al., 2013), can make this task easier. Simply put, the searcher uses the seven approaches captured by the CLUSTER mnemonic – Citations, Lead authors, Unpublished materials, Google Scholar, tracking Theories, ancestry searching for Early examples and follow up of Related projects – to compile a set of documents related to each project.

A 'realist search' involves six principal elements (Booth, Wright and Briscoe, 2018), some parallel to the systematic review process while others are demonstrably different:

1 **Formulating specific questions** as lines of inquiry (Denyer and Tranfield, 2009).
2 Exploring a proposed area for previously published research and, if necessary, refining the research question (**the Background Search**) (Pawson, 2006).
3 Identifying theories for how an intervention works (**the Search for Programme Theories**) (Pawson, 2006).
4 Identifying empirical evidence to test and refine the programme theories (**the Search for Empirical Evidence**) (Pawson, 2006).
5 Responding to new information needs that emerge during testing and refining of the initial programme theory (**the Final Search to refine programme theories**) (Pawson, 2006).
6 **Documenting the search process** in an explicit and transparent manner (Wong et al., 2013).

A search for theories combines keywords for the subject area with purpose-specific terms such as 'theor* OR concept* OR framework* OR model*' (Booth and Carroll, 2015). Testing of theories requires use of subject keywords combined with terms identifying study designs such as 'randomised controlled trial' or 'qualitative study'.

Perhaps the biggest difference is that the entire realist search process is iterative, involving multiple feedback loops between the requester and the searcher. Unlike conventional intervention searches, which are largely predictable and may be specified after an initial scoping search, mechanisms that explain how participants respond to a particular intervention or policy (for example, how smokers respond to health warnings or to the creation of smoker-only zones) may surface during the course of the review, requiring 'forays' into other disciplines. This presents several challenges, not least in how to document a transparent and comprehensible search strategy. Review teams are becoming increasingly interested in how to document search strategies across multiple review types with the information specialist playing an important role as the guarantor of search quality (Meert, Torabi and Costella, 2016; Rethlefsen et al., 2015).

Mixed methods reviews

Mixed methods reviews include reviews that examine 'all types of empirical research (qualitative, quantitative, or mixed methods) concurrently to develop a breadth and depth of understanding of scientific knowledge' (El Sherif et al., 2016, 47). They can also refer to reviews that synthesise and analyse only mixed methods studies. The popularity of mixed methods studies reviews can, in part, be attributed to their usefulness in addressing complex research questions (Petticrew et al., 2013). The past decade has witnessed rapid developments within qualitative synthesis, coupled with increased use of frameworks to combine quantitative and qualitative methods, reviews or data, contributing to the popularity of the mixed methods review.

Question structures

Question structures offer a framework for formulating a problem statement and communicating this within the review team and with wider stakeholders. From the initial PICO format, a plethora of question structure formats have been developed. Instrumentally, question structures help the team to conceptualise the literature search, specify inclusion/exclusion criteria and structure the data extraction form. Boolean OR logic is used to combine items within a component (so, synonyms and variants, for example schools OR colleges) while the Boolean AND is typically used to connect items across components (for example, schools AND exercise). Formulating questions in this manner gives the review team a foundation for the subsequent review and encourages them to reflect on what review method to use, what literature to review and what data to consider (see Table 2.3).

Table 2.3 *Some alternative question formats*

Question Formulation	Elements	Application	Review Types
BeHEMoTh (Booth and Carroll, 2015)	Behaviour, Health context, Exclusions, Models or Theories	Theory-informed reviews	Realist Synthesis Framework Synthesis
CIMO (Denyer and Tranfield, 2009)	Context, Intervention, Mechanism, Outcome	Management Health services delivery Education topics	Reviews of Complex Interventions Realist Synthesis
PerSPE(C)TiF (Booth, Noyes and Flemming, 2018)	Perspective, Setting, Phenomenon of Interest, Environment, (Comparison – optional) Time/Timing Findings	Mixed methods questions	Mixed Methods Reviews
PICo (Stern, Jordan and McArthur, 2014)	Population, Interest, phenomenon of, Context	Qualitative questions	Qualitative Evidence Syntheses
PICOC (Petticrew and Roberts, 2006)	Population, Intervention, Comparison, Outcome, Context	Social science topics	Systematic Reviews of Complex Interventions
SPICE (Booth, 2006a)	Setting, Perspective, Interest, phenomenon of, Comparison (optional), Evaluation	Qualitative questions	Qualitative Evidence Syntheses
SPIDER (Cooke, Smith and Booth, 2012)	Sample, Phenomenon of Interest, Design, Evaluation, Research type	Qualitative questions Mixed methods questions	Qualitative Evidence Syntheses Mixed Methods Reviews

Qualitative syntheses may define the question, not as a starting point but as an intermediate outcome of the review process (Harris et al., 2018). Reviews of complex interventions (Squires, Valentine and

Grimshaw, 2013) and realist syntheses (Harris et al., 2018) may seek to explore multiple questions; for example, a realist synthesis may pursue an understanding of how different interventions, policies or programmes may trigger a common response or reaction in those receiving or delivering a programme.

The CIMO question formulation, which originates within management and is now being applied to such fields as education, can extend the search boundaries beyond a specific intervention to a family of interventions that share a common mechanism (for example, a set of group-based interventions). CIMO can similarly be used in constructing multiple questions to populate a diagrammatic representation of how a complex intervention is believed to work (known as a 'logic model').

Controversy and debate

Current controversy and debate centres on sampling issues and search efficiency. Even an 'exhaustive' search aspires more to representativeness than to completeness. Within primary qualitative research, at least 16 sampling strategies have been identified, with many offering an appropriate basis for literature search strategies (Suri, 2011). Indeed 'snowball sampling', in the form of citation searching, has been a staple of the systematic review search for many years. When should we select particularly rich and informative cases from our wider sampling frame (known as 'intensity sampling') or select widely contrasting cases (known as 'maximum variation sampling') in order to deliver a review that best addresses a decision-maker's review question? Limited evidence exists to address this issue (Benoot, Hannes and Bilsen, 2016).

Interest in search efficiency has two current stimuli: first, the facility to interrogate and download large datasets has resulted in impossibly large results sets. Given the time reviewers take to screen bibliographic records, savings made in retrieval time may end up being offset by larger numbers needing to be retrieved to identify each potentially relevant study. Review teams differ in what they consider a 'reasonable' number of records to process, prompting concerns that excessively large datasets may constitute 'research waste'. Increasingly, investigators explore whether a small number of high-yield databases might be sufficient (Aagaard, Lund and Juhl, 2016; Booth, 2016b; Hartling et al.,

2016) and the quest has become to optimise rather than to maximise (Bramer et al., 2017).

Secondly, producers of evidence-based guidance cannot afford to have the credibility of their searches undermined by the omission of relevant items (Delaney and Tamás, 2017). A further prompt for examining search efficiency comes from the developing area of rapid reviews. Rather than thinking in terms of how many records are 'enough', information specialists are starting to consider such metrics as 'the number needed to read/retrieve' (Bachmann et al., 2002; Booth, 2006b). How many titles and abstracts does a review team need to read in order to identify an additional relevant reference? More critically, does the additional relevant reference hold the potential to provide a 'tipping point' by overturning the result of a current review? Similarly, the dialogue on what is the optimal number of databases starts to focus on the unique contribution of references ('Unique Hits Retrieved') from each database rather than the absolute number of hits.

Techniques first developed within health research are now paralleled by other disciplines, with information retrieval experts from health sciences contributing to developments in domains such as environmental science (Livoreil et al., 2017). The Campbell Collaboration has developed guidance for searching for reviews of social interventions (i.e. for crime and justice, disability, education, international development, knowledge translation and implementation, nutrition and social welfare) (Kugley et al., 2017) comparable to that from its health counterpart, Cochrane. Social care has demonstrated that a shorter list of database sources may be sufficient, although indexing of such databases remains suboptimal (McGinn et al., 2016). The potential value of methodological filters has also been explored in social care (Shlonsky, Baker and Fuller-Thomson, 2011). Crime prevention literature exhibits similar diversity in the terminology used but manifests a proportionately higher dependence upon grey literature (Tompson and Belur, 2016). Greater use of linguistic analysis when developing search strategies has been proposed for conservation biology (Westgate and Lindenmayer, 2017). Such fields occupy an earlier stage of development compared to health care, with much variability in knowledge of database coverage and features among scholars and students (Calver et al., 2017).

Case studies

Case study 2.1 applies these issues to realist synthesis and Case study 2.2 explores the issues in mixed methods reviews.

Case study 2.1: Examples of a realist synthesis

Initial work on identifying explanations ('programme theories' or 'theories of change') for how interventions to enable evidence-informed health care work (Rycroft-Malone et al., 2012) identified four 'theory areas': change agency; technology; education and learning strategies; and systems change. The realist synthesis team produced a list of relevant search terms to guide searches for each theory area. Six online databases were searched over a ten-year period and 14 key journals were reviewed to identify relevant articles missed by the initial strategy. The team would have liked to use snowballing and consulting experts within their realist review process but did not have the resources to extend beyond the database search. Over 24,000 electronic references were returned from the largest of the four searches, illustrating the choice between database searching and complementary searching described earlier. The team erred on the side of inclusivity, retrieving all seemingly relevant papers as full-text prior to a relevance test: 'Is the evidence provided in this theory area good and relevant enough to be included in the synthesis?'.

In contrast, a review of community engagement initiatives narrowed its initial trawl of over 13,000 references down to about 140 projects conducted in the UK (Harris et al., 2015). Ten projects were purposively selected against different populations, settings and target conditions. Each index study was used as the starting point for CLUSTER searching to retrieve associated reports. The narrative of searching for just one of these initiatives is described in detail in the CLUSTER methodology paper (Booth et al., 2013). This approach extends the role of the searcher beyond the painstaking 'fingertip combing' of the comprehensive search to intuitive follow up of leads and associated 'detective' work.

As a further example, a search on group clinics sought to supplement the US-dominated research literature with context-sensitive examples of UK practice by searching the '.nhs.uk' internet domain (Booth et al., 2015). The literature search process confirmed contextual differences in that UK patients were more likely to expect to see a medical consultant than a managed care population in the USA, leading to hybrid clinic approaches. Geographic filters, as recently developed for the UK (Ayiku et al., 2017) and previously for Spain (Valderas et al., 2006), and country-specific database sources (Stansfield et al., 2012) may also prove valuable in identifying context-specific material.

Case study 2.2: Example of a mixed methods review

A mixed methods review examining the information needs of young people with epilepsy (Lewis, Noyes and Mackereth, 2010) used a simple qualitative filter, having formulated the subject search around SPICE elements. No specific details are given of the search string for the quantitative or mixed methods studies. This review predated the 2016 mixed method study filter which essentially involves adding the following search string to existing qualitative filters on the Ovid platform:

'(mixed adj5 method*).mp. OR multimethod*.mp. OR (multiple adj5 method*).mp.'.

However, this filter has not been validated and appears to miss obvious variants such as 'multiple approaches' and 'mixed research approaches' (El Sherif et al., 2016). The search included specialist Cochrane trial registers and databases, supplemented by handsearching of key epilepsy journals. Study types included mixed method studies, randomised controlled trials and quantitative and qualitative studies that broadly reported young people or parent perspectives on their information needs. This review used the method of conducting separate quantitative and qualitative reviews and then integrating them in a third and final review (Harden et al., 2004).

Strategically, a review team could conduct searches for quantitative and qualitative evidence separately, supplemented by a search for mixed methods studies. Alternatively, they could identify relevant studies from a single topic-based pass through the database, unrestricted by search filters, thereby passing the workload to the screening stage. The former runs the risk of studies falling down the gaps between filters due to indexing or retrieval inadequacies, while the latter may result in retrieval of large numbers of non-empirical studies, such as opinion pieces and commentaries.

Future directions

The examples described in the case studies either required the development of tailored search methods or would have benefited from methods that have been developed subsequent to their publication. This emphasises that the field of emerging review methods is particularly volatile, requiring information specialists to develop strategies to keep up to date with current research and practice.

As previously mentioned, it is increasingly important to identify sibling studies (linked publications, published or unpublished, that share a study context). Leading figures in the systematic review movement are vocal in their support of the need to identify linked studies (Altman et al., 2014). Researchers are also recognising that the validity of a review is just as likely, if not more likely, to be undermined by the omission of unpublished studies as it is by failure to retrieve difficult-to-identify published studies (Golder, Loke and Bland, 2010). Effective retrieval and the ability to follow up links between different publication types from the same project are important skills and information specialists continue at the forefront of such initiatives. Technological improvements are likely to facilitate cross-database searching (Smalheiser et al., 2014) and the use of text mining (for search strategy development) (Hausner et al., 2015) and data mining (for study selection) (Paynter et al., 2016; Shemilt et al., 2014; Shemilt et al., 2016). Tools for translating search strategies across databases have been devised by information specialists through collaborative or individual initiatives (Bramer et al., 2018) and these need to be evaluated across a wide range of circumstances.

Systematic searching of full-text offers a more nuanced analysis of a topic than that afforded by title and abstract searches. Tools such as Publish or Perish (https://harzing.com/resources/publish-or-perish) offer the same facility to perform structured searches as Google Scholar (https://scholar.google.co.uk), and to download retrieved results that have long been available for bibliographic databases (Harzing, 2010). It is now possible to access tables embedded within articles and assess relevance and to extract data automatically from full-text articles.

With it being possible to identify more information at the point of searching, rather than only from retrieval of full-text, the separation between the searcher (who assesses topic relevance) and the review team (who judge the relevance of individual items) becomes blurred. Use of relevance ranking in many databases removes the simple Boolean division of relevant versus non-relevant. Instead, the team must consider degrees of relevance and relevance thresholds; coverage of a topic may be determined by an arbitrary relevance value rather than by an exhaustive list of decreasingly relevant keywords. It becomes possible to compare 'sort by relevance' functions across databases and web search engines, allowing a team to agree how they are going to define 'good enough rigour' (Bates et al., 2017). Instead of 'reasonableness' being defined by how many (and which) databases to search and the amount of time and specialist expertise used in constructing search strategies, a review team could agree the number of hits sorted by relevance that they are willing to consider. This approach is similar to the 'stopping rules' previously proposed for methodological or social science reviews (Petticrew and Roberts, 2006). However, the authors also observe that many researchers remain uncertain about the value of automated approaches and are understandably suspicious of cut-offs determined by an algorithm rather than by expert knowledge.

Improvements in current awareness services offer the prospect of real time harvesting of studies as they are published. Study classifiers are being developed to make semi-automated identification of study types easier (Thomas et al., 2017). Identifying studies 'upstream' (as new papers appear) could completely revolutionise a landscape occupied for the last 25 years by 'downstream' development of methodological filters (for use at the time of searching), as described in Chapter 9. Living reviews, continually refreshed with emerging studies, already exist for conventional systematic reviews (Elliott et al., 2014) and it seems simply a matter of time before these extend to such areas as qualitative evidence syntheses. Given the existence of increasing numbers of quantitative and qualitative systematic reviews, the prospect of integrating both streams of evidence into live mixed methods reviews becomes a real possibility.

Developments in open access have seen the dominance of publishers within the publication cycle being challenged by academics, funders and the public alike. Never before has such a high proportion of published literature been available open access; 60% of global journal output and 70% of UK-authored journal output is available open access rather than behind paywalls (Jubb et al., 2017). The 'currency' of literature searches is likely to transfer from bibliographic records to full-text articles, requiring new search techniques and retrieval technologies. Against such a backdrop, developments such as peer review of electronic search strategies (PRESS) (McGowan et al., 2016) to ensure quality control, self-audit and peer review and to encourage reflective learning, become even more important.

Conclusion

Generally speaking, information specialists across a wide range of disciplines and sectors continue to rise to the challenge posed by different review types, different question structures and diverse information sources. They tend to devise new ways of working and new techniques opportunistically, meaning that many procedures are supported by a limited number of case studies within health and even fewer examples within other developing disciplines. Guidance and documentation, already noted as absent for innovative review methods in general (Tricco et al., 2016a), is lacking for search processes and procedures. The evidence base for innovative searching is scattered and largely devoid of underpinning theory, resulting in considerable variation in practice. For example, information specialists from three national centres for excellence have worked together to compare and contrast three very different, yet equally valid, approaches to supporting realist reviews (Booth, Wright and Briscoe, 2018).

Such diversity is both a strength and a weakness. Searchers in a wide range of disciplines continue to explore innovative techniques and technologies to address new and demanding questions from research commissioners presented via their local review teams. The plethora of review methods offers information specialists the opportunity to extend their role from literature search consultant to include literature review advisor. Emerging technologies, and a more critical examination of search yields and search efficiency, are likely to free the searcher from the routine demands of study identification to become an informed consumer of systematic approaches to the literature. Such a transition offers a further opportunity to confirm and strengthen the role of the expert searcher (Zhang, Sampson and McGowan, 2006).

Suggestions for further reading

Booth, A. (2016) Searching for Qualitative Research for Inclusion in Systematic Reviews: a structured methodological review, *Systematic Reviews*, **5** (1), 74.

Booth, A. and Carroll, C. (2015) Systematic Searching for Theory to Inform Systematic Reviews: is it feasible? Is it desirable?, *Health Information and Libraries Journal*, **32** (3), 220-235.

Buchberger, B., Krabbe, L., Lux, B. and Mattivi, J. T. (2016) Evidence Mapping for Decision Making: feasibility versus accuracy – when to abandon high sensitivity in electronic searches, *GMS German Medical Science*, **14**.

Cooper, C., Booth, A., Britten, N. and Garside, R. (2017) A Comparison of Results of Empirical Studies of Supplementary Search Techniques and Recommendations in Review Methodology Handbooks: a methodological review, *Systematic Reviews*, **6** (1).

Cooper, C., Lovell, R., Husk, K., Booth, A. and Garside, R. (2017) Supplementary Search Methods were more Effective and Offered Better Value than Bibliographic Database Searching: a case study from public health and environmental enhancement, *Research Synthesis Methods*, **9** (2), 195-223.

Lefebvre, C., Glanville, J., Wieland, L. S., Coles, B. and Weightman, A. L. (2013) Methodological Developments in Searching for Studies for Systematic Reviews: past, present and future?, *Systematic Reviews*, **2**, 78.

O'Mara-Eves, A., Brunton, G., McDaid, D., Kavanagh, J., Oliver, S. and Thomas, J. (2014) Techniques for Identifying Cross-disciplinary and 'Hard-to-detect' Evidence for Systematic Review, *Research Synthesis Methods*, **5** (1), 50-59.

Paynter, R., Bañez, L. L., Berliner, E., Erinoff, E., Lege-Matsuura, J., Potter, S. and Uhl, S. (2016) EPC Methods: an exploration of the use of text-mining software in systematic reviews, Research White Paper, Agency for Healthcare Research and Quality (USA). https://www.ncbi.nlm.nih.gov/books/NBK362044

Stansfield, C., Brunton, G. and Rees, R. (2014) Search Wide, Dig Deep: literature searching for qualitative research: an analysis of the publication formats and information sources used for four systematic reviews in public health, *Research Synthesis Methods*, **5** (2), 142-151.

References

Aagaard, T., Lund, H. and Juhl, C. (2016) Optimizing Literature Search in Systematic Reviews – are MEDLINE, EMBASE and CENTRAL enough for identifying effect studies within the area of musculoskeletal disorders?, *BMC Medical Research Methodology*, **16** (1), 161.

Aguirre, R. and Bolton, K. (2014) Qualitative Interpretive Meta-synthesis in Social Work Research: uncharted territory, *Journal of Social Work*, **14** (3), 279-294.

Altman, D. G., Furberg, C. D., Grimshaw, J. M. and Shanahan, D. R. (2014) Linked Publications from a Single Trial: a thread of evidence, *Trials*, **15** (1), 369.

Ayiku, L., Levay, P., Hudson, T., Craven, J., Barrett, E., Finnegan, A. and Adams, R. (2017) The MEDLINE UK Filter: development and validation of a geographic search filter to retrieve research about the UK from

OVID MEDLINE, *Health Information and Libraries Journal*, **34** (3), 200-216.

Bachmann, L. M., Coray, R., Estermann, P. and Ter Riet, G. (2002) Identifying Diagnostic Studies in MEDLINE: reducing the number needed to read, *Journal of the American Medical Informatics Association*, **9** (6), 653-658.

Bates, J., Best, P., McQuilkin, J. and Taylor, B. (2017) Will Web Search Engines Replace Bibliographic Databases in the Systematic Identification of Research?, *The Journal of Academic Librarianship*, **43** (1), 8-17.

Belter, C. W. (2016) Citation Analysis as a Literature Search Method for Systematic Reviews, *Journal of the Association for Information Science and Technology*, **67** (11), 2766-2777.

Benoot, C., Hannes, K. and Bilsen, J. (2016) The Use of Purposeful Sampling in a Qualitative Evidence Synthesis: a worked example on sexual adjustment to a cancer trajectory, *BMC Medical Research Methodology*, **16,** 21.

Booth, A. (2006a) Clear and Present Questions: formulating questions for evidence based practice, *Library Hi Tech*, **24** (3), 355-368.

Booth, A. (2006b) The Number Needed to Retrieve: a practically useful measure of information retrieval?, *Health Information and Libraries Journal*, **23** (3), 229-232.

Booth, A. (2010) How Much Searching is Enough? Comprehensive Versus Optimal Retrieval for Technology Assessments, *International Journal of Technology Assessment in Health Care*, **26** (4), 431-435.

Booth, A. (2016a) Searching for Qualitative Research for Inclusion in Systematic Reviews: a structured methodological review, *Systematic Reviews*, **5** (1), 74.

Booth, A. (2016b) Over 85% of Included Studies in Systematic Reviews are on MEDLINE, *Journal of Clinical Epidemiology*, **79**, 165.

Booth, A., Cantrell, A., Preston, L., Chambers, D. and Goyder, E. (2015) What is the Evidence for the Effectiveness, Appropriateness and Feasibility of Group Clinics for Patients with Chronic Conditions? A Systematic Review, *Southampton (UK): NIHR Journals Library*, Dec 2015.

Booth, A. and Carroll, C. (2015) Systematic Searching for Theory to Inform Systematic Reviews: is it feasible? Is it desirable?, *Health Information and Libraries Journal*, **32** (3), 220-235.

Booth, A., Harris, J., Croot, E., Springett, J., Campbell, F. and Wilkins, E. (2013) Towards a Methodology for Cluster Searching to Provide Conceptual and Contextual 'Richness' for Systematic Reviews of

Complex Interventions: case study (CLUSTER), *BMC Medical Research Methodology*, **13** (1), 118.

Booth, A., Noyes, J. and Flemming, K. (2018) Formulating Questions to Address the Acceptability and Feasibility of Complex Interventions in Qualitative Evidence Synthesis, *BMJ Global Health*, in press.

Booth, A., Noyes, J., Flemming, K., Gerhardus, A., Wahlster, P., van der Wilt, G. J., Mozygemba, K., Refolo, P., Sacchini, D. and Tummers, M. (2016) Guidance on Choosing Qualitative Evidence Synthesis Methods for Use in Health Technology Assessments of Complex Interventions, INTEGRATE-HTA. https://www.integrate-hta.eu/downloads

Booth, A., Wright, J. and Briscoe, S. (2018) Scoping and Searching to Support Realist Approaches to Doing Realist Research. In Emmel, N., Greenhalgh, J., Manzano, A., Monaghan, M. and Dalkin, S. (eds), *Doing Realist Research*, SAGE Publishing.

Bramer, W. M., Rethlefsen, M. L., Kleijnen, J. and Franco, O. H. (2017) Optimal Database Combinations for Literature Searches in Systematic Reviews: a prospective exploratory study, *Systematic Reviews*, **6** (1), 245.

Bramer, W. M., Rethlefsen, M. L., Mast, F. and Kleijnen, J. (2018) Evaluation of a New Method for Librarian-mediated Literature Searches for Systematic Reviews, *Research Synthesis Methods*, **9** (4), 510-520.

Briner, R. B. and Denyer, D. (2012) Systematic Review and Evidence Synthesis as a Practice and Scholarship Tool. In Rousseau, D. M. (ed), *The Oxford Handbook of Evidence-based Management*, Oxford University Press, 112–129.

Briscoe, S. (2017) A Review of the Reporting of Web Searching to Identify Studies for Cochrane Systematic Reviews, *Research Synthesis Methods*, **9** (1), 89-99.

Calver, M. C., Goldman, B., Hutchings, P. A. and Kingsford, R. T. (2017) Why Discrepancies in Searching the Conservation Biology Literature Matter, *Biological Conservation*, **213**, 19-26.

Challen, K., Lee, A. C., Booth, A., Gardois, P., Woods, H. B. and Goodacre, S. W. (2012) Where is the Evidence for Emergency Planning: a scoping review, *BMC Public Health*, **12** (1), 542.

Cooke, A., Smith, D. and Booth, A. (2012) Beyond PICO: the SPIDER tool for qualitative evidence synthesis, *Qualitative Health Research*, **22** (10), 1435-1443.

Cooper, C., Booth, A., Britten, N. and Garside, R. (2017a) A Comparison of Results of Empirical Studies of Supplementary Search Techniques and Recommendations in Review Methodology Handbooks: a methodological review, *Systematic Reviews*, **6** (1), 234.

Cooper, C., Lovell, R., Husk, K., Booth, A. and Garside, R. (2017b) Supplementary Search Methods were More Effective and Offered Better Value than Bibliographic Database Searching: a case study from public health and environmental enhancement, *Research Synthesis Methods*, **9** (2), 195-223.

Counsell, C. (1997) Formulating Questions and Locating Primary Studies for Inclusion in Systematic Reviews, *Annals of Internal Medicine*, **127** (5), 380-387.

Davidoff, F., Dixon-Woods, M., Leviton, L. and Michie, S. (2015) Demystifying Theory and its Use in Improvement, *BMJ Quality and Safety*, **24** (3), 228-238.

Davies, K. S. (2011) Formulating the Evidence Based Practice Question: a review of the frameworks, *Evidence Based Library and Information Practice*, **6** (2), 75-80.

Delaney, A. and Tamás, P. A. (2017) Searching for Evidence or Approval? A Commentary on Database Search in Systematic Reviews and Alternative Information Retrieval Methodologies, *Research Synthesis Methods*, **9** (1), 124-131.

Denyer, D. and Tranfield, D. (2009) Producing a Systematic Review. In Buchanan, D. A. and Bryman, A. (eds), *The SAGE Handbook of Organizational Research Methods*, SAGE Publishing.

El Sherif, R., Pluye, P., Gore, G., Granikov, V. and Hong, Q. N. (2016) Performance of a Mixed Filter to Identify Relevant Studies for Mixed Studies Reviews, *Journal of the Medical Library Association*, **104** (1), 47-51.

Elliott, J. H., Turner, T., Clavisi, O., Thomas, J., Higgins, J. P., Mavergames, C. and Gruen, R. L. (2014) Living Systematic Reviews: an emerging opportunity to narrow the evidence-practice gap, *PLOS Medicine*, **11** (2), e1001603.

France, E. F., Ring, N., Noyes, J., Maxwell, M., Jepson, R., Duncan, E., Turley, R., Jones, D. and Uny, I. (2015) Protocol-developing Meta-ethnography Reporting Guidelines (eMERGe), *BMC Medical Research Methodology*, **15** (1), 103.

Golder, S., Loke, Y. K. and Bland, M. (2010) Unpublished Data can be of Value in Systematic Reviews of Adverse Effects: methodological overview, *Journal of Clinical Epidemiology*, **63** (10), 1071-1081.

Hannes, K., Booth, A., Harris, J. and Noyes, J. (2013) Celebrating Methodological Challenges and Changes: reflecting on the emergence and importance of the role of qualitative evidence in Cochrane reviews, *Systematic Reviews*, **2**, 84.

Harden, A., Garcia, J., Oliver, S., Rees, R., Shepherd, J., Brunton, G. and Oakley, A. (2004) Applying Systematic Review Methods to Studies of People's Views: an example from public health research, *Journal of Epidemiology and Community Health*, **58** (9), 794-800.

Harris, J. L., Booth, A., Cargo, M., Hannes, K., Harden, A., Flemming, K., Garside, R., Pantoja, T., Thomas, J. and Noyes, J. (2018) Cochrane Qualitative and Implementation Methods Group Guidance Series - Paper 2: Methods for question formulation, searching and protocol development for qualitative evidence synthesis, *Journal of Clinical Epidemiology*, **97**, 39-48.

Harris, J., Springett, J., Croot, L., Booth, A., Campbell, F., Thompson, J., Goyder, E., Van Cleemput, P., Wilkins, E. and Yang, Y. (2015) Can Community-based Peer Support Promote Health Literacy and Reduce Inequalities? A Realist Review, *Public Health Research*, **3** (3).

Hartling, L., Featherstone, R., Nuspl, M., Shave, K., Dryden, D. M. and Vandermeer, B. (2016) The Contribution of Databases to the Results of Systematic Reviews: a cross-sectional study, *BMC Medical Research Methodology*, **16** (1), 127.

Harzing, A-W. K. (2010) *The Publish or Perish Book*, Tarma Software Research Pty Ltd.

Hausner, E., Guddat, C., Hermanns, T., Lampert, U. and Waffenschmidt, S. (2015) Development of Search Strategies for Systematic Reviews: validation showed the noninferiority of the objective approach, *Journal of Clinical Epidemiology*, **68** (2), 191-199.

Jubb, M., Plume, A., Oeben, S., Brammer, L., Johnson, R., Bütün, C. and Pinfield, S. (2017) *Monitoring the Transition to Open Access*, Universities UK.

Kugley, S., Wade, A., Thomas, J., Mahood, Q., Jørgensen, A-M. K., Hammerstrøm, K. and Sathe, N. (2017) *Searching for Studies: a guide to information retrieval for Campbell Systematic Reviews - Campbell Methods Series Guide 1*, The Campbell Collaboration. www.campbellcollaboration.org/library/searching-for-studies-information-retrieval-guide-campbell-reviews.html

Lefebvre, C., Manheimer, E. and Glanville, J. (2011) Searching for Studies. In Higgins, J. P. T. and Green, S. (eds), *Cochrane Handbook for Systematic Reviews of Interventions (version 5.1.0)*, The Cochrane Collaboration. http://handbook-5-1.cochrane.org

Lewis, S. A., Noyes, J. and Mackereth, S. (2010) Knowledge and Information Needs of Young People with Epilepsy and their Parents: mixed-method systematic review, *BMC Pediatrics*, **10**, 103.

Livoreil, B., Glanville, J., Haddaway, N. R., Bayliss, H., Bethel, A., de Lachapelle, F. F., Robalino, S., Savilaakso, S., Zhou, W., Petrokofsky, G. and Frampton, G. (2017) Systematic Searching for Environmental Evidence Using Multiple Tools and Sources, *Environmental Evidence*, **6** (1), 23.

McGinn, T., Taylor, B., McColgan, M. and McQuilkan, J. (2016) Social Work Literature Searching: current issues with databases and online search engines, *Research on Social Work Practice*, **26** (3), 266-277.

McGowan, J., Sampson, M., Salzwedel, D. M., Cogo, E., Foerster, V. and Lefebvre, C. (2016) PRESS Peer Review of Electronic Search Strategies: 2015 guideline statement, *Journal of Clinical Epidemiology*, **75**, 40-46.

Meert, D., Torabi, N. and Costella, J. (2016) Impact of Librarians on Reporting of the Literature Searching Component of Pediatric Systematic Reviews, *Journal of the Medical Library Association*, **104** (4), 267-277.

Miake-Lye, I. M., Hempel, S., Shanman, R. and Shekelle, P. G. (2016) What is an Evidence Map? A Systematic Review of Published Evidence Maps and their Definitions, Methods, and Products, *Systematic Reviews*, **5**, 28.

Munn, Z., Stern, C., Aromataris, E., Lockwood, C. and Jordan, Z. (2018) What Kind of Systematic Review Should I Conduct? A Proposed Typology and Guidance for Systematic Reviewers in the Medical and Health Sciences, *BMC Medical Research Methodology*, **18** (1), 5.

Noyes, J., Hendry, M., Lewin, S., Glenton, C., Chandler, J. and Rashidian, A. (2016) Qualitative 'Trial-sibling' Studies and 'Unrelated' Qualitative Studies Contributed to Complex Intervention Reviews, *Journal of Clinical Epidemiology*, **74**, 133-143.

Ogilvie, D., Hamilton, V., Egan, M. and Petticrew, M. (2005) Systematic Reviews of Health Effects of Social Interventions: 1. Finding the evidence: how far should you go?, *Journal of Epidemiology and Community Health*, **59** (9), 804-808.

Oxman, A. D. and Guyatt, G. H. (1988) Guidelines for Reading Literature Reviews, *CMAJ: Canadian Medical Association Journal*, **138** (8), 697.

Paez, A. (2017) Gray Literature: an important resource in systematic reviews, *Journal of Evidence-based Medicine*, **10** (3), 233-240.

Pawson, R. (2006) Evidence-based Policy: the promise of systematic review. In Pawson, R., *Evidence-Based Policy: a realist perspective*, SAGE Publishing.

Pawson, R., Boaz, A., Grayson, L., Long, A. and Barnes, C. (2003) Types and Quality of Knowledge in Social Care, *Knowledge Review*, **3**, 1-84.

Paynter, R., Bañez, L. L., Berliner, E., Erinoff, E., Lege-Matsuura, J., Potter, S. and Uhl, S. (2016) *EPC Methods: an exploration of the use of text-mining software in systematic reviews*, Research White Paper, Agency for Healthcare Research and Quality (USA). www.ncbi.nlm.nih.gov/books/NBK362044

Pearson, A., Wiechula, R., Court, A. and Lockwood, C. (2007) A Re-consideration of What Constitutes 'Evidence' in the Healthcare Professions, *Nursing Science Quarterly*, **20** (1), 85-88.

Petticrew, M. (2015) Time to Rethink the Systematic Review Catechism? Moving from 'What Works' to 'What Happens', *Systematic Reviews*, **4**, 36.

Petticrew, M., Anderson, L., Elder, R., Grimshaw, J., Hopkins, D., Hahn, R., Krause, L., Kristjansson, E., Mercer, S., Sipe, T., Tugwell, P., Ueffing, E., Waters, E. and Welch, V. (2015) Complex Interventions and their Implications for Systematic Reviews: a pragmatic approach, *International Journal of Nursing Studies*, **52** (7), 1211-1216.

Petticrew, M., Rehfuess, E., Noyes, J., Higgins, J. P., Mayhew, A., Pantoja, T., Shemilt, I. and Sowden, A. (2013) Synthesizing Evidence on Complex Interventions: how meta-analytical, qualitative, and mixed-method approaches can contribute, *Journal of Clinical Epidemiology*, **66** (11), 1230-1243.

Petticrew, M. and Roberts, H. (2003) Evidence, Hierarchies, and Typologies: horses for courses, *Journal of Epidemiology and Community Health*, **57** (7), 527-529.

Petticrew, M. and Roberts, H. (2006) *Systematic Reviews in the Social Sciences: a practical guide*, Blackwell Publishing.

Rethlefsen, M. L., Farrell, A. M., Trzasko, L. C. O. and Brigham, T. J. (2015) Librarian Co-authors Correlated with Higher Quality Reported Search Strategies in General Internal Medicine Systematic Reviews, *Journal of Clinical Epidemiology*, **68** (6), 617-626.

Richardson, W. and Wilson, M. C. (1997) On Questions, Background and Foreground, *Evidence Based Healthcare Newsletter*, **17**, 8-9.

Roth, S. (2017) A Team-based Approach to the Library Systematic Review Service Model [Preprint]. https://doi.org/10.17605/OSF.IO/HMQJZ

Rycroft-Malone, J., McCormack, B., Hutchinson, A. M., DeCorby, K., Bucknall, T. K., Kent, B., Schultz, A., Snelgrove-Clarke, E., Stetler, C. B., Titler, M., Wallin, L. and Wilson, V. (2012) Realist Synthesis: illustrating the method for implementation research, *Implementation Science*, **7**, 33.

Schryen, G., Wagner, G. and Benlian, A. (2015) Theory of Knowledge for Literature Reviews: an epistemological model, taxonomy and empirical analysis of IS literature, *International Conference on Information Systems*.

Shemilt, I., Khan, N., Park, S. and Thomas, J. (2016) Use of Cost-effectiveness Analysis to Compare the Efficiency of Study Identification Methods in Systematic Reviews, *Systematic Reviews*, **5** (1), 140.

Shemilt, I., Simon, A., Hollands, G., Marteau, T., Ogilvie, D., O'Mara-Eves, A., Kelly, M. and Thomas, J. (2014) Pinpointing Needles in Giant Haystacks: use of text mining to reduce impractical screening workload in extremely large scoping reviews, *Research Synthesis Methods*, **5** (1), 31-49.

Shepherd, J. (2013) Judgment, Resources, and Complexity: a qualitative study of the experiences of systematic reviewers of health promotion, *Evaluation and the Health Professions*, **36** (2), 247-267.

Shlonsky, A., Baker, T. M. and Fuller-Thomson, E. (2011) Using Methodological Search Filters to Facilitate Evidence-based Social Work Practice, *Clinical Social Work Journal*, **39** (4), 390-399.

Smalheiser, N. R., Lin, C., Jia, L., Jiang, Y., Cohen, A. M., Yu, C., Davis, J. M., Adams, C. E., McDonagh, M. S. and Meng, W. (2014) Design and Implementation of Metta, a metasearch engine for biomedical literature retrieval intended for systematic reviewers, *Health Information Science and Systems*, **2** (1), 1.

Squires, J. E., Valentine, J. C. and Grimshaw, J. M. (2013) Systematic Reviews of Complex Interventions: framing the review question, *Journal of Clinical Epidemiology*, **66** (11), 1215-1222.

Stansfield, C., Dickson, K. and Bangpan, M. (2016) Exploring Issues in the Conduct of Website Searching and Other Online Sources for Systematic Reviews: how can we be systematic? *Systematic Reviews*, **5** (1), 191.

Stansfield, C., Kavanagh, J., Rees, R., Gomersall, A. and Thomas, J. (2012) The Selection of Search Sources Influences the Findings of a Systematic Review of People's Views: a case study in public health, *BMC Medical Research Methodology*, **12**, 55.

Stern, C., Jordan, Z. and McArthur, A. (2014) Developing the Review Question and Inclusion Criteria, *American Journal of Nursing*, **114** (4), 53-56.

Suri, H. (2011) Purposeful Sampling in Qualitative Research Synthesis, *Qualitative Research Journal*, **11** (2), 63-75.

Thomas, J., Noel-Storr, A., Marshall, I., Wallace, B., McDonald, S., Mavergames, C., Glasziou, P., Shemilt, I., Synnot, A., Turner, T. and

Elliott, J. (2017) Living Systematic Reviews: 2. Combining human and machine effort, *Journal of Clinical Epidemiology*, **91**, 31-37.

Tompson, L. and Belur, J. (2016) Information Retrieval in Systematic Reviews: a case study of the crime prevention literature, *Journal of Experimental Criminology*, **12** (2),187-207.

Tricco, A. C., Langlois, E. V. and Straus, S. E. (2017) Rapid Reviews to Strengthen Health Policy and Systems: a practical guide, World Health Organization. www.who.int/alliance-hpsr/resources/publications/methodsreaders/en/

Tricco, A. C., Lillie, E., Zarin, W., O'Brien, K., Colquhoun, H., Kastner, M., Levac, D., Ng, C., Sharpe, J. P., Wilson, K., Kenny, M., Warren, R., Wilson, C., Stelfox, H. T. and Straus, S. E. (2016a) A Scoping Review on the Conduct and Reporting of Scoping Reviews, *BMC Medical Research Methodology*, **16** (1), 15.

Tricco, A. C., Soobiah, C., Antony, J., Cogo, E., MacDonald, H., Lillie, E., Tran, J., D'Souza, J., Hui, W., Perrier, L., Welch, V., Horsley, T., Straus, S. E. and Kastner, M. (2016b) A Scoping Review Identifies Multiple Emerging Knowledge Synthesis Methods, but few Studies Operationalize the Method, *Journal of Clinical Epidemiology*, **73**, 19-28.

Valderas, J. M., Mendivil, J., Parada, A., Losada-Yáñez, M. and Alonso, J. (2006) Development of a Geographic Filter for PubMed to Identify Studies Performed in Spain, *Revista Española de Cardiología (English Edition)*, **59** (12), 1244-1251.

Westgate, M. J. and Lindenmayer, D. B. (2017) The Difficulties of Systematic Reviews, *Conservation Biology*, **31** (5), 1002-1007.

Whittemore, R. and Knafl, K. (2005) The Integrative Review: updated methodology, *Journal of Advanced Nursing*, **52** (5), 546-553.

Wong, G., Greenhalgh, T., Westhorp, G., Buckingham, J. and Pawson, R. (2013) RAMESES Publication Standards: realist syntheses, *BMC Medicine*, **11**, 21.

Zhang, L., Sampson, M. and McGowan, J. (2006) Reporting of the Role of the Expert Searcher in Cochrane Reviews, *Evidence Based Library and Information Practice*, **1** (4), 3-16.

3

Searching for broad-based topics

Claire Stansfield

Introduction

A range of research is often required to address a specific research need. This chapter draws on examples of systematic searches used for systematic reviews that inform public policy decisions. Systematic reviews used to inform public policy are driven by practice needs, rather than neatly centred on discrete areas of research. Literature searches for these reviews are often required to capture samples of research studies that both span across a variety of topics and research fields and provide sufficient depth of research for each topic area (Francis et al., 2015; Oliver, Dickson and Bangpan, 2015).

This research might cross a range of subject domains, use a variety of approaches to address similar issues, or be described by diverse terminology. The diversity and fragmentation of the relevant literature poses challenges for literature searching using a systematic approach and this may affect our confidence that the studies collected are representative of the research that exists. There is no clear uniform solution to finding information in broad research fields such as public health (Bayliss Davenport and Pennant, 2014; Levay, Raynor and Tuvey, 2015).

At its heart, a manageable search strategy requires careful choices of where and how to locate research. This chapter is relevant to anyone supporting or undertaking systematic literature searches and other stakeholders involved in undertaking or using systematic reviews. It focuses on key aspects in planning a literature search for a broad-based topic, highlights challenges and provides examples of various approaches. This chapter closely relates to Chapter 2, on innovative and iterative approaches to systematic searching, and Chapter 4 on choosing the right sources and techniques. A discussion of broad-based topics is followed by examples of how different approaches have been used.

Overview of the topic

Systematic searching involves applying a clear rationale to seek out the best available evidence to address a research question. It aims to obtain research that is either a comprehensive collection or a representative sample of the available evidence (Brunton et al., 2017, 96-98). In practice, it is impossible to know the total universe of relevant studies and search strategies are unlikely to retrieve every relevant reference (Brettle et al., 1998; Brunton et al., 2017, 98). We introduce our own biases as to which resources we decide to search and how we search them. We are also constrained by our access to specific databases and journals and how much time we have available. The resources themselves vary in their content, how they are organised, how they process user queries and their searching functionality. The controlled vocabularies available on databases differ in a number of ways, including their specificity, accuracy and consistency (Lancaster and Warner, 1993, 206). Some journals might only be partially indexed within a resource. Searching databases using free-text elements, such as titles and abstracts, can be challenging where authors use ambiguous terms that change frequently and where abstracts may have limited detail (Papaioannou et al., 2010). It is difficult to design precise searches where there is a lack of distinctive terminology that separates relevant from irrelevant literature.

These challenges can arise when literature searching within discrete topics from a narrow research field, but the challenges are magnified for broader-based topics (Stansfield, 2018). Broad topics require a range of techniques to be used to counter the challenges (Grayson and Gomersall, 2003; Papaioannou et al., 2010) and help produce reliable and high-quality reviews. Transparency in reporting the methods enables others to critique the appropriateness of the search, its likely impact on the studies included (Booth, Papaioannou and Sutton, 2016,

20) and the limitations of the review. Some large systematic reviews utilise an advisory group consisting of a range of stakeholders and they can provide input into the search strategy and other areas to help strengthen the reliability of a review.

Discussion

Planning the search

Two key aspects in planning a search are choosing which resources to search and making decisions on how to search them in the context of the anticipated volume and breadth of search results. Chapter 4 has an in-depth discussion on choosing sources. These decisions are made according to the research question, the purpose and the type of review that is being conducted and the resources available.

Choosing the sources

For broad-based topics, it is important to consider the subject domain and how the relevant research is published (for example, journals, standalone reports and working papers, surveys or other formats) and the resource types that may locate this research (for example, databases, websites, specialist repositories). This includes thinking about particular study designs, geographical areas and stakeholder populations, as the resources searched should be suitable for capturing them. For example, systematic reviews are published in a range of formats, such as standalone reports or journal articles, and to find these an information specialist might:

- search suitable databases of systematic reviews.
- review the websites of funders of systematic reviews or review-producing organizations (such as Cochrane and the Campbell Collaboration).
- use topic-relevant bibliographic databases.
- browse the websites of organizations relevant to the topic.
- use web search engines.

This approach considers the sources from both a study type (in this case, systematic reviews) and a topic-based perspective.

International development topics (which are relevant to the context of developing economies) are a good example of literature that is scattered across resources. The relevant research may not be published in journals and may be disseminated across the websites of development agencies and non-governmental organizations that fund, undertake or disseminate research (Stansfield, Dickson and Bangpan, 2016; Stewart, van Rooyen and de Wet, 2012). For these reviews, a variety of resources need to be searched, including topic-based resources, resources that focus on international development research and appropriate international and regional resources, including both databases and websites.

Any review centred on a particular geographical region will draw on searches from international and suitable regional resources. Similarly, for reviews with a focus on the views of particular populations, such as clinicians, teachers or user groups, the information specialist needs to consider where research relating to these stakeholders is usually found. Resource lists and subject gateways produced by libraries or research groups can inform where to search (Brunton et al., 2017, 107). As well as searching databases and websites, other techniques such as reference checking, handsearching, citation searching or contact with authors and experts may be useful (Harris et al., 2018).

Social media is potentially a useful resource (see Chapter 6). Stewart, van Rooyen and de Wet (2012) cite participation in informal microfinance networks via Twitter as a source of identifying relevant research papers for their review on this topic. Adams et al. (2016) indicate that Twitter requests relating to their review were widely re-tweeted. There can be uncertainty on the best places to search in the time available to the review, but the information specialist who considers and understands the options to inform their choices will have an increased awareness of the limitations of their chosen approach.

Deciding how to search the sources

Searching resources involves thinking about the shared aspects of the literature required that can be described by a set of search terms, for example, populations, settings, contexts. This yields a set of studies that can be screened or assessed for relevance. Where some characteristics of the literature are difficult to define through a set of search terms, these could be filtered during screening rather than through searching (such as the concept of 'care', described later in this chapter). Therefore, there are decisions on which concepts to use in a search and which need to be screened.

Related to this is ensuring the search is broad and sensitive enough to capture the range of research on the topic of interest. The volume of results from the search is unlikely to be a problem for a topic with a distinct vocabulary because a search concept and the terms describing it may easily distinguish between the relevant and irrelevant literature, though this might vary between different resources. It is more common to find that there is a wide variation of vocabulary in the literature of interest (such as health inequalities or community development) and it is difficult to distinguish it from literature that is not of interest. There seem to be three ways to address the problems of the volume and breadth of search results (Stansfield, 2018):

- Creating a search that aims for a high sensitivity for finding relevant studies and at the same time aims for a manageable precision by reducing the number of irrelevant studies within a resource.
- Using selective searches, which aim for high precision and may also aim for breadth, through a series of selective searches that are focused on a range of concepts.
- Developing searches that are deliberately sensitive and then applying machine learning to automate or prioritise the search results for screening (see Chapter 7).

In practice, a combination of these approaches might be used and there should be a clear rationale for using them that is informed by considerable testing and iteration. Examples are provided in the case studies described later in this chapter.

Research question

The extent of the sources and approaches chosen depends on the research question and scope of the literature sought and how comprehensive or selective the literature review is intended to be

(Stansfield, 2018). This is underpinned by the purpose and use of the completed systematic review. The search methods used will vary according to the type of review, for example a scoping review of key research in a topic area might only use databases that are key to the discipline areas covered, whereas a mapping review covering the nature and extent of the literature may use a broader range of sources and techniques (Booth, Papaioannou and Sutton, 2016, 127). The clear understanding of the sources and approaches may not emerge until later in development for reviews that are undertaken iteratively. For other reviews, the search approach is often informed by a preliminary searching phase, followed by implementing the search in a more linear way. They differ from iterative approaches as the results of the search used for the final systematic review are not assessed to reformulate a new search.

The familiarisation with the research question and the scope of the literature often takes place while the protocol for the systematic review is being developed. The process of understanding the literature might be through searching databases or using search engines and other search tools to optimise finding relevant and diverse literature related to the topic. It might also involve consulting other information specialists, researchers and topic experts (see Chapter 11).

It can take time to design and test suitable combinations of search terms for broad-based topics. Helpful starting points can be drawing on existing search filters if they are available, using approaches described in the literature or adapting search concepts from systematic reviews on similar topics. However, it is worth bearing in mind that a search strategy reported in a systematic review serves as a description of what was done at the time and may not be what the authors would choose to re-run with the benefit of hindsight (Brunton et al., 2017, 110). Furthermore, within the same domain, search terms may behave differently, as shown in the following examples:

- A search strategy identifying studies on the prognosis of work disability had varied performance across different health conditions (Kok et al., 2015).
- A set of search terms to find health-related values differed depending on whether the focus was on dementia, diabetes, obesity or schizophrenia (Petrova et al., 2012).

Although bibliographic database searching is often considered a main component of a systematic review, the same principles apply to those supplementary techniques used in searching for other types of evidence or choosing resources. This means that a thoughtful, reasoned approach should be taken in deciding which sources to use and how they are searched or browsed.

Guidance and different approaches to searching

Guidance, commentaries, research studies and networks with information specialists can help inform choices of where and how to search. There is, though, a paucity of literature that is focused on broad-based topics, particularly outside searching for reviews of effectiveness (Stansfield, 2018). The literature tends to focus on particular subject areas, study types (such as qualitative research) or searching techniques. The Campbell Collaboration has published guidance on literature searching for reviews on education, social welfare and crime and justice (Kugley et al., 2017) and it is supplemented by a 'methods note' on databases and other online resources to search for reviews of interventions in international development (Campbell Collaboration, 2014). General guidance on reviews of health promotion and public health interventions is set out in Cochrane guidelines (Armstrong, Waters and Doyle, 2011).

Books or book chapters that cover systematic searching across discipline areas include: Booth, Papaioannou and Sutton (2016), Brunton et al. (2017), White (2009) and Petticrew and Roberts (2006), though they generally use examples from health, education, social welfare and social science. Examples of methodology-related reviews are: a review on the search methods of qualitative systematic reviews (Booth, 2016); methods for checking reference lists (Horsley, Dingwall and Sampson, 2011); methods for searching for quasi-experimental studies (Glanville et al., 2017); methods covering supplementary search methods (Cooper et al., 2017); and methods focusing on searching for environmental evidence (Livoreil et al., 2017). There is a resource list for health resources in international development developed collaboratively by information specialists (https://epoc.cochrane.org/lmic-databases) which provides hints on using individual resources (Stansfield et al., 2013).

There are a variety of approaches described in the literature on searching for broad-based topics. Sandieson (2006) describes a process of 'pearl harvesting' in which a comprehensive set of synonyms is generated and tested for identifying relevant articles for specific topics; these are maintained via a wiki (https://sites.google.com/view/pearl-harvesting-search/home). Finfgeld-Connett and Johnson (2013) used an approach to searching described by Boell and Cecez-Kecmanovic (2010) that involves using selective search terms to identify a small set of relevant literature, which is used for further targeted searches to locate additional publications. Booth et al. (2013) propose a set of systematic procedures, described as 'CLUSTER searching', for realist reviews, where the type and focus of the literature sought potentially changes throughout the review (see Chapter 2). There is appeal in avoiding a long list of similar databases to facilitate using a range of search techniques, such as citation searching and website searching, and this has been explored in public health intervention reviews (Morgan et al., 2015; Tuvey et al., 2018).

There are a range of potential influences on the nature of individual search strategies that can help in designing a search strategy (Stansfield, 2018). Understanding these influences provides for flexibility in a systematic process and in developing approaches that are suitable for a particular research problem. These influences include:

1   The input of people from the review team and topic experts.
2   The range of processes and approaches used from testing to documenting the search strategies.
3   Drawing on library resources and websites to inform on sources to search and, where available, similar systematic reviews and external research registers of likely relevant studies.
4   Research evidence on information retrieval methods.
5   Using technology such as text mining and utilising available functionality in databases.
6   Specific standards and expectations for the literature search that are required by an organization or services.
7   Considering information seeking as problem-solving activity (Hung et al., 2008) and a creative process (Zins, 2000).

Information specialists who are able to engage with and reflect on these influences will have an increased understanding of searching systematically and improved awareness of the opportunities and limitations of the process (Stansfield, 2018).

The current practice of designing search strategies is underpinned by generic guidance on searching processes, some empirical literature on methods and on practical experience (Stansfield, 2018). There is a limited evidence-base on the value and the suitability of different information retrieval methods (Booth, 2016; Delaney and Tamás, 2018; Glanville et al., 2017). Furthermore, each literature search presents a unique challenge to working out ways of searching systematically and efficiently (Stansfield, 2018). Each time an information specialist starts a new search there will be decisions to make about translating the research question into searchable concepts, prioritising where to search and in navigating and using resources to find evidence. Overall, it is tackling these challenges that can ease the tension between being efficient and sensitive in searching systematically.

Practical examples of approaches to take

The examples of approaches described here are selected to illustrate a variety of processes and techniques that can be used to search systematically for broad-based topics. Searching for broad-based topics might utilise a similar approach to discrete topics, although it would probably require more time to develop and test the search strategy. For example, the database searching could use a wider range of sources from different disciplines, while the search strategy itself could encompass many variants of terminology (Golder, Mason and Spilsbury, 2008). Considering suitable ways to restrict a search might involve, for example, only searching for studies published in a recent timeframe. There may be clear ways to safely exclude studies from a search without inadvertently excluding relevant studies; for example, it might be appropriate to exclude studies indexed with 'child' from a review about older adults (while taking care to retain studies indexed with both child and adult).

Alternatively, other techniques are more appropriate for broad-based topics. The examples below are highlighted for their novelty and focus in tackling a variety of challenges. These methods show how information specialists reflect on the overall approach they take to the search and do not just focus on making small tweaks to database strategies.

Test searches

Having a varied pool of references relevant to the topic can inform the search, while being careful that the search is not designed around locating *only* those studies. The pool of references might be sourced from focused or iterative searching using search engines, specialised registers, systematic reviews and bibliographic databases, and from utilising functions to find cited papers and related items. The aim is to quickly build up a varied sample of relevant studies on which to help expand ways of thinking about where to search, appropriate search concepts and search terms. The samples of studies may also be used as a way of testing the retrieval within individual databases and may improve the choice of search terms used. Case studies 3.1 and 3.2 help to illustrate how these ideas might be put into practice.

> **Case study 3.1: Testing and refining the scope of a multi-faceted review**
>
> In a review on self-care of minor ailments, designing the search strategy involved several iterations of running test searches and screening for two purposes: it gave the authors an understanding of the range of literature potentially available for each research question, and it helped to guide decisions on how this evidence might be captured by database search strategies (Richardson et al., 2018).

> **Case study 3.2: Standalone report not published in a journal**
>
> A standalone report not published in a journal was found on Google Scholar during an exploratory search. Search strategies were then designed for Google Scholar (Haddaway et al., 2015) but testing showed the report would not be retrieved again as it was too low down the list of search results. The report was not located on the other databases that were planned to be searched. However, it was found to be discoverable on the Bielefeld Academic Search Engine (BASE), prompting BASE to be added to the review protocol specifically for identifying possible non-journal reports that might not be found from the other sources (Lorenc and Lester, 2018).

Conceptualising the search

Structuring the research question into searchable concepts can be challenging and it is informed by testing. Some concepts may be too broad for the context they are intended, for example in a search about risk communication and risk concepts in dementia care, Stevenson, Taylor and Knox (2016) chose to focus on terms for risk and dementia.

They avoided using 'care' as a concept as it was found to be too diffuse to define within the contexts they were interested in. They observe that 'care' includes, amongst others, location of care, types of carers and other professionals, services and service policies.

Some concepts may be definable but broad. Their combination with other concepts is needed to specify their meaning. Some concepts need to be very specific in order to be distinguished from irrelevant literature. For example, for a guideline on care and support for older people with learning disabilities (NICE, 2018), the population terms for specific conditions were required to be in close proximity to certain population or service user terms to reduce the volume of unwanted clinical studies, for example, the terms 'adult' and 'service' had to be within five words of 'learning disability' (Stansfield, O'Mara-Eves and Thomas, 2017). If there are several research questions that need to be addressed on the same topic with concepts common to each review question, it may be more appropriate to develop a collective search strategy than to develop separate strategies to address each question in turn (see Case study 3.3).

> **Case study 3.3: Collective search strategies for multiple questions**
> A collective search strategy was used for sets of reviews that informed the development of social care guidelines as each had common populations and settings with no clear outcomes (Stansfield and Liabo, 2017). Using this approach made the search inclusive, though It may have increased the effort needed to screen the results as each paper had to be examined for its suitability for multiple questions. For one set of reviews, a broad study design filter was used (covering trials, cost-effectiveness, qualitative studies and other research on people's views) because the test searching had shown it would be beneficial to reduce the yield of studies on prevalence or describing the characteristics of a population (Stansfield and Liabo, 2017).

Developing sets of search terms

Developing sets of search terms can involve both considering ways to increase precision and increase sensitivity. This can involve knowledge of the literature, published pre-existing searches in related areas, topic expertise, database thesauri, iterative searching, browsing citations within databases and text mining (Stansfield, O'Mara-Eves and Thomas, 2017). The search terms used on individual databases might vary depending on the subject coverage and indexing, search functionality and size.

The value of relying on controlled vocabulary terms could vary between databases. Bayliss, Davenport and Pennant (2014) found, when searching for studies on public health intervention programmes, that some index terms could improve search precision in MEDLINE, while the same approach had poor sensitivity in Embase. Another consideration is that the indexing terms may not match the focus of the review question and may be too broad or narrowly focused. For a review on self-care for minor ailments (Richardson et al., 2018), a range of conceptual perspectives were relevant and so 'self care' was one of many indexing terms used, alongside 'consumer health information', 'remote consultation' and 'pharmacies'.

Search strategies are often run across several databases and one useful approach is to develop a set of free-text terms that can be used on similar types of databases, while using indexing terms specific to an individual resource. Proximity searching (where two free-text search terms are within a specific proximity of each other) is useful to increase precision, though it may miss some studies (see Case study 3.4).

Case study 3.4: Proximity searching
Databases that generate a relatively small volume of references provide an opportunity to search more sensitively than in other databases. Proximity phrase searching missed at least one study on the large nursing database Cumulative Index to Nursing and Allied Health Literature (CINAHL), which was found on the smaller database British Nursing Index (BNI) because a more sensitive strategy (using AND rather than proximity) was used (Stansfield and Liabo, 2017). The searches again emphasise the need to test search strategies and to adapt them to the database being searched.

High volume versus stepped searches

Two contrasting approaches by different research teams towards processing high volumes of literature on broad topics are illustrated in the following case studies. Case study 3.5 uses sensitive searches and applies automation to aid screening. In the stepped approaches in Case

Case study 3.5: Extreme reviewing
Shemilt et al. (2014) describe a case of 'extreme reviewing', using text mining to prioritise the references that were manually screened for two scoping reviews where the literature searches collected over 800,000 records. These reviews had ill-defined boundaries relating to behaviour change interventions. (See Chapter 7 for further discussion on text mining.)

studies 3.6 and 3.7, relevant literature from the initial searches are incorporated into the review and then used to inform subsequent searches.

Case study 3.6: Iterative and selective searches
A review on whole-systems approaches to obesity (Garside et al., 2010) was undertaken iteratively to build a series of results as the scope of whole-systems approaches was ill-defined at the start of the project and was developed as the initial evidence was reviewed (Levay, Raynor and Tuvey 2015). This approach, as discussed in Chapter 1, led in unexpected directions as it followed leads on the use of whole-systems approaches to smoking cessation, which helped to inform the understanding of the concept.

Case study 3.7: A stepped approach to searching
A stepped approach to searching was undertaken for two systematic reviews on interventions for preventing drug misuse (NICE, 2017), comprising: searching for systematic reviews; backward citation and forward citation searches; database searches for primary studies limited to a recent timeframe; website searches; database searches specifically on named intervention programmes; and references from previous NICE guidelines. This stepped approach was used to mitigate a high volume of search results and the broad scope of the review. The review focused on drug misuse, with no discrete boundaries on the population or setting, and covered a range of study designs to answer questions on effectiveness of interventions and acceptability and perspectives of interventions.

Using existing systematic reviews

Systematic reviews and a research register were used to identify diffuse primary research in Case study 3.8.

Case study 3.8: Review of community engagement and health inequalities
O'Mara-Eves et al. (2014) describe using a sample of systematic reviews to find primary studies for obtaining a purposive sample of studies for a review on community engagement for reducing health inequalities. They used a sample of systematic reviews of public health interventions and sought further primary studies from a research register of health promotion trials (Trials Register of Promoting Health Interventions (TRoPHI)), which itself is populated from systematic searching and screening (Brunton et al., 2017, 103; O'Mara-Eves et al., 2014).

The population focus was on people with health inequalities but the studies were only screened for their focus on health inequalities at the full-text screening stage. This is because studies that contain data on subgroups do not always refer to these in the abstract and using inequalities filters can exclude relevant studies, since authors used a wide range of terms to describe a population (Oliver et al., 2008). There were benefits in searching the evidence tables and reference lists of the full-text publications but it is also important to consider the time and costs involved in taking this approach (Brunton et al., 2015).

Full-text searches

Sometimes full-text searching may be an appropriate and feasible option in conjunction with searching abstracting and indexing databases (as in Case study 3.9).

Case study 3.9: Tracking research from the Millennium Cohort Study

This approach was used in order to locate research that utilised the data of a UK-wide cohort study, the Millennium Cohort Study. While the search only used the concept Millennium Cohort Study and some word variations, full-text searching was found to be feasible and necessary for locating some research as the name of the cohort study was not always mentioned in the titles and abstracts of relevant studies (Kneale et al., 2016). A challenge with full-text databases is that they may be publisher-specific or contain less search functionality than abstract and indexing databases.

Future directions

There seems to be an increasing need for systematic searching for literature on broad-based topics. The widening range of information resources available to search, along with increased functionality and information content, looks set to continue. This, coupled with changes in how research is published and disseminated, will influence how this evidence is located. Chapters 7 to 9 discuss the role of text mining, linked data and automated evidence surveillance systems. These technologies and systems are likely to alter some of the processes in identifying studies. Furthermore, information specialists will need to contribute to an increasing variety of products that require systematic searching techniques.

While the resources, tools, processes and outputs may change, information specialists will still need to design and implement systematic search strategies addressing specific research questions. The challenges of finding a representative sample of a diverse range of relevant literature will remain, and information specialists will hopefully share and collaborate on ways to address these. Research ought to continue into developing and evaluating different approaches for searching, and how they impact on both the review processes and the set of relevant studies used in reviews. Different perspectives gained from the adoption of systematic searching methods across various subject domains can contribute to this.

Conclusion

Systematic literature searching for broad-based topics is undertaken in a variety of ways. Particular attention is needed to plan an approach appropriate to the research question that chooses the right sources and searches them effectively for the topic and format of evidence required. This chapter has discussed a range of search techniques that seek to be systematic and sensitive, while being efficient in the volume of irrelevant literature that needs to be manually screened. Understanding the influences on searching can provide for more flexibility and facilitate the iterative approaches discussed in Chapter 1. Information specialists need to combine an understanding of systematic searching with information-seeking skills to address these challenges. The use of new technologies, reflective practice and research evidence can contribute to improving methods in this area.

Suggestions for further reading

Adams, J., Hillier-Brown, F. C., Moore, H. J., Lake, A. A., Araujo-Soares, V., White, M. and Summerbell, C. (2016) Searching and Synthesising 'Grey Literature' and 'Grey Information' in Public Health: critical reflections on three case studies, *Systematic Reviews*, **5**, 164.

Bayliss, H. R. and Beyer, F. R. (2015) Information Retrieval for Ecological Syntheses, *Research Synthesis Methods*, **6** (2), 136-148.

Booth, A., Papaioannou, D. and Sutton, A. (2016) *Systematic Approaches to a Successful Literature Review*, 2nd edn, SAGE Publishing.

Brunton, G., Stansfield, C., Caird, J. and Thomas, J. (2017) Finding Relevant Studies. In Gough, D., Oliver, S. and Thomas, J. (eds), *An Introduction to Systematic Reviews*, 2nd edn, SAGE Publishing.

Delaney, A. and Tamás, P. A. (2018) Searching for Evidence or Approval? A

Commentary on Database Search in Systematic Reviews and Alternative Information Retrieval Methodologies, *Research Synthesis Methods*, **9**, 124-131.

Grayson, L. and Gomersall, A. (2003) *A Difficult Business: finding the evidence for social science reviews*, ESRC UK Centre for Evidence Based Policy and Practice, Working Paper 19.

McGinn, T., Taylor, B., McColgan, M. and McQuilkan, J. (2016) Social Work Literature Searching: current issues with databases and online search engines, *Research on Social Work Practice*, **26** (3), 266-277.

Papaioannou, D., Sutton, A., Carroll, C., Booth, A. and Wong, R. (2010) Literature Searching for Social Science Systematic Reviews: consideration of a range of search techniques, *Health Information and Libraries Journal*, **27** (2), 114-122.

Schucan Bird, K. and Tripney, J. (2011) Systematic Literature Searching in Policy Relevant, Inter-disciplinary Reviews: an example from culture and sport, *Research Synthesis Methods*, **2** (3), 163-173.

Stansfield, C., Dickson, K. and Bangpan, M. (2016) Exploring Issues in the Conduct of Website Searching and Other Online Sources for Systematic Reviews: how can we be systematic?, *Systematic Reviews*, **5** (1), 191.

Tompson, L. and Belur, J. (2016) Information Retrieval in Systematic Reviews: a case study of the crime prevention literature, *Journal of Experimental Criminology*, **12** (2), 187–207.

References

Adams, J., Hillier-Brown, F. C., Moore, H. J., Lake, A. A., Araujo-Soares, V., White, M. and Summerbell, C. (2016) Searching and Synthesising 'Grey Literature' and 'Grey Information' in Public Health: critical reflections on three case studies, *Systematic Reviews*, **5**, 164.

Armstrong, R., Waters, E. and Doyle, J. (2011) Reviews in Health Promotion and Public Health. In Higgins, J. P. T. and Green, S. (eds), *Cochrane Handbook for Systematic Reviews of Interventions (version 5.1.0)*, The Cochrane Collaboration. http://handbook-5-1.cochrane.org

Bayliss, S. E., Davenport, C. F. and Pennant, M. E. (2014) Where and How to Search for Information on the Effectiveness of Public Health Interventions - a Case Study for Prevention of Cardiovascular Disease, *Health Information and Libraries Journal*, **31** (4), 303-313.

Boell, S. K. and Cecez-Kecmanovic, D. (2010) Literature Reviews and the Hermeneutic Circle, *Australian Academic and Research Libraries*, **41** (2), 129-144.

Booth, A. (2016) Searching for Qualitative Research for Inclusion in Systematic Reviews: a structured methodological review, *Systematic Reviews*, **5**, 74.

Booth, A., Harris, J., Croot, E., Springett, J., Campbell, F. and Wilkins, E. (2013) Towards a Methodology for Cluster Searching to Provide Conceptual and Contextual 'Richness' for Systematic Reviews of Complex Interventions: case study (CLUSTER), *BMC Medical Research Methodology*, **13**, 118.

Booth, A., Papaioannou, D. and Sutton, A. (2016) *Systematic Approaches to a Successful Literature Review*, 2nd edn, SAGE Publishing.

Brettle, A. J., Long, A. F., Grant, M. J. and Greenhalgh, J. (1998) Searching for Information on Outcomes: do you need to be comprehensive? *Quality in Health Care*, **7** (3), 163-167.

Brunton, G., Stansfield, C., Caird, J. and Thomas, J. (2017) Finding Relevant Studies. In Gough, D., Oliver, S. and Thomas, J. (eds), *An Introduction to Systematic Reviews*, 2nd edn, SAGE Publishing.

Brunton, G., Stokes, G., Shemilt, I., Caird, J., Sutcliffe, K., Stansfield, C. and Thomas, J. (2015) Searching for Trials in Systematic Reviews Versus a Specialist Trials Register: a case study comparison of source, time and costs, paper presented at Cochrane Colloquium, Vienna, Austria, 7 October 2015. https://abstracts.cochrane.org/2015-vienna/searching-trials-systematic-reviews-versus-specialist-trials-register-case-study

Campbell Collaboration (2014) Systematic Reviews in International Development: key online databases. https://www.campbellcollaboration.org/images/id/Database_Guide_for_SRs_in_International_Development.pdf

Cooper, C., Lovell, R., Husk, K., Booth, A. and Garside, R. (2017) Supplementary Search Methods were More Effective and Offered Better Value than Bibliographic Database Searching: a case study from public health and environmental enhancement, *Research Synthesis Methods*, **9** (2), 195-223.

Delaney, A. and Tamás, P. A. (2018) Searching for Evidence or Approval? A Commentary on Database Search in Systematic Reviews and Alternative Information Retrieval Methodologies, *Research Synthesis Methods*, **9** (1), 124-131.

Finfgeld-Connett, D. and Johnson, E. D. (2013) Literature Search Strategies for Conducting Knowledge-building and Theory-generating Qualitative Systematic Reviews, *Journal of Advanced Nursing*, **69** (1), 194-204.

Francis, D., Turley, R., Thomson, H., Weightman, A., Waters, E. and Moore, L. (2015) Supporting the Needs of Public Health Decision-makers and Review Authors in the UK, *Journal of Public Health*, **37** (1), 172-174.

Garside, R., Pearson, M., Hunt, H., Moxham, T. and Anderson, R. (2010) *Identifying the key elements and interactions of a whole system approach to obesity prevention*, Peninsula Technology Assessment Group. https://www.nice.org.uk/guidance/ph42/evidence/review-1-identifying-the-key-elements-and-interactions-of-a-whole-system-approach-to-obesity-prevention-pdf-69056029

Glanville, J., Eyers, J., Jones, A. M., Shemilt, I., Wang, G., Johansen, M., Fiander, M. and Rothstein, H. (2017) Quasi-experimental Study Designs Series - Paper 8: identifying quasi-experimental studies to inform systematic reviews, *Journal of Clinical Epidemiology*, **89**, 67-76.

Golder, S., Mason, A. and Spilsbury, K. (2008) Systematic Searches for the Effectiveness of Respite Care, *Journal of the Medical Library Association*, **96** (2), 147-152.

Grayson, L. and Gomersall, A. (2003) *A Difficult Business: finding the evidence for social science reviews*, ESRC UK Centre for Evidence Based Policy and Practice, Working Paper 19.

Haddaway, N. R., Collins, A. M., Coughlin, D. and Kirk, S. (2015) The Role of Google Scholar in Evidence Reviews and its Applicability to Grey Literature Searching, *PLOS ONE*, **10** (9), e0138237.

Harris, J. L., Booth, A., Cargo, M., Hannes, K., Harden, A., Flemming, K., Garside, R., Pantoja, T., Thomas, J. and Noyes, J. (2018) Cochrane Qualitative and Implementation Methods Group Guidance Series - Paper 2: methods for question formulation, searching, and protocol development for qualitative evidence synthesis, *Journal of Clinical Epidemiology*, **97**, 39-48.

Horsley, T., Dingwall, O. and Sampson, M. (2011) Checking Reference Lists to Find Additional Studies for Systematic Reviews, *Cochrane Database of Systematic Reviews*, **8**, MR000026.

Hung, P. W., Johnson, S. B., Kaufman, D. R. and Mendonça, E. A. (2008) A Multi-level Model of Information Seeking in the Clinical Domain, *Journal of Biomedical Informatics*, **41** (2), 357-370.

Kneale, D., Patalay, P., Khatwa, M., Stansfield, C., Fitzsimons, E. and Thomas, J. (2016) *Piloting and Producing a Map of Millennium Cohort Study Data Usage: where are data underutilized and where is granularity lost?*, EPPI-Centre, Social Science Research Unit, UCL Institute of Education,

University College London.
https://eppi.ioe.ac.uk/cms/Default.aspx?tabid=3502

Kok, R., Verbeek, J. A., Faber, B., van Dijk, F. J. and Hoving, J. L. (2015) A Search Strategy to Identify Studies on the Prognosis of Work Disability: a diagnostic test framework, *BMJ Open*, **5** (5), e006315.

Kugley, S., Wade, A., Thomas, J., Mahood, Q., Jørgensen, A-M. K., Hammerstrøm, K. and Sathe, N. (2017) *Searching for Studies: a guide to information retrieval for Campbell Systematic Reviews - Campbell Methods Series Guide 1*, The Campbell Collaboration.
www.campbellcollaboration.org/library/searching-for-studies-information-retrieval-guide-campbell-reviews.html

Lancaster, F. W. and Warner, A. J. (1993) *Information Retrieval Today*, Information Resources Press.

Levay, P., Raynor, M. and Tuvey, D. (2015) The Contributions of MEDLINE, Other Bibliographic Databases and Various Search Techniques to NICE Public Health Guidance, *Evidence Based Library and Information Practice*, **10** (1), 50-68.

Livoreil, B., Glanville, J., Haddaway, N. R., Bayliss, H., Bethel, A., de Lachapelle, F. F., Robalino, S., Savilaakso, S., Zhou, W., Petrokofsky, G. and Frampton, G. (2017) Systematic Searching for Environmental Evidence Using Multiple Tools and Sources, *Environmental Evidence*, **6**, 23.

Lorenc, T. and Lester, S. (2018) Adverse Childhood Experiences (ACEs): systematic review of reviews of effectiveness and qualitative data. PROSPERO, CRD42018092192.
www.crd.york.ac.uk/prospero/display_record.php?RecordID=92192

Morgan, H. E., Klerings, I., Searchfield, L. E., Demeyin, W., Burns, L., Griebler, U., Levay, P. and Weightman, A. L. (2015) Systematic Reviews of Public Health Interventions to Support Practice and Policy: where should you look?, Poster, Evidence Based Library and Information Practice (EBLIP8), Queensland University of Technology, Brisbane, Australia, 6-8 July 2015.

NICE (2017) *Drug Misuse Prevention: targeted interventions - Appendix 2 to Evidence Review 1*, NICE Guideline (NG64).
www.nice.org.uk/guidance/ng64/documents/evidence-review-3

NICE (2018) *NICE Guideline: Care and support of older people with learning disabilities.* NICE guideline (NG96). www.nice.org.uk/guidance/ng96

Oliver, S., Dickson, K. and Bangpan, M. (2015) *Systematic Reviews: making them policy relevant. A briefing for policy makers and systematic reviewers,*

EPPI-Centre, Social Science Research Unit, UCL Institute of Education, University College London. www.who.int/alliance-hpsr/projects/eppi/en

Oliver, S., Kavanagh, J., Caird, J., Lorenc, T., Oliver, K., Harden, A., Thomas, J., Greaves, A. and Oakley, A. (2008) *Health Promotion, Inequalities and Young People's Health: a systematic review of research*, EPPI-Centre, Social Science Research Unit, UCL Institute of Education, University College London. https://eppi.ioe.ac.uk/cms/Default.aspx?tabid=2410

O'Mara-Eves, A., Brunton, G., McDaid, D., Kavanagh, J., Oliver, S. and Thomas, J. (2014) Techniques for Identifying Cross-disciplinary and 'Hard-to-detect' Evidence for Systematic Review, *Research Synthesis Methods*, **5** (1), 50-59.

Papaioannou, D., Sutton, A., Carroll, C., Booth, A. and Wong, R. (2010) Literature Searching for Social Science Systematic Reviews: consideration of a range of search techniques, *Health Information and Libraries Journal*, **27** (2), 114-122.

Petrova, M., Sutcliffe, P., Fulford, K. W. M. and Dale, J. (2012) Search Terms and a Validated Brief Search Filter to Retrieve Publications on Health-related Values in MEDLINE: a word frequency analysis study, *Journal of the American Medical Informatics Association*, **19** (3), 479-488.

Petticrew, M. and Roberts, H. (2006) How to Find the Studies: the literature search. In Petticrew, M. and Roberts, H., *Systematic Reviews in the Social Sciences: a practical guide*, Wiley-Blackwell.

Richardson, M., Khouja, C., Sutcliffe, K., Hinds, K., Stansfield, C. and Thomas, J. (2018) *Decision-making and Behaviour Change in Self-care for Minor Ailments: a systematic review to evaluate how people decide, and how they can be directed, to use the most appropriate service*, EPPI-Centre, Social Science Research Unit, UCL Institute of Education, University College London.

Sandieson, R. (2006) Pathfinding in the Research Forest: the Pearl Harvesting method for effective information retrieval, *Education and Training in Developmental Disabilities*, **41** (4), 401-409.

Shemilt, I., Simon, A., Hollands, G. J., Marteau, T. M., Ogilvie, D., O'Mara-Eves, A., Kelly, M. P. and Thomas, J. (2014) Pinpointing Needles in Giant Haystacks: use of text mining to reduce impractical screening workload in extremely large scoping reviews, *Research Synthesis Methods*, **5** (1), 31-49.

Stansfield, C. (2018) *Exploring Search Strategy Design to Identify Diverse Literature for Inclusion in Systematic Reviews*, PhD Thesis, University College London. http://discovery.ucl.ac.uk/10053319

Stansfield, C., Dickson, K. and Bangpan, M. (2016) Exploring Issues in the Conduct of Website Searching and Other Online Sources for Systematic Reviews. How can we be systematic?, *Systematic Reviews*, **5** (1), 191.

Stansfield, C. and Liabo, K. (2017) Identifying Social Care Literature: case studies from guideline development, *Evidence Based Library and Information Practice*, **12** (3), 114-131.

Stansfield, C., O'Mara-Eves, A. and Thomas, J. (2017) Text Mining for Search Term Development in Systematic Reviewing: a discussion of some methods and challenges, *Research Synthesis Methods*, **8** (3), 355-365.

Stansfield, C., Weightman, A., Kavanagh, J. and Johansen, M. (2013) Cochrane Update: identifying health related research resources relevant to low and middle income countries, *Journal of Public Health*, **35** (3), 477-480.

Stevenson, M., Taylor, B. J. and Knox, J. (2016) Risk in Dementia Care: searching for the evidence, *Health, Risk and Society*, **18** (1-2), 4-20.

Stewart, R., van Rooyen, C. and de Wet, T. (2012) Purity or Pragmatism? Reflecting on the Use of Systematic Review Methodology in Development, *Journal of Development Effectiveness*, **4** (3), 430-444.

Tuvey, D., Walton, L., Levay, P. and Heath, A. (2018) Efficient Searching for Public Health: can we search fewer sources?, presentation at *NICE Joint Information Day*, London, 28 February 2018. https://medicinesevents.nice.org.uk/NPC/media/uploaded/EVNPC/event_272/P2_Efficient_choice_of_sources_for_PHGs_-_JID_2018_-_FINAL_for_website.pdf

White, H. (2009) Scientific Communication and Literature Retrieval. In Cooper, H., Hedges, L. V. and Valentine, J. C. (eds), *The Handbook of Research Synthesis and Meta-Analysis*, 2nd edn, Russell Sage Foundation.

Zins, C. (2000) Success, a Structured Search Strategy: rationale, principles, and implications, *Journal of the American Association for Information Science*, **51** (13), 1232-1247.

4

Choosing the right databases and search techniques

Alison Bethel and Morwenna Rogers

Introduction

In this chapter we will explore how to choose resources and techniques to provide the best results. Systematic searching is most often associated with systematic reviews in health care. However, systematic searching is also a key element of scoping reviews, systematic maps and realist reviews. The issues we describe here will certainly be useful when undertaking literature searching in any subject field including health, education and environment. By the end, you will have confidence in how to plan for your search, how to select the best sources to search and the best way to utilise those resources to maximise returns without increasing time pressures or workload.

The often cited rule for systematic review searching is that searches should be comprehensive and find all the available evidence relating to the research question. Chapters 2 and 3 have shown that a search may actually aim for representativeness rather than completeness. Focusing on the sensitivity of electronic database searches assumes that the best evidence is available on bibliographic databases. An important first step to take, therefore, is to ask which other techniques we might need to find the evidence, as well as deciding which databases we will search.

Advice on the most effective sources and best search techniques is readily available from librarians and other information specialists and it is particularly useful from those who have expertise in the relevant topic area. There are a number of studies comparing the content and functionality of different databases, comparing which method of searching finds the most relevant studies, or those examining different searches across databases. Despite this, the choice of resources to use in a search requires a combination of knowledge, intuition, availability and occasionally luck.

A rapidly changing world

Traditionally, systematic searching on health topics has focused on finding the best evidence, usually in the form of randomised controlled trials (RCTs), either published in journals or unpublished in registries of clinical trials. This model makes resource selection relatively straightforward. It is becoming increasingly common to see reviews take new approaches (see Chapter 2), include a variety of study types (for example, qualitative evidence) or synthesise reports and other documents often found in the grey literature (see Chapter 5). Grant and Booth (2009) categorised 14 types of review, each with associated methodologies, and it is important to apply the techniques appropriate to the study that is being undertaken. This ballooning of the review world means that identifying and choosing resources is not as straight-forward as perhaps it once was.

The rapid explosion in the amount and type of information available online (see Chapter 6) has led to an emergence of new technologies such as text mining to find related or similar studies (see Chapter 7), and machine learning to reduce the screening burden (see Chapter 9). However, until databases become more closely integrated with text mining software, reference management systems and software for machine learning, and while the publishing world is made up of many organizations with their multitude of journals, databases and interface products, information specialists will need to choose carefully the databases and search techniques appropriate to their review.

Choosing the right sources

Choosing which resources should be searched, and what techniques should be used, is dependent primarily on three factors:

1   The research question.
2   The time and resources available.
3   Access to information sources.

The research question

A well-structured research question is invaluable when choosing databases and search techniques. It will tell you whether you need to focus on databases covering health, social sciences, education or a combination of these, if the question traverses disciplines. The research question will tell you whether the focus is on a profession (for example, nurses or teachers) or on 'clients' (for example, patients or school pupils), or on a condition (for example, research on mental health). It will tell you whether location is important: is it a setting such as a hospital or care home, or a country or geographical region?

The research question will also tell you what type of evidence is required. The information specialist needs to consider the best places to find that type of evidence. Is the evidence available on bibliographic databases or would searching those waste our time when we could concentrate on something more productive? Questions that are seeking qualitative evidence about experiences or barriers to change may not need the same databases as when we need to answer a question asking if one medical intervention is more effective than another.

The time and resources available

It is important to prioritise your choice of databases and search techniques when resources are limited:

> Comprehensive searching is resource intensive, due not only to the time and cost required to physically carry out the searches, but also to the work invested in preparing the search strategies and managing and screening the results. If each source used produces unique eligible studies for the systematic review, then this represents an efficient use of resources, but may otherwise be a source of inefficiency.
>
> (Beyer and Wright, 2013, 50)

To help with this planning process, experienced information specialists will carry out extensive scoping searches during the review planning stage. Scoping searches are a way of finding out:

- what literature is out there.
- how much of it there is.
- broadly the number of records to screen.
- some key papers on a topic.
- useful free-text search terms.
- appropriate headings from the controlled vocabulary.
- relevant systematic reviews.
- other related studies.
- relevant databases to search.
- ideas on which supplementary search techniques to employ.

TIP:
Seek out high-quality evidence first in scoping searches, i.e. systematic reviews, either by searching databases of systematic reviews or using limits or filters in databases in the field of interest. Finding a number of systematic reviews could indicate there is a large body of primary studies; finding no existing systematic reviews may indicate a lack of evidence or gaps in our knowledge of the topic.

The information gathered during the scoping searches will provide details of how long the search could take and, therefore, the cost. Decisions can then be made on resource (time and cost) availability when planning the next steps.

Access to information sources

An information specialist is limited by the tools available: the choice of resources used in a systematic review will always be restricted by access to them. Organizations do not always have access to all of the databases that might be identified during the scoping searches. The information specialist needs to understand the issues this may cause and consider whether a comprehensive search could still be performed. For example, a review examining the effects of healthy eating incentives in schools would benefit from using the freely accessible PubMed, but it could be severely limited if the team did not also have access to education and social science databases.

Databases and journals are often supplied by subscription to institutions via an intermediate provider or multiple providers. It is not unusual therefore for institutions to not have access to particular databases or journals and the choices faced by the reviewer are subsequently curbed. This will be a limitation of the review that the information specialist will need to discuss with the rest of the review team (see Chapter 11).

Advice on sources

Handbooks and guidelines in specific fields can be useful in helping to choose your databases and search techniques. In health care, where Cochrane reviews are considered to be high quality, there is plenty of advice. The *Cochrane Handbook* chapter on searching (Lefebvre, Manheimer and Glanville, 2011) says this on source selection:

> The Cochrane Central Register of Controlled Trials (CENTRAL), MEDLINE and Embase (if access is available to either the review author or the trials search co-ordinator) should be searched for all Cochrane reviews.   (Lefebvre, Manheimer and Glanville, 2011)

The Centre for Reviews and Dissemination Handbook (2009, 17) states: 'MEDLINE and Embase are the databases most commonly used to identify studies'.

In the area of social sciences, the Campbell Collaboration (Kugley et al., 2017) are more general with their advice:

> ... decisions related to which subject-specific databases are to be searched, in addition to the main field-related databases, will be influenced by the topic of the review, access to specific databases, and budget considerations.   (Kugley et al., 2017, 11)

In the environmental field the Collaboration for Environmental Evidence Guidelines (Pullin et al., 2018, 5.2.1) suggest: '... start the search using the source where the largest number of relevant papers are likely to be found'.

These recommendations obviously require the information specialist to have done some scoping searches and to have some prior knowledge of the topic area. The review team needs an information specialist because it is unlikely that a core set of resources can be defined for all searches and it needs the appropriate expertise to test and define a suitable list for the particular research question.

Of course, guidelines are just that and there is no better substitute for knowing your own area and having a broad experience of a selection of databases and what they contain. Published guidance can therefore be quite general. The Joanna Briggs Institute (www.joannabriggs.org) recommends that a search should be 'as broad and as inclusive as possible' and observes that there is 'insufficient evidence to suggest that searching a particular number or even particular databases will identify all of the evidence on a particular topic'. The number of databases to search is just as important as choosing the right ones and deciding how best to find grey literature and other information sources (Booth, 2010). We should never search a database just because we have access to it without thinking about its relevance to our research question, the type of evidence we need and the time available for the project. The number of databases that should be searched is covered in more detail later.

The key to choosing the best resources is good preparation. It is to be hoped that by the time of the main searches, the information specialist will have helped the review team to reach a well-defined research question with clear expectations of the search. Scoping searches will have indicated how much literature might be returned

Case study 4.1: Experiences of carers

Sandra is carrying out a qualitative evidence synthesis about the experiences of people who care for those with dementia. She carries out extensive scoping searches, initially using PubMed, and finds a handful of useful studies. However, when she searches on Google Scholar she finds many studies that are not present on PubMed and a rich source of information in the form of blogs and book chapters. On the advice of an information specialist she extends her search to PsycINFO, which includes books, and Cumulative Index to Nursing and Allied Health Literature (CINAHL), which has several subject headings for qualitative research. She finds many more relevant studies.

In the subsequent protocol, the search methods state that the databases MEDLINE, PsycINFO and CINAHL will be searched, along with blog sites, websites relevant to dementia and other sources of grey literature about carers. The protocol also shows that experts in the field will be consulted for additional studies and sources.

by the searches. Experts will have been consulted on the key papers in the topic and the types of evidence required. Review authors should not proceed beyond this point without consulting an information specialist on what databases are relevant to the topic and whether they will return the study types required. Case study 4.1 describes in more detail how this process might actually work in practice.

Practical issues to consider

We have discussed some of the principles underlying the choice of sources. The next section will look at some of the practical issues in selecting how to find the best evidence according to the topic and type of information required for the research question, the time and resources available and the access you have.

Topic area of the question

The database has to be relevant to the topic of the research question. There is no point searching a database just because you have used it before on a different review. A review on a surgical procedure would probably use MEDLINE but that does not mean it should automatically be added to the list of sources for a review on promoting physical activity in schools. In this example, the scoping search should establish the usefulness of MEDLINE and then consider whether it needs to be supplemented with education databases (such as Education Resources Information Center (ERIC)) or the sports science database SPORTDiscus (Hollis et al., 2017).

Type of information required

A research question that needs evidence from randomised controlled trials (RCTs) will not need the same sources as one that needs to understand qualitative evidence. A review requiring RCTs will certainly require a search of CENTRAL, along with MEDLINE and Embase and clinical trials registries. However, qualitative evidence syntheses or mixed methods reviews will also require a search of CINAHL and possibly PsycINFO (if the question relates to mental health or psychology). This is why the information specialist should be tailoring the list of sources: a search for evidence on the clinical effectiveness of tests for HIV will not provide us with the evidence describing the barriers faced by service providers promoting HIV testing to vulnerable populations.

Time and resources available

There is no point planning a search that cannot be completed in the time available to the project. There is also no value in planning a search that would require the team to pay for more subscriptions, article downloads or other resources than the budget will allow. These factors must be balanced against the risk of not finding the appropriate evidence. This section sets out some factors for information specialists to consider.

Functionality of the search platform and interface

If a database cannot be adequately searched because of poor functionality, then is it worth searching at all? This is worth considering, especially if the database is relatively small and unspecialised with no reason to suppose it has any unique content. Some database platforms are not designed for complex searching (Bethel and Rogers, 2014) and searching the same database on different platforms may provide different results (Younger and Boddy, 2009).

There is little doubt that most expert searchers have strong feelings about the functionality of the platforms they use and it is possible that databases are omitted because searching them in a systematic way is simply not possible via particular interfaces. At the time of writing there are no published studies investigating whether the functionality of the interface actually has a real impact on database selection but it is not a scenario that is difficult to imagine. Whether or not to search in these situations requires a little balancing of priorities. Does the possibility of finding relevant studies outweigh the difficulties faced with searching the database? If so, you could compromise by running a quick and simple search, for example by searching a few keywords in the title field, rather than by translating a long complex set of search strings from MEDLINE.

How many databases should we search?

It is usual to see a variation in the number of databases included in different reviews. Specific topics with well-defined inclusion criteria may find sufficient evidence from searching only two or three databases. A study by Vassar et al. (2017) found an average of 2.59 databases were used in clinical neurology reviews. Other subject areas are more diverse and multidisciplinary and the selection of databases will need careful consideration. We found (Bethel and Rogers, 2018) that, on average, 8.9 databases were searched for environmental systematic reviews, suggesting the subject area can affect the number of databases searched. Interestingly, Vassar et al. also found that more databases were usually searched when an information specialist was on the review team, reflecting perhaps increased knowledge and expertise about which resources were best to use. Case study 4.2 describes the typical process of testing out sources and adapting a list of databases for a new review.

Case study 4.2: The physical health of surfers

Finlay is working on a review of the effect of pollution on the physical health of surfers. He plans to search PubMed but is unsure what other databases should be searched. He finds Environment Complete and CAB Abstracts via his university library so adds them too. Following some extensive scoping searches, he identifies some reviews in related areas of environmental research that searched BIOSIS, Web of Science, Scopus, GreenFILE, Aquatic Sciences and Fisheries Abstracts (ASFA) and GEOBASE. He realises he doesn't have any sport databases listed but is not sure whether this is important. Finlay is short of time and there are only two reviewers to help with screening.

   After consultation with a librarian and investigation of coverage of the databases, he decides to search PubMed, Environment Complete, Web of Science, BIOSIS and CAB Abstracts. He decides not to retain ASFA but will include website searching. As Web of Science and Scopus are also citation databases, he uses them to carry out citation searching of key references.

Other studies have looked at what was missed when just one database was searched, concluding that MEDLINE alone, for example, was not sufficient (Betran et al., 2005; Sampson et al., 2003). To add to the uncertainty, studies examined whether it was necessary to search both PubMed and MEDLINE (Damarell, Tieman and Sladek, 2013; Duffy et al., 2016), because PubMed had more content and was updated in advance of MEDLINE. Such decisions must be made bearing in mind time constraints, ease of adapting the search strategy from one database to another and the probability of retrieving unique studies rather than just additional 'noise'.

Lists of valuable databases describing subjects and geographic coverage are easy to locate, for example in the *Cochrane Handbook* chapter on searching (Lefebvre, Manheimer and Glanville, 2011). The University of Massachusetts Medical School Lamar Soutter Library also produces a useful A-Z list of databases and descriptions (https://library.umassmed.edu/resources/databases).

Non-English language and regional databases

It is worth remembering that MEDLINE is produced in the USA and Embase in Europe, even though they are both international in their scope. Geographically relevant databases also play a vital role in reviews that either focus on a specific country or region or which are about subjects that are more pertinent to specific regions. Examples of regional databases include African Index Medicus, IndMed (India) and KoreaMed.

The database LILACS (Latin American and Caribbean Health Sciences Literature) contains scientific and technical literature on health published by Latin American and Caribbean authors and so would be integral in a review of a treatment for an illness predominant in South America. CNKI (China National Knowledge Infrastructure) is the largest, continuously updated Chinese journals database in the world and contains many studies in Chinese that are not present on databases more commonly used in the USA and Europe. LILACS and CNKI both contain non-English language content but they are searchable in English. Cohen et al. (2015) compared two different systematic reviews on diagnosing rheumatoid arthritis and found there was little overlap in the studies they had included since one had used Chinese databases and the other had not done so.

The jury is still out as to whether a failure to include non-English language papers in reviews has a negative impact on their findings. Interestingly, most reviews do not restrict by language when searching, but non-English papers are then rarely included (Hartling et al., 2017) either because far fewer are found or because they are later dropped due to lack of translation resources. Is it worth searching a database if the review team cannot read its results? This is the kind of question that the information specialist needs to be raising with the review team in the early planning stages and not when the searches are underway. On the other hand, it may be costly to ignore databases because their content is predominantly non-English language, such as reviews of the effectiveness of Chinese medicine or treatments for diseases prevalent in tropical regions. It might be advisable to include a researcher on the team that can speak the language used in the databases vital to the research question.

Regional databases also play a role in non-health-related fields and where contextual evidence is required. ERIC, which is sponsored by the Institute of Education Sciences of the US Department of Education, claims to be the largest education database and, as expected, returns a vast amount of literature pertaining to research carried out in schools in the USA. In education, and other fields, culture and policy may mean interventions that are successful in the USA may have different effects when they are applied elsewhere. It would be advisable therefore to include the British Education Index or the Australian Education Index if the findings of the review are intended to be implemented in those countries. It is the responsibility of the information specialist to be thinking about the appropriate sources for the evidence required instead of just using the biggest or the most well-known databases.

Topic-focused databases

Topic-focused databases can be incredibly useful. Operating like a large scale search filter, they often index only those journals that are relevant to their domain, meaning that relatively simple searches can be run without generating too much 'noise'. Examples of small useful databases are Physiotherapy Evidence Database (PEDro) (www.pedro.org.au), which contains randomised trials, systematic reviews and practice guidelines for evidence-based physiotherapy or physical therapy, and OT seeker (www.otseeker.com), holding similar records in the field of occupational therapy. Similar small databases may be both topic-focused and geographically relevant, which can make them particularly useful in reviews that focus on practices or conventions held within a particular country. An example is the British Nursing

Index (BNI), which would be useful in a review of nursing practices specific to the National Health Service in the UK. Allied and Complementary Medicine Database (AMED) is a useful source when reviewing topics in complementary medicine.

Databases with grey literature

Smaller databases can also be a rich source of grey literature, indexing reports, occasional papers, conference proceedings and government documents. One example in the UK is the Health Management Information Consortium (HMIC) database, which contains reports from the government, hospitals, charities and advocacy groups as well as from conventional peer-reviewed journals. Another is Social Policy and Practice (SPP), which is made up of five social policy collections covering topics such as ageing, child health and social care.

These are particularly useful sources to provide contextual information for qualitative reviews. In-house surveys, reports of findings from questionnaires or focus groups may never be published in journals and so they are often unlikely to be indexed on conventional databases. If the review question, for example, is about ways to improve a health service, then a valuable piece of evidence might come from a survey of how people from ethnic minority groups have experienced the current services. Collections of small databases which index this type of data can suddenly seem a lot more useful than at first glance. The results would be much richer and more meaningful than a search that had used a standard list of, say, MEDLINE and CENTRAL.

Access to databases

Databases are often supplied by subscription to libraries as part of a package and not all intermediaries have access to all databases. Other databases may be purchased only as part of a bundle with others and cannot be accessed individually. Libraries make decisions based on cost of the database, availability through existing suppliers and the likely benefits to their core users (who might be students rather than review teams with an interest in a particular topic).

Some information specialists will be able to access resources from outside their own organization, such as from national libraries, networks of researchers or by contacting other review teams. Chapter 11 provides further details on the importance of collaboration to systematic searching. The collaboration must always comply with licensing, copyright and other restrictions when accessing resources provided by other organizations.

To summarise, deciding what databases to choose is a trade-off between time and resources. It is worth keeping these questions in mind when making these decisions:

- Will I find anything unique on this database?
- Does it hold vital information that I won't find easily by searching one large database?
- Will the results be accessible to the review team?
- Do I have access to the database?
- Can I search it effectively?

If the answer to all of these questions is yes, the database should be included in your list.

Other search techniques

It is commonly accepted that searching bibliographic databases alone is not enough to allow a search to be considered properly 'systematic'. Supplementary searching may be considered to be so crucial to the review process that the term supplementary is misguided, and individual non-database search techniques such as citation searching, handsearching or pearl growing, should be referred to alongside database searching as methods in their own right. A case study by Cooper et al. (2017) found that from the 21,409 references identified by database searching for a systematic review on public health and environmental enhancement, only two were included in the qualitative synthesis, whereas the supplementary search techniques found an additional four qualitative papers out of 453 screened.

Studies can be picked up by supplementary search techniques for several reasons, including:

1 The reference is not indexed on the databases searched.
2 The reference has a descriptive or 'non-scientific' title, e.g. qualitative studies often use a quotation from a study participant so free-text searching does not pick it up.
3 The study is inaccurately indexed so using controlled vocabulary searching does not pick it up.
4 The database searching was kept precise rather than sensitive for a valid reason, e.g. time or cost constraints, therefore potentially includable studies might have been missed.

The choice of other techniques is influenced by the same factors as when we are choosing databases. The technique has to return evidence relevant to the research question in the time available and be accessible to the review team. The information specialist also needs to get the balance right between the databases and the other techniques so that they complement each other effectively. It might be tempting to search one more database just in case it finds another study but what if that uses up the time that might have been available for a different technique? The aim of each database and each technique should be to find something new and not to duplicate what has already been found. The scoping searches will be a guide to the gaps in the evidence that the non-database techniques could aim to fill. It can be time consuming to use the other techniques and the information specialist needs to accommodate this when they are planning the searches. Examples of non-database search techniques are as follows.

Citation searching

Citation searching is a commonly used search technique and it can be done 'forwards' or 'backwards'. Forwards citation searching means looking for references that cite key references; this can be done using resources such as Google Scholar, Web of Science or Scopus, which provide links to papers that have cited the publication of interest.

Backwards citation searching can be carried out by scrolling through reference lists at the end of studies, using citation databases such as Web of Science or Scopus, or via the website hosting the journal.

Related techniques include 'pearl growing' (Ramer, 2005) and 'snowballing' (Greenhalgh and Peacock, 2005), techniques whereby the researcher starts with one or two key papers and seek citations from those papers via references lists and website links. Further details of the reviews where this might be a particularly fruitful approach are provided in Chapter 2.

Handsearching

Handsearching is an extremely useful technique if a journal or a number of journals are pertinent in the topic area, particularly if the journal is not indexed in any of the databases being searched. Although the term brings up the image of hours in the library searching through rows of old bound journals and their indexes, in reality and thanks to technology, handsearching usually involves scrolling through the online contents of the relevant journals. This is particularly useful for finding studies that appear in journal supplements or special editions that might not make it onto databases.

Web searching

The internet hosts a wide variety of information not available to us via databases and provides a point of access to useful organizations that might publish relevant papers or documents. Despite this, there is little guidance available as to how to incorporate it into a systematic search. Guidelines are vague; the relevant Cochrane standard states:

> … report the search terms used to search any sources other than bibliographic databases (e.g. trials registers, the web), and the dates of the searches.   (Churchill et al., 2016, 46)

Web searching is perhaps trickier than this recommendation suggests. The process is often exploratory, starting with one or two search terms in a search engine and then maybe clicking on a relevant link, finding one or two names, then searching for them until eventually you happen upon a key document with only the vaguest idea of how you eventually came upon it. Nevertheless, in the interests of keeping the process fully transparent, it is advisable to record at the very least the initial terms typed into a search engine, the date searched, the browser used, the number of results, the number of pages scrolled through and any subsequent websites that were used to access relevant information. Further information on the details to record from websites and search engines is available in Briscoe (2015).

Recording the sources and techniques

It is important to record the sources and techniques used to retrieve the evidence for a review (Rader et al., 2014). It is generally understood that literature search methods should be explicit and replicable (Lefebvre, Manheimer and Glanville, 2011). They should therefore be written as such. When recording search methods it is always worth bearing this in mind: 'could someone else do what I have done based on what I have recorded and get the same result?' The PRISMA (Preferred Reporting Items for Systematic Reviews and Meta-Analyses) checklist advises: 'describe all information sources (for example, databases with dates of coverage, contact with study authors to identify additional studies) in the search and date last searched' and 'present full electronic search strategy for at least one database, including any limits used, such that it could be repeated' (Liberati et al., 2009, item 7, item 8). The whole review risks being less transparent if it is not known how the included studies were located because the search methods are not adequately reported. Atkinson and colleagues (2015) have attempted to produce their own guidelines for search reporting.

It is advisable for the information specialist to retain the results of their scoping searches, test searches and anything else that might help to justify their choice of databases and search techniques. It is unlikely that all of these details would be reported in the review itself, but they are useful if the review team receives any queries about its methods for how the evidence was identified and selected. The notes are also useful in the future if the evidence is to be updated or a new review in a similar topic area is being planned.

Future directions

It would be helpful if information specialists assessed the impact of their decisions on the outcomes of the review. How do we know if we searched the right sources? Should we search a different set of sources next time we update this review? Can we learn any lessons from the reviews that have been done in this topic area before?

The transparency and reproducibility of reviews is greatly aided by the use of search summary tables (Bethel and Rogers, 2015). The template enables the information specialist to log which databases and other techniques were used and which ones retrieved studies that were included in the final review. The completed template shows which sources retrieved unique studies, which ones found relevant studies that were already known and which ones did not lead to any relevant studies. The completed template in Figure 4.1 shows that in this project on outdoor spaces (Whear et al., 2014), 6 of the 17 publications included in the systematic review were found on MEDLINE out of the 180 records downloaded from this database.

Included references	Format	Databases searched February 2013					Supplementary	
		ASSIA	Embase	MEDLINE	PscyINFO	Social Care Online	Backwards citation search	Contact with experts
Bengtsson 2006	Jnl	x						x
Calkins 2007	Jnl							
Cohen-Mansfield 1998	Book							x
Connell 2007	Book						x	
Cox 2004	Jnl		x	x				
Detweller 2009	Jnl	x	x	x	x			
Detweller 2008	Jnl	x	x	x	x			
Edwards 2013	Jnl							x
Hernandez 2007	Jnl	x						
Innes 2011	Jnl	x		x	x			
Luk 2011	Jnl	x	x	x	x			
Mather 1997	Jnl	x			x			
Mooney 1992	Jnl						x	
Morgan 1999	Jnl	x	x	x	x			
Rappe 2007	Jnl						x	
Raske 2010	Jnl					x		
Vuolo 2003	Report							x
No. of included refs		7	5	6	6	1	3	4
No. of unique refs		1	0	0	0	1	3	4
No. of refs downloaded		48	548	180	288	243		
No. of refs screened		24	382	176	212	237		
Sensitivity (%)		41.18	29.41	35.29	35.29	5.88		
Precision (%)		14.58	0.91	3.33	2.08	0.41		

Figure 4.1 *Example of a completed search summary table*

In the future, search summary tables will allow searchers to streamline the resources they choose based on previous reviews and will cut down the time and costs wasted searching resources unlikely to contribute to the review. In other words, the choices we make become more evidence based, transparent and reliable. This is the kind of data we need to be able to strike the right balance between databases and other search techniques when time and resources are limited. The long-term aim would be to move towards a repository of completed search summary tables that can be consulted by any information specialist.

Advances in text mining and machine learning are likely to impact on the way information specialists practice searching in the future. Factors about which databases to choose may become less about context and content and more about their compatibility with other software, for example for reference management or automated screening. In practice, we should continue to share, train and work collaboratively. Specifically, we could share and cite our search strategies more widely, work collaboratively with database providers to ensure our voice is heard as they develop new tools and technologies and take on new tasks such as peer reviewing. These actions will help us to develop our collective knowledge about resources and our continued influence over their development.

It is safe to suppose that, for some time at least, expert information specialists will continue to be required to navigate through the selection of databases and their hosts and other online sources. Supplementary search techniques such as checking reference lists and handsearching key journals remains imperative as all content cannot be found by database searching alone.

Conclusion

It would come as no surprise that a novice to the search process would feel utterly daunted by the selection of databases available, confounded by their content and unable to comprehend why in the age of digital data there isn't a straightforward algorithm or automated search process using one interface that would just return the studies required. This is an exciting time to be an information specialist with the knowledge and skills to carry out complex searching and to influence the development of new technologies such as text mining and machine learning. As a professional group we need to keep up the dialogue with providers and continue to share and publish our research and findings.

Suggestions for further reading

Gough, D., Oliver, S. and Thomas, J. (eds) (2017) *An Introduction to Systematic Reviews*, 2nd edn, SAGE Publishing.

Petticrew, M. and Roberts, H. (2005) *Systematic Reviews in the Social Sciences: a practical guide*, Wiley-Blackwell.

References

Atkinson, K. M., Koenka, A. C., Sanchez, C. E., Moshontz, H. and Cooper, H. (2015) Reporting Standards for Literature Searches and Report Inclusion Criteria: making research syntheses more transparent and easy to replicate, *Research Synthesis Methods*, **6** (1), 87-95.

Bethel, A. and Rogers, M. (2014) A Checklist to Assess Database-hosting Platforms for Designing and Running Searches for Systematic Reviews, *Health Information and Libraries Journal*, **31** (1), 43-53.

Bethel, A. and Rogers, M. (2015) Search Summary Tables. Cochrane Colloquium, Vienna, Austria, 3-7 October 2015. https://abstracts.cochrane.org/2015-vienna/search-summary-table-systematic-reviews-srs

Bethel, A. and Rogers, M. (2018) Search Methods in Environmental Systematic Reviews: which databases have been searched?, Collaboration for Environmental Evidence, Paris, 16-20 April 2018. https://cee2018.sciencesconf.org/189073/document

Betran, A. P., Say, L., Gulmezoglu, A. M., Allen, T. and Hampson, L. (2005) Effectiveness of Different Databases in Identifying Studies for Systematic Reviews: experience from the WHO systematic review of maternal morbidity and mortality, *BMC Medical Research Methodology*, **5** (1), 6.

Beyer, F. R. and Wright, K. (2013) Can We Prioritise which Databases to Search? A Case Study Using a Systematic Review of Frozen Shoulder Management, *Health Information and Libraries Journal*, **30** (1), 49-58.

Booth, A. (2010) How Much Searching is Enough? Comprehensive Versus Optimal Retrieval for Technology Assessments, *International Journal of Technology Assessment in Health Care*, **26** (4), 431-435.

Briscoe, S. (2015) Web Searching for Systematic Reviews: a case study of reporting standards in the UK Health Technology Assessment programme, *BMC Research Notes*, **8**, 153.

Centre for Reviews and Dissemination (2009) *Systematic Reviews: CRD's guidance for undertaking reviews in health care*, Centre for Reviews and

Dissemination University of York. www.york.ac.uk/crd/guidance

Churchill, R., Lasserson, T., Chandler, J., Tovey, D. and Higgins, J. P. T. (2016) Standards for the Conduct of New Cochrane Intervention Reviews. In Higgins, J. P. T., Lasserson, T., Chandler, J., Tovey, D. and Churchill R. (eds), *Methodological Expectations of Cochrane Intervention Reviews*, Cochrane. www.community.cochrane.org/mecir-manual/standards-reporting-new-cochrane-intervention-reviews-r1-109/reporting-review-conduct-r1-55/search-methods-identification-studies-r33-38

Cohen, J. F., Korevaar, D. A., Wang, J., Spijker, R. and Bossuyt, P. M. (2015) Should We Search Chinese Biomedical Databases When Performing Systematic Reviews?, *Systematic Reviews*, **4**, 23.

Cooper, C., Lovell, R., Husk, K., Booth, A. and Garside, R. (2017) Supplementary Search Methods Were More Effective and Offered Better Value than Bibliographic Database Searching: a case study from public health and environmental enhancement, *Research Synthesis Methods*, **9** (2), 195-223.

Damarell, R. A., Tieman, J. J. and Sladek, R. M. (2013) OvidSP MEDLINE-to-PubMed Search Filter Translation: a methodology for extending search filter range to include PubMed's unique content, *BMC Medical Research Methodology*, **13**, 86.

Duffy, S., de Kock, S., Misso, K., Noake, C., Ross, J. and Stirk, L. (2016) Supplementary Searches of PubMed to Improve Currency of MEDLINE and MEDLINE In-Process Searches via Ovid, *Journal of the Medical Library Association*, **104** (4), 309-312.

Grant, M. J. and Booth, A. (2009) A Typology of Reviews: an analysis of 14 review types and associated methodologies, *Health Information and Libraries Journal*, **26** (2), 91-108.

Greenhalgh, T. and Peacock, R. (2005) Effectiveness and Efficiency of Search Methods in Systematic Reviews of Complex Evidence: audit of primary sources, *BMJ*, **331** (7524), 1064-1065.

Hartling, L., Featherstone, R., Nuspl, M., Shave, K., Dryden, D. M. and Vandermeer, B. (2017) Grey Literature in Systematic Reviews: a cross-sectional study of the contribution of non-English reports, unpublished studies and dissertations to the results of meta-analyses in child-relevant reviews, *BMC Medical Research Methodology*, **17** (1), 64.

Hollis, J. L., Sutherland, R., Williams, A. J., Campbell, E., Nathan, N., Wolfenden, L., Morgan, P. J., Lubans, D. R., Gilham, K. and Wiggers, J.

(2017) A Systematic Review and Meta-analysis of Moderate-to-vigorous Physical Activity Levels in Secondary School Physical Education Lessons, *International Journal of Behavioral Nutrition and Physical Activity*, **14** (1), 52.

Kugley, S., Wade, A., Thomas, J., Mahood, Q., Jørgensen, A-M. K., Hammerstrøm, K. and Sathe, N. (2017) *Searching for Studies: a guide to information retrieval for Campbell Systematic Reviews - Campbell Methods Series Guide 1*, The Campbell Collaboration. www.campbellcollaboration.org/library/searching-for-studies-information-retrieval-guide-campbell-reviews.html

Lefebvre, C., Manheimer, E. and Glanville, J. (2011) Searching for Studies. In Higgins, J. P. T. and Green, S. (eds) *Cochrane Handbook for Systematic Reviews of Interventions (version 5.1.0)*, The Cochrane Collaboration. http://handbook-5-1.cochrane.org

Liberati, A., Altman, D. G., Tetzlaff, J., Mulrow, C., Gøtzsche, P. C., Ioannidis, J. P., Clarke, M., Devereaux, P. J., Kleijnen, J. and Moher, D. (2009) The PRISMA Statement for Reporting Systematic Reviews and Meta-analyses of Studies that Evaluate Healthcare Interventions: explanation and elaboration, *BMJ*, **339**, b2700.

Pullin, A. S., Frampton, G. K., Livoreil, B. and Petrokofski, G. (eds) (2018) *Guidelines and Standards for Evidence Synthesis in Environmental Management: Version 5.0*, Collaboration for Environmental Evidence. www.environmentalevidence.org/information-for-authors

Rader, T., Mann, M., Stansfield, C., Cooper, C. and Sampson, M. (2014) Methods for Documenting Systematic Review Searches: a discussion of common issues, *Research Synthesis Methods*, **5** (2), 98-115.

Ramer, S. L. (2005) Site-ation Pearl Growing: methods and librarianship history and theory, *Journal of the Medical Library Association*, **93** (3), 397-400.

Sampson, M., Barrowman, N. J., Moher, D., Klassen, T. P., Pham, B., Platt, R., St John, P. D., Viola, R. and Raina, P. (2003) Should Meta-analysts Search Embase in Addition to MEDLINE?, *Journal of Clinical Epidemiology*, **56** (10), 943-955.

Vassar, M., Yerokhin, V., Sinnett, P. M., Weiher, M., Muckelrath, H., Carr, B., Varney, L. and Cook, G. (2017) Database Selection in Systematic Reviews: an insight through clinical neurology, *Health Information and Libraries Journal*, **34** (2), 156-164.

Whear, R., Coon, J. T., Bethel, A., Abbott, R., Stein, K. and Garside, R. (2014) What is the Impact of Using Outdoor Spaces such as Gardens on the

Physical and Mental Well-being of those with Dementia? A Systematic Review of Quantitative and Qualitative Evidence, *Journal of the American Medical Directors Association*, **15** (10), 697-705.

Younger, P. and Boddy, K. (2009) When is a Search Not a Search? A Comparison of Searching the AMED Complementary Health Database via EBSCOhost, OVID and DIALOG, *Health Information and Libraries Journal*, **26** (2),126-135.

5

Gathering evidence from grey literature and unpublished data

Shannon Kugley and Richard Epstein

Introduction

The objectives of this chapter are to describe sources of unpublished data and grey literature, review the challenges associated with finding and using these sources, and highlight the current tools and strategies to efficiently use them to strengthen systematic reviews and other information retrieval tasks.

Grey literature is defined by the *Cochrane Handbook for Systematic Reviews of Interventions* as '... literature that is not formally published in sources such as books or journal articles' (Lefebvre, Manheimer and Glanville, 2011, 6.2.1.8). Another source provides a more qualitative description of grey literature as various document types that are 'protected by intellectual property rights, of sufficient quality to be collected and preserved by library holdings or institutional repositories, but not controlled by commercial publishers' (Schöpfel, 2011, 5). Grey literature may be in print or electronic format and sources include government reports, technical reports, theses and conference proceedings, among others.

We have chosen to adapt the definition for 'unpublished sources' as used by Su Golder and her colleagues in a study comparing the reporting of adverse events in published and unpublished sources (Golder et al., 2016a). Published papers typically are disseminated by peer-reviewed journals, whereas unpublished data is maintained by regulatory agencies, stored in trial registries or owned by industry (for example, pharmaceutical companies) or individual researchers.

Background

Scientific literature is critical to the documentation and dissemination of academic scholarship and scientific knowledge. Historically, the knowledge acquired from empirical and theoretic enquiry has been shared via print formats, which permits an accumulation of observations that can be retrieved, reviewed and revisited over time. When information from individual reports is consolidated with similar and contradicting reports, bodies of evidence emerge with the potential to dispel outdated beliefs and cultivate new knowledge.

Commercial publishers, academic journals and bibliographic databases make it possible for researchers and information specialists to search efficiently the vast collection of accumulating data and documents using controlled vocabularies and tailored search strategies. Systematic searching is the requisite step for the targeted collection of data from various sources. In recent years, researchers and information scientists have devised and refined nomenclature, processes and methods to locate, compile and evaluate data from multiple sources. These processes and methods have culminated in a set of best practices that comprise the steps to conduct a systematic review or meta-analysis. Systematic reviews are recognised as the gold standard for comparing the benefits and harms of interventions by pooling data from individual studies and subjecting those data to critical appraisal, synthesis and qualitative or quantitative analyses. A systematic literature search is a crucial and fundamental step in the conduct of a systematic review.

To conduct a high-quality systematic review, the information specialist must identify the most relevant information from a large corpus of documents. Published study reports in scholarly journals and other commercial formats are important but not sufficient for a comprehensive and accurate estimation of the evidence. Research suggests that estimates of treatment effects based on published studies tend to be more positive than those that have also derived evidence from the grey literature or unpublished data (Balshem et al., 2013; Hartung et al., 2014; Song et al., 2009; Song et al., 2010; Vedula, Li and Dickersin, 2013; Wieland et al., 2014).

Recent developments

A quick scoping search of PubMed was done on 9 July 2018 for publications entered by the end of 2017 with the following terms:

> ("grey literature" OR "gray literature" OR "unpublished data") AND ("systematic review" OR "literature search" OR "meta-analysis" OR "evidence synthesis")

Figure 5.1 shows that about 90% of the records retrieved on grey literature or unpublished data in relation to systematic reviews were published in the last 10 years.

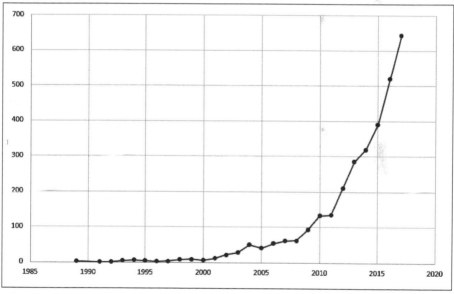

Figure 5.1 *Number of publications relevant to grey literature and unpublished data in PubMed*

A shift from print to digital media, the emergence of open access journals and mandates to make information on trials and government-funded studies available to the public are a few of the factors that have facilitated expanded access to unpublished data and information that was otherwise difficult to obtain. Electronic versions of study reports may include details and additional information as supplemental data that were not possible to include in print versions (Doshi, Jones and Jefferson, 2012).

Other sources of unpublished data are increasingly accessible due to clinical trial and research study reporting requirements that were established to elevate standards of accountability and transparency, especially for trials funded in whole or in part by tax-payers. The Food and Drug Administration (FDA) in the USA requires studies of all drugs, biologics and devices be publicly accessible via ClinicalTrials.gov, while the European Medicines Agency (EMA) stipulates that all trials carried out in the European Union are registered in the European Clinical Trials database (EudraCT). The World Health Organization (WHO) maintains the International Clinical Trials Registry Platform to promote transparency and strengthen the validity of the scientific evidence base by encouraging clinical trial registration at the study inception (Gülmezoglu et al., 2005).

Tackling publication bias

Studies with positive, statistically significant results may be more appealing for publication and consequently more likely to be accepted for publication than studies that fail to demonstrate that an intervention or programme produces a desired effect (Hopewell et al., 2009). This bias, sometimes referred to as the file drawer effect, can lead to an overestimation of the benefits of an intervention and an underestimation of harms (Rosenthal, 1979). To provide an accurate and representative profile of information on a given topic, it is equally important to include data from studies that found an intervention to be ineffective as it is to include data from studies that demonstrate a significant positive effect. Furthermore, it has been suggested that much of the information on adverse events and other study data may be unpublished. To ensure a reliable estimate of harms from analyses of pooled data, reviewers should seek and include data from unpublished sources (Golder et al., 2016b).

In a comparison of reporting completeness among a sample (n = 202) of drug trials in the USA registered with ClinicalTrials.gov, reporting of adverse events was significantly more complete in the trial registry than in the study publications indexed in PubMed (73% versus 45%) (Riveros et al., 2013). Authors from the Nordic Cochrane Centre acquired clinical study reports for the obesity drug orlistat from the European Medicines Agency through the Freedom of Information Act and concluded that the adverse effects were substantially under-reported in published papers (Schroll, Penninga and Gøtzsche, 2016).

Beyond intentional or unintentional misreporting, there are also inherent limitations of the gold-standard study design for establishing the effectiveness of an intervention. Randomised controlled trials (RCTs) that are conducted to establish the efficacy or non-inferiority of an intervention are not an optimal source of information on potential harms. Harms and adverse events are infrequent and so the duration of follow-up and/or numbers of participants needed to detect harms is often not feasible. Therefore, surveillance data from regulatory agencies or other sources that collect and capture long-term outcomes are important sources of information to include when collecting evidence to inform policies and recommendations (Chou and Helfand, 2005; Golder, Loke and Bland, 2010).

Challenges

Systematic searching of grey literature and unpublished data is challenging for several reasons. In addition to the obvious challenge related to the volume and variable quality of information retrieved from internet searches, the search features can make it difficult to replicate a search. Advanced algorithms mean that searches conducted just minutes apart by different people, especially if they are in different geographic locations, will probably not return the same results. Information maintained by organizations and agencies may be replaced or removed without notice, which also affects the replicability of web searches. A study identified through a grey literature search will often be identified by a link; however searchers must be cautious in documentation as the link may expire after a period of time leading to an 'error' message. It is better practice to document the steps and search queries conducted in order to permit replication of the process.

Once grey literature sources are identified, what is the best approach to evaluating the source? Unlike other literature sources that are frequently shaped by the publishing platform or dissemination strategy, the grey literature may come in multiple formats and varied 'designs'. Specific tools to assess the reporting and methodologic rigour of other publication types and study designs abound (Bossuyt et al., 2015; Juni, Altman and Egger, 2001; Juni et al., 1999; Karlsson and Takahashi, 2017; Olivo et al., 2008; Shea et al., 2009; Sterne et al., 2016; Whiting et al., 2006; Whiting et al., 2016), whereas there are few, if any, validated and widely available options for grey literature and unpublished data. Other minor impediments are the absence of export features, a lack of standardised metadata and the tendency for the content to become obsolete.

To mitigate these challenges, there are several recommended approaches to improving the reliability and reproducibility of grey literature searching:

1 Scan and pre-specify sources in advance.
2 Review search sources and strategies with stakeholders and experts who are likely to be familiar with the trends and sources of information. Case study 5.1 illustrates the benefits of this process in more detail.
3 Document strategies and keep clear explanations of decision points and any limitations.

Case study 5.1: Initiating personal contacts to identify key information sources

For some topics, grey literature is likely to yield more representative and useful information than the indexed literature. For example, a technical brief of interventions to support the transition of young people with special health needs to adult care relied heavily upon information from model programmes and approaches obtained from non-traditional sources. The investigators consulted key informants to identify organizations and provider services, which included, among others, the National Center for Medical Home Implementation (a national network providing families with tools to make informed decisions), a collaborative on workforce and disability, a special council for children with disabilities, as well as transition services and programmes administered by individual states and local governments in the USA. Investigators contacted, searched and catalogued the retrievals systematically to augment the comprehensive literature review of evaluation studies (Davis et al., 2014; McPheeters et al., 2014).

Discussion

Theory and practice

In 2007, it was reported that over a half of studies reported in conference abstracts never reach full publication and those that are eventually fully published have been shown to be systematically different from those that are never published in full (Scherer, Langenberg and von Elm, 2007). More recent reports confirm that many studies reported in abstracts do not go on to be reported as complete publications, although there is wide variation in the rate of non-publication (Egloff et al., 2017; Gregory et al., 2012; Lim et al., 2013; Prohaska et al., 2013). This variation across disciplines reinforces the importance of developing an intentional and tailored approach to the selection and prioritisation of sources for each review. It is also important to identify ongoing studies for reference in the review and for inclusion in subsequent updates. Extracting information, if only study characteristics and metadata, from ongoing studies is particularly useful for identifying future research recommendations, as well as anticipating the data and study results for a systematic review update (Brasure et al., 2010). Although it can be challenging to identify studies conducted but not completed, trial registries are useful resources and they are easily searched.

Existing guidance

A summit held in 2014 at the Italian National Council of Research in Pisa culminated in 15 recommendations for policy development and recognition of the value of grey literature to a diverse group of stakeholders (Savić et al., 2017). Additionally, there are numerous empirical evaluations that address the benefits and challenges of finding and using unpublished data for evidence reviews (Balshem et al., 2013; Golder, Loke and Bland, 2010; Halfpenny et al., 2016; Hartling et al., 2017; Hartung et al., 2014; Mahood, Van Eerd and Irvin, 2014; Quigley et al., 2015; Relevo and Balshem, 2011; Saleh, Ratajeski and Bertolet, 2014; Turner, Knoepflmacher and Shapley, 2012; Vedula, Li and Dickersin, 2013) but, to our knowledge, no formalised, consolidated guidelines for searching, using and documenting grey literature and unpublished data exist.

Information retrieval guides from several reputable groups that have a long history of commissioning systematic reviews or issuing evidence-based policy and practice guidelines are a useful source of further reading (Balshem et al., 2013; Canadian Agency for Drugs and

Technologies in Health, 2015; Institute of Medicine Committee on Standards for Systematic Reviews of Comparative Effectiveness Research et al., 2011; Joanna Briggs Institute, 2011; Kugley et al., 2017; National Institute for Health and Care Excellence, 2013; Relevo and Balshem, 2011; Rutter et al., 2010).

Sources, approaches and techniques

In addition to guidance and review manuals, the 2011 search standards from the Committee on Standards for Systematic Reviews of Comparative Effectiveness Research at the National Academies in the USA, which incorporates the Institute of Medicine (IOM), state that systematic review authors should:

- include grey literature databases, clinical trial registries and other sources of unpublished information about studies (IOM Standard 3.2.1).
- invite study sponsors to submit unpublished data, including unreported outcomes (IOM Standard 3.2.3).
- conduct a web search (IOM Standard 3.2.3).

Colleagues can be an important source of information about unpublished studies and informal channels of communication can sometimes be the only means of identifying unpublished data. The systematic review team may choose to send requests for information to the first author of reports of included studies to clarify and obtain missing data and ask if the author is aware of potentially relevant published or unpublished studies (Centre for Reviews and Dissemination, 2009; Kugley et al., 2017; Relevo and Balshem, 2011). Contacting authors by e-mail results in the greatest response rate with the fewest number of attempts and the shortest time to respond (Young and Hopewell, 2011).

To obtain more accurate results when conducting searches of online content, use the advanced features and other tools provided by the web search service. For example, the search engine Google includes an optional setting 'verbatim' which limits the query to the entry terms only, as opposed to variants and synonyms. This is particularly useful when the user does not want the search engine to personalise the search results, identify synonyms or otherwise modify the initial search criteria. To use Google's verbatim, perform a search and select the 'Search tools' to reveal the 'verbatim' option.

Sources

A detailed review of specific sources of unpublished data is beyond the scope of this work, however many academic libraries and consortiums that conduct systematic reviews offer guidance and training to help information specialists learn how to tailor search strategies and use sources to find unpublished data (Balshem et al., 2013). Information specialists should advocate for their role on the research team as experts who can provide technical assistance and recommendations for selecting the most appropriate sources. If possible, the information specialist should engage the research team in the initial stages of planning for an evidence review and draft a broad list of potential sources of data. These may include:

- regulatory agencies
- professional, private and non-profit organizations
- product manufacturers
- business, industry and trade groups
- academic institutions.

Some of the common types of literature that may contain unpublished data are:

- conference proceedings
- graduate dissertations and theses
- technical reports
- clinical trial summaries.

With a properly scoped research topic that is appropriately framed for a systematic investigation, using a 'population', 'intervention', 'comparator', 'outcome', 'timing' and 'setting' (PICOTS) framework for preliminary literature searches will reveal the extent of coverage in published sources (Schardt et al., 2007).

Table 5.1 on the next page provides a selected sample of sources to give readers a starting point for the literature search strategy, which includes key regulatory sources from the USA, European Union and Canada, guidance resources, registries and grey literature databases. Notable grey literature databases include the Grey Literature Report, Open Grey and Grey Net. Until January 2017, the New York Academy of Medicine published bimonthly the *Grey Literature Report* to alert readers to new grey literature publications in health services research and selected public health topics. The System for Information on Grey Literature in Europe, via Open Grey, is an open access database of grey literature from many research disciplines. The Grey Literature Network Service (Grey Net) was founded in 1992 and provides a rich forum for communication, distribution and innovation in the field of grey literature.

Table 5.1 *Sample of key sources for grey literature and unpublished data in the USA, European Union and Canada*

Source Type	Name	URL	Description
Database	Grey Literature Report	www.greylit.org	A bi-monthly publication of the New York Academy of Medicine. The database is keyword searchable and serves as an archive for the catalogued reports. As of January 2017, the Grey Literature Report website and database will be discontinued and will no longer be updated, but the resources will still be accessible.
Database	GreyNet	www.greynet.org/home.html	A portal of research and information in the field of grey literature. GreyNet hosts OpenGrey, a system for information on grey literature and the successor to OpenSIGLE, a repository of research originating from the International Conference Series on Grey Literature.
Database	SciTech Connect	www.osti.gov/scitech	A portal that provides access to a publicly-available collection of US Department of Energy sponsored research and development results, including technical reports, bibliographic references, journal articles, conference papers, books, multimedia, software and data information.
Database	Open Grey	www.opengrey.eu	Provides access to bibliographical references of grey literature produced in Europe.

(Continued)

Table 5.1 *Continued*

Source Type	Name	URL	Description
Guidance	Grey Matters: A practical search tool for evidence-based medicine	www.cadth.ca/resources/finding-evidence/grey-matters	Online manual from the Canadian Agency for Drugs and Technologies in Health (CADTH) providing a thorough list of sources for grey literature in medicine and a helpful checklist to help systematise your process.
Guidance	Finding Grey Literature Evidence and Assessing for Outcome and Analysis Reporting Biases When Comparing Medical Interventions	www.effectivehealthcare. ahrq.gov/topics/methods-guidance-reporting-bias/ methods	Methods guide chapter authored by methodologists at the Agency for Healthcare Research and Quality (AHRQ) Effective Healthcare Program.
Registry	ClinicalTrials. gov	www.clinicaltrials.gov	USA-based trial registry of federal and private funded clinical trials for a wide range of diseases and conditions conducted in all 50 States and in more than 100 countries.
Registry	ISRCTN	www.isrctn.com	A registry and curated database containing data items to meet the requirements of the World Health Organization (WHO), International Clinical Trials Registry Platform (ICTRP) and the International Committee of Medical Journal Editors (ICMJE) guidelines. The scope of the registry has expanded beyond RCTs to include any study designed to assess the efficacy of health interventions in a human population.
Registry	World Health Organization (WHO) International Clinical Trials Registry	www.who.int/ictrp/en	A meta-registry of international content.
Regulatory	Food and Drug Administration Drugs@FDA	www.accessdata.fda.gov/scripts/cder/daf/index.cfm	Includes most of the drug products approved for use in the USA since 1939. The majority of patient information, labels, approval letters, reviews and other information are available for drug products approved since 1998.

(Continued)

Table 5.1 *Continued*

Source Type	Name	URL	Description
Regulatory	Food and Drug Administration Devices@FDA	www.accessdata.fda.gov/scripts/cdrh/devicesatfda	Includes regulatory information for cleared and approved medical devices and links to device summary information, manufacturer, approval date, user instructions and other consumer information.
Regulatory	Health Canada Drug Product Database	www.canada.ca/en/health-canada/services/drugs-health-products/drug-products/drug-product-database.html	Includes regulatory information on human pharmaceutical and biological drugs and contains approximately 47,000 products that are currently approved or marketed in Canada.
Regulatory	European Medicines Agency	www.ema.europa.eu	Provides information on the regulation of medicines for human use in the European Union.

Controversies and developments

Although there is widespread recognition that literature search strategies must be comprehensive in order to reduce the risk of bias in the conduct of systematic reviews, most methods guidance does not provide detailed directions on how to search for grey literature, how to screen or otherwise decide about the relevance of grey literature to a particular systematic review or how to incorporate grey literature that has been identified as relevant into a systematic review. To some degree, at least, this is understandable given the nature of grey literature means it is often unindexed. At the same time, although there is widespread agreement that grey literature might contain potentially important information to multiple steps in the process, from scoping a review to interpreting results, it is unclear how these sources actually do, in fact, contribute to systematic reviews.

The rationale for including grey literature is theoretically sound, although the empirical value of including it is unclear. Methods experts at the Agency for Healthcare Research and Quality (AHRQ) Effective Healthcare Program in the USA examined a subset of systematic reviews (n = 129) in child health from three Cochrane Review Groups and found that most searched for grey literature but only 6% of the reviews included studies from grey sources and only nine of the 129 reviews included dissertations (Hartling et al., 2017). Of the minority that did include data from grey literature sources, the impact of the unpublished studies on the overall results was minimal (Hartling et al., 2017). Case study 5.2 discusses one systematic review where the inclusion of previously unpublished data had an important effect on the findings of the systematic review, which had far-reaching consequences for public policy.

Case study 5.2: Inconsistent reporting of harms in published and unpublished sources

A Cochrane review update of the evidence for the effectiveness for a class of early antivirals, neuraminidase inhibitors, following an outbreak of the A/H1N1 viral strain of influenza in April 2009, led to a controversy in which unpublished data was the pivotal source of debate. The review update included 25 RCTs, of which many were incompletely reported. The review authors' attempts to obtain complete study reports from the pharmaceutical companies were unsuccessful initially. Later, the companies supplied review authors with hundreds of pages of report data which the authors analysed to assess risks of harm and comment on the discrepancies between the published and unpublished study reports. The review and its subsequent critiques and author responses affirms the need for transparency in clinical trials and access to data for public health decisions (Doshi, Jefferson and Del Mar, 2012; Jefferson et al., 2012; Jefferson et al., 2014).

A partial response to this dilemma would be to use the grey literature results as an indicator that relevant data from published reports has been missed. The discovery of a relevant grey literature source may provide preliminary information and contact details that can be used to track down data that has been conventionally published in a peer-reviewed article. For example, a relevant doctoral thesis might not be incorporated into the systematic review in its own right, rather it may lead to the discovery of a subsequently published but previously unidentified trial.

It is also reasonable to believe that for certain vulnerable or difficult to study populations (for example, homeless youth) or for interventions tailored to meet the unique and real-world needs of a local dilemma, the grey literature is likely to provide information otherwise unobtainable. In these cases, non-profit organizations and funding agencies may be more likely to host these data. The incentive for scholarly publication may be reduced as compared with research that is conducted to establish the widespread value of an intervention or to market a medical product. Although these trends may be shifting as the digital age and open access publishing provide more opportunities for dissemination and easier access to research data, the contextual details remain critical to prioritising approaches and allocating resources in the initial planning stages of the review.

An active controversy regards how much time and other resources to invest in identifying relevant grey literature and unpublished data. The strategies and tools noted above are options to make searching of grey literature more efficient. This is important because conducting systematic reviews is a resource-heavy endeavour. Particularly in the absence of clear guidance about how to search for, screen and appraise grey literature, it seems possible, if not probable, that efforts to incorporate grey literature have the potential to consume already limited resources quite quickly.

It is unclear whether investing resources in searching grey literature provides a return on the investment. For example, if searching grey literature identifies relevant and unique data (from published or unpublished sources) the additional time and resources to conduct a grey literature search are justified. Data derived from grey literature has the potential to minimise publication and/or selective reporting bias in a systematic review. On the other hand, if searching grey literature provides information only cited in the background section or identifies data already captured by a standard search of the published literature, the information specialist may consider focusing information retrieval efforts in subsequent similar reviews.

The ideal information retrieval strategy may be more apparent to a seasoned systematic review methodologist or information specialist than to the content experts who are less likely to recognise the trends in information dissemination across disciplines. Therefore, it is critical for systematic review authors and information specialists to probe the content experts early and recursively in the initial stages of protocol development for the usual sources of information within their field, as well as introduce alternate strategies to ensure comprehensive retrieval. The relative value of grey literature and sources of unpublished data will vary by topic and review types. Adhering to the core principles of systematic literature searching of documenting the retrieval and adopting standards for assessment of relevance and quality, is a sound and flexible strategy for meeting a diverse range of information needs.

Quality and reporting

There are several factors that contribute to the difficulty of appraising the quality of grey literature sources. The underlying motivations for limiting a research output to unpublished sources and the lack of uniform standards for research conduct, analysis and reporting encompass most, if not all, the inherent shortcomings of grey literature. Ulrich's authoritative source of bibliographic and publisher information for more than 300,000 periodicals identifies peer-reviewed journals as being 'refereed' and states that refereed journals 'include articles that have been reviewed by experts and respected researchers in specific fields of study including the sciences, technology, the social sciences, and arts and humanities' (www.ulrichsweb.com/ulrichsweb/faqs.asp). Thus, one can assume that a research article published in a refereed source is of a minimum degree of quality owing to the peer-review process.

Not only are grey literature reports prone to not meeting a minimum threshold of quality, they do not adhere to a uniform or consistent format such as IMRaD (Introduction, Methods, Results and Discussion), the predominant article layout among scholarly biomedical articles, which can impede the screening and data extraction process (Sollaci and Pereira, 2004). Various layouts and organization of grey literature, especially reports from well-funded projects, are often visually pleasing and effectively convey key outcomes and salient points but they can be difficult to navigate and it can be time consuming to find the information needed to evaluate the research. For example, the Consolidated Standards of Reporting Trials (CONSORT) strongly recommends that RCTs report a flow diagram to account for the recruitment, allocation and follow-up of individual participants (Moher et al., 2010; Shamseer et al., 2016).

CONSORT and other standards, such as those endorsed by the International Committee of Medical Journal Editors (ICMJE) introduce a quality check to promote consistent and transparent reporting which permits a reader to more easily discern information needed to assess risk of bias (De Angelis et al., 2004). There exists a potential for poorer quality reporting in the grey literature, although poor reporting does not necessarily equate to poorly conducted research. Verification of methods in the absence of clear descriptions is, at minimum, time consuming and at worst impossible. Research reports from indexed, conventional sources are not immune from these shortcomings, but these deficiencies are usually easier to spot and are subject to self-correction through a culture of discourse among colleagues and academic competitors by submitting letters to the editor (Gøtzsche et al., 2010).

Reviews in multiple disciplines

Initially, systematic reviews were commissioned to gauge the effectiveness of medical, behavioural and educational interventions by identifying, extracting, appraising and consolidating data from existing research. By employing reproducible methods and a structured process, the systematic review has become the 'go-to' model for evaluating questions across other fields of study (for example, management science, information science, social science, agriculture and engineering) and to address questions other than effectiveness. Systematic reviews often examine cross-cutting themes requiring multidisciplinary sources, for example quality improvement to reduce disparities in delivery of care.

Unpublished data and grey literature sources may hold key insights, otherwise not represented in conventional outlets, for certain populations and specific topics. Examples include:

- Information on applied public health may be predominantly, or only, held in grey literature and grey information (Adams et al., 2016).
- To identify the most relevant studies of religion and mental health, the optimal strategies and sources were searching specialised health, social science and grey literature databases in addition to citation searching and researchers' personal libraries (Wright, Cottrell and Mir, 2014).
- Systematic review search methods applied to a review of grey literature for school-based breakfast programmes in Canada was warranted because guidelines for breakfast programmes are typically released by government and non-government organizations and not published in academic journals (Godin et al., 2015).

Across the spectrum of knowledge needs and inquiry, the importance and availability of unpublished data varies. For example, the relative value of unpublished data is likely to be much greater for a review of a medical device used off-label than for a review of well-studied and academically sourced interventions. Case study 5.3 details one area where unpublished data has played a key role in understanding and preventing suicidal behaviour.

Case study 5.3: Novel use of unpublished data to address a research question

Suicide is a leading cause of death worldwide with significant social and economic impacts from an estimated 800,000 deaths annually (World Health Organization, 2014). To address this public health dilemma, evidence-based suicide prevention interventions must target individuals who are at risk of suicide as many people who attempt suicide do not receive prior treatment (Demyttenaere et al., 2004; Nock et al., 2008; Rivero et al., 2014).

A 2014 report describes an example of using unpublished data from a national sample of Veterans' Administration (USA) electronic health records to estimate the risk of subsequent suicide. Using an administrative dataset, researchers describe the development of a language-based model that used keyword analysis and themes from physician notes. Researchers analysed medical notes for individuals who received mental health treatment and did or did not die by suicide and a control group of individuals who did not use mental health services to identify predictive words and classify text-based signals of suicidality (Poulin et al., 2014). Subsequent similar studies have used electronic health record data to develop predictive models for suicide risk with improved classification accuracy (Barak-Corren et al., 2016; Fernandes et al., 2018; Walsh, Ribeiro and Franklin, 2017).

Future directions

Attention to using and finding grey literature and unpublished data for systematic reviews and evidence-based research has grown in the last two decades. However, there has been little focus on how to appropriately and reliably select, appraise and integrate unpublished data with traditional research findings. There are virtually no recommendations for the transparent and standard reporting of grey literature and unpublished data included in systematic reviews or for evidence-based recommendations.

Future research efforts should aim to help researchers decide when and how to include unpublished data and support efforts to create and maintain curated access to indexed pharmaceutical and industry documents (Wieland et al., 2014). Information specialists across disciplines can play an active role in research to evaluate the effect of prospective registration of studies, explore the role of open access policy and develop guidelines for retrieval, management and integration of unpublished data into evidence reviews, as well as develop methods to assess qualitatively the risk of publication bias in systematic reviews (Song et al., 2009; Song et al., 2010).

Future work should focus on adapting the established best practices derived from experience with published data to retrieving and using grey literature and extending those practices to novel and evolving sources of unpublished data, for example health data from electronic medical records and administrative databases. Although, as yet, not an unequivocal category of unpublished data, social media and cloud computing give rise to a new kind of data, user-generated content and large datasets that can be easily accessed and analysed. Insights derived from aggregate social media data has the potential to inform early identification of disease (for example, influenza) (Allen et al., 2016; Santillana et al., 2015; Woo et al., 2016; Yang, Horneffer and DiLisio, 2013; Zuccon et al., 2015) or reveal health-related risks (Ayers et al., 2016) or behaviours responsive to early or targeted intervention (Castro and Osório, 2012; Kalyanam et al., 2016; Scott et al., 2015; Sofean and Smith, 2013).

Genomic and medical datasets offer enormous potential for researchers to explore large amounts of data in digital format. Information generated by individuals and comprised of personal beliefs and behaviours may serve as alternate sources of data. Using application programming interfaces (APIs), researchers can access user-supplied online content in blogs, tweets and other social networks to discover attitudinal and explore social determinants of health (see Chapter 6).

Conclusion

Grey literature, broadly, is a body of information that may not be published in conventional sources such as books or journal articles or is not indexed in a manner that makes the information readily identifiable using a standard search strategy. Important research provided in grey literature by or for governmental and public organizations may be overlooked if the search is not extended beyond bibliographic databases. Some of the specific approaches to identifying grey literature include contacting authors and researchers directly, conducting searches of web-based content and consulting resources that contain or point to appropriate sources of data. The final selection of grey literature sources should take into account the team's experience with conducting systematic searches, the funder's expectations and the actual resources available to the review authors.

Academic journals and the scientific publishing community have tended to favour studies that demonstrate a significant effect. Studies that do not show an effect from an intervention are more likely to remain unpublished. Some data, such as harms and unanticipated events, may not be reported but are critically important to decisions on practice and policy. Investigators should adopt a deliberate strategy to seek out unpublished data, especially when they suspect there may be a mismatch between the published and unpublished sources. Clinical trial registration is a step towards minimising the bias associated with selective outcome reporting in published reports and it is mandatory in some countries. This means that the public can see which outcomes were measured and analysed in the clinical trial and it is clear if the investigator has only chosen to report a selection of them (presumably those most favourable to the desired outcome, for example the effectiveness of a new drug).

Trial registries support transparency in research and are valuable tools to confirm the completeness of evidence included in reviews and may help review authors identify deviations from planned statistical analyses. Data obtained from regulatory agencies or pharmaceutical companies may provide missing information, confirm that results reported in published papers are accurate or reveal potential biases in the published literature due to selective outcome reporting. Identifying ongoing studies is important to future research recommendations and planned review updates. Regulatory agencies such as the FDA and the EMA have access to comprehensive datasets from individual trials, as well as post-marketing surveillance data and adverse events (Halfpenny et al., 2016).

Information specialists and review teams who use grey literature and unpublished data must evaluate the quality and reliability of the information relative to the research question. At minimum, they should assess the credibility of the author or publication source, the currency of the information, the quality and accuracy of the cited sources and whether or not the methods of knowledge synthesis are appropriate to the questions and conclusions.

The ways in which grey literature and unpublished data will contribute to new knowledge remain unclear, though it is likely that data mining, machine learning and other computational techniques will comprise a set of new skills that information specialists and systematic review methodologists seek to employ. There is a risk that without new knowledge and skills, reviews will not be able to make effective use of the deluge of data that digital and technological advances will create. It will be important to extend our understanding of these challenges and to develop robust methods for finding and integrating grey literature and unpublished data.

Suggestions for further reading

Canadian Agency for Drugs and Technologies in Health (2015) *Grey Matters: a practical tool for searching health-related grey literature.* www.cadth.ca/resources/finding-evidence/grey-matters

Institute of Medicine (USA) Committee on Standards for Systematic Reviews of Comparative Effectiveness Research; Eden, J., Levit, L., Berg, A. and Morton, S. (eds) (2011) *Finding What Works in Health Care: standards for systematic reviews*, The National Academies Press. www.nationalacademies.org/hmd/Reports/2011/Finding-What-Works-in-Health-Care-Standards-for-Systematic-Reviews
Two of the six required elements defined by the Institute of Medicine to address reporting bias of research results (Standard 3.2) concern unpublished data. A third element, conduct a web search, is related to unpublished data.

Jørgensen, A. W., Hilden, J. and Gøtzsche, P. C. (2006) Cochrane Reviews Compared with Industry Supported Meta-analyses and Other Meta-analyses of the Same Drugs: systematic review, *BMJ*, **333** (7572), 782.
The report that differences in conclusions and estimates of effect independently varied by sponsorship status prompted a series of comments.

Saleh, A. A., Ratajeski, M. A. and Bertolet, M. (2014) Grey Literature Searching for Health Sciences Systematic Reviews: a prospective study of time spent and resources utilized, *Evidence Based Library and Information Practice*, **9** (3), 28-50.
A survey of 17 individuals reported that time spent searching for grey

literature for systematic reviews ranged from 20 to 3,480 minutes.
TrialsTracker (https://trialstracker.ebmdatalab.net/#/)

Identifies trials registered in ClinicalTrials.gov that have not published results two years after the end of the trial. Information is current as of April 2017.

Tyndall, J. (2010) *AACODS Checklist*, Flinders University, Australia. Available from https://dspace.flinders.edu.au/xmlui/bitstream/handle/ 2328/3326/AACODS_Checklist.pdf.

Jessica Tyndall developed a checklist for grey literature consisting of multiple items across six domains: Authority, Accuracy, Coverage, Objectivity, Date, Significance (AACODS). The tool seems promising but lacks the necessary information to confirm its validity. The tool is currently archived in the Flinders University open digital repository.

Vedula, S. S., Bero L., Scherer R. W. and Dickersin, K. (2009) Outcome reporting in industry-sponsored trials of gabapentin for off-label use, *New England Journal of Medicine*, **361** (20), 1963-1971.

Authors report how published endpoints and planned analyses differed from those in the internal documents among ten industry sponsored trials of off-label uses of the drug gabapentin.

References

Adams, J., Hillier-Brown, F. C., Moore, H. J., Lake, A. A., Araujo-Soares, V., White, M. and Summerbell, C. (2016) Searching and Synthesising 'Grey Literature' and 'Grey Information' in Public Health: critical reflections on three case studies, *Systematic Reviews*, **5**, 164.

Allen, C., Tsou, M. H., Aslam, A., Nagel, A. and Gawron, J. M. (2016) Applying GIS and Machine Learning Methods to Twitter Data for Multiscale Surveillance of Influenza, *PLOS ONE*, **11** (7), e0157734.

Ayers, J. W., Westmaas, J. L., Leas, E. C., Benton, A., Chen, Y., Dredze, M. and Althouse, B. M. (2016) Leveraging Big Data to Improve Health Awareness Campaigns: a novel evaluation of the Great American Smokeout, *JMIR Public Health and Surveillance*, **2** (1), e16.

Balshem, H., Stevens, A., Ansari, M., Norris, S., Kansagara, D., Shamliyan, T., Chou, R., Chung, M., Moher, D. and Dickersin K. (2013) *Finding Grey Literature Evidence and Assessing for Outcome and Analysis Reporting Biases When Comparing Medical Interventions: AHRQ and the Effective Health Care Program, Methods Guide for Effectiveness and Comparative Effectiveness*

Reviews, Agency for Healthcare Research and Quality (USA).
https://effectivehealthcare.ahrq.gov/topics/methods-guidance-reporting-bias/methods

Barak-Corren, Y., Castro, V. M., Javitt, S., Hoffnagle, A. G., Dai, Y., Perlis, R. H., Nock, M. K., Smoller, J. W. and Reis, B. Y. (2016) Predicting Suicidal Behavior from Longitudinal Electronic Health Records, *American Journal of Psychiatry*, **174** (2), 154-162.

Bossuyt, P. M., Reitsma, J. B., Bruns, D. E., Gatsonis, C. A., Glasziou, P. P., Irwig, L., Lijmer, J. G., Moher, D., Rennie, D., de Vet, H. C., Kressel, H. Y., Rifai, N., Golub, R. M., Altman, D. G., Hooft, L., Korevaar, D. A. and Cohen, J. F. (2015) Stard 2015: an updated list of essential items for reporting diagnostic accuracy studies, *BMJ*, **351**, h5527.

Brasure, M., Shamliyan, T., Butler, M. and Kane, R. L. (2010) *Finding Evidence on Ongoing Studies, Methods Future Research Needs Reports, No. 1*, Agency for Healthcare Research and Quality (USA). www.ncbi.nlm.nih.gov/books/NBK52886

Canadian Agency for Drugs and Technologies in Health (2015) *Grey Matters: a practical tool for searching health-related grey literature.* www.cadth.ca/resources/finding-evidence/grey-matters

Castro, T. S. and Osório, A. (2012) Online Violence: not beautiful enough … not thin enough. Anorectic testimonials in the web, *PsychNology Journal*, **10** (3), 169-186.

Centre for Reviews and Dissemination (2009) *Systematic Reviews: CRD's guidance for undertaking reviews in health care*, Centre for Reviews and Dissemination University of York. www.york.ac.uk/crd/guidance

Chou, R. and Helfand, M. (2005) Challenges in Systematic Reviews that Assess Treatment Harms, *Annals of Internal Medicine*, **142** (12 Pt 2), 1090-1099.

Davis, A. M., Brown, R. F., Taylor, J. L., Epstein, R. A. and McPheeters, M. L. (2014) Transition Care for Children with Special Health Care Needs, *Pediatrics*, **134** (5), 900-908.

De Angelis, C., Drazen, J. M., Frizelle, F. A., Haug, C., Hoey, J., Horton, R., Kotzin, S., Laine, C., Marusic, A., Overbeke, A. J., Schroeder, T. V., Sox, H. C. and Van Der Weyden, M. B. (2004) Clinical Trial Registration: a statement from the International Committee of Medical Journal Editors, *The Lancet*, **364** (9438), 911-912.

Demyttenaere, K., Bruffaerts, R., Posada-Villa, J. and the WHO World Mental Health Survey Consortium (2004) Prevalence, Severity, and

Unmet Need for Treatment of Mental Disorders in the World Health
Organization World Mental Health Surveys, *JAMA*,
291 (21), 2581-2590.

Doshi, P., Jefferson, T. and Del Mar, C. (2012) The Imperative to Share
Clinical Study Reports: recommendations from the Tamiflu experience,
PLOS Medicine, **9** (4), e1001201.

Doshi, P., Jones, M. and Jefferson, T. (2012) Rethinking Credible Evidence
Synthesis, *BMJ*, **344**, d7898.

Egloff, H. M., West, C. P., Wang, A. T., Lowe, K. M., Edakkanambeth
Varayil, J., Beckman, T. J. and Sawatsky, A. P. (2017) Publication Rates of
Abstracts Presented at the Society of General Internal Medicine Annual
Meeting, *Journal of General Internal Medicine*, **32** (6), 673-678.

Fernandes, A. C., Dutta, R., Velupillai, S., Sanyal, J., Stewart, R. and
Chandran, D. (2018) Identifying Suicide Ideation and Suicidal Attempts
in a Psychiatric Clinical Research Database Using Natural Language
Processing, *Scientific Reports*, **8** (1), 7426.

Godin, K., Stapleton, J., Kirkpatrick, S. I., Hanning, R. M. and Leatherdale,
S. T. (2015) Applying Systematic Review Search Methods to the Grey
Literature: a case study examining guidelines for school-based breakfast
programs in Canada, *Systematic Reviews*, **4** (1), 138.

Golder, S., Loke, Y. K. and Bland, M. (2010) Unpublished Data can be of
Value in Systematic Reviews of Adverse Effects: methodological
overview, *Journal of Clinical Epidemiology*, **63** (10), 1071-1081.

Golder, S., Loke, Y. K., Wright, K. and Norman, G. (2016a) Reporting of
Adverse Events in Published and Unpublished Studies of Health Care
Interventions: a systematic review, *PLOS Medicine*, **13** (9), e1002127.

Golder, S., Loke, Y. K., Wright, K., Norman, G. and Bland, M. (2016b) P18
the Extent of Hidden or Unpublished Adverse Events Data: a methodological review, *Journal of Epidemiology and Community Health*, **70**
(Suppl 1), A61.

Gøtzsche, P. C., Delamothe, T., Godlee, F. and Lundh, A. (2010) Adequacy
of Authors' Replies to Criticism Raised in Electronic Letters to the Editor:
cohort study, *BMJ*, **341**, c3926.

Gregory, T. N., Liu, T., Machuk, A. and Arneja, J. S. (2012) What is the
Ultimate Fate of Presented Abstracts? The Conversion Rates of
Presentations to Publications Over a Five-year Period from Three North
American Plastic Surgery Meetings, *The Canadian Journal of Plastic Surgery
(Journal Canadien de Chirurgie Plastique)*, **20** (1), 33-36.

Gülmezoglu, A. M., Pang, T., Horton, R. and Dickersin, K. (2005) WHO Facilitates International Collaboration in Setting Standards for Clinical Trial Registration, *The Lancet*, **365** (9474), 1829-1831.

Halfpenny, N. J. A., Quigley, J. M., Thompson, J. C. and Scott, D. A. (2016) Value and Usability of Unpublished Data Sources for Systematic Reviews and Network Meta-analyses, *Evidence Based Medicine*, **21** (6), 208.

Hartling, L., Featherstone, R., Nuspl, M., Shave, K., Dryden, D. M. and Vandermeer, B. (2017) Grey Literature in Systematic Reviews: a cross-sectional study of the contribution of non-English reports, unpublished studies and dissertations to the results of meta-analyses in child-relevant reviews, *BMC Medical Research Methodology*, **17** (1), 64.

Hartung, D. M., Zarin, D. A., Guise, J. M., McDonagh, M., Paynter, R. and Helfand, M. (2014) Reporting Discrepancies Between the ClinicalTrials.gov Results Database and Peer-reviewed Publications, *Annals of Internal Medicine*, **160** (7), 477-483.

Hopewell, S., Loudon, K., Clarke, M. J., Oxman, A. D. and Dickersin, K. (2009) Publication Bias in Clinical Trials Due to Statistical Significance or Direction of Trial Results, *Cochrane Database of Systematic Reviews*, **1**, MR000006.

Institute of Medicine (USA) Committee on Standards for Systematic Reviews of Comparative Effectiveness Research; Eden, J., Levit, L., Berg, A. and Morton, S. (eds), (2011) *Finding What Works in Health Care: standards for systematic reviews*, The National Academies Press. www.nap.edu/catalog/13059/finding-what-works-in-health-care-standards-for-systematic-reviews

Jefferson, T., Jones, M. A., Doshi, P., Del Mar, C. B., Hama, R., Thompson, M. J., Onakpoya, I. and Heneghan, C. (2014) Risk of Bias in Industry-funded Oseltamivir Trials: comparison of core reports versus full clinical study reports, *BMJ Open*, **4** (9), e005253.

Jefferson, T., Jones, M. A., Doshi, P., Del Mar, C. B., Hama, R., Thompson, M. J., Spencer, E. A., Onakpoya, I., Mahtani, K. R., Nunan, D., Howick, J. and Heneghan, C. (2012) Neuraminidase Inhibitors for Preventing and Treating Influenza in Healthy Adults and Children, *Cochrane Database of Systematic Reviews*, **4**, CD008965.

Joanna Briggs Institute (2011) *Joanna Briggs Institute Reviewers' Manual: 2011 edition*, The Joanna Briggs Institute. http://joannabriggs.org/assets/docs/sumari/reviewersmanual-2011.pdf

Juni, P., Altman, D. G. and Egger, M. (2001) Systematic Reviews in

Health Care: assessing the quality of controlled clinical trials, *BMJ*, **323**, 42.

Juni, P., Witschi, A., Bloch, R. and Egger, M. (1999) The Hazards of Scoring the Quality of Clinical Trials for Meta-analysis, *JAMA*, **282** (11), 1054-1060.

Kalyanam, J., Katsuki, T., Lanckriet, G. R. G. and Mackey, T. K. (2016) Exploring Trends of Nonmedical Use of Prescription Drugs and Polydrug Abuse in the Twittersphere Using Unsupervised Machine Learning, *Addictive Behaviors*, **65**, 289-295.

Karlsson, L. E. and Takahashi, R. (2017) *A Resource for Developing an Evidence Synthesis Report for Policy-making. Health Evidence Network Synthesis Report, No. 50*, WHO Regional Office for Europe. www.ncbi.nlm.nih.gov/books/NBK453541

Kugley, S., Wade, A., Thomas, J., Mahood, Q., Jørgensen, A-M. K., Hammerstrøm, K. T. and Sathe, N. (2017) *Searching for Studies: a guide to information retrieval for Campbell Systematic Reviews - Campbell Methods Series Guide 1*, The Campbell Collaboration. www.campbellcollaboration.org/library/searching-for-studies-information-retrieval-guide-campbell-reviews.html

Lefebvre, C., Manheimer, E. and Glanville, J. (2011) Searching for Studies. In Higgins, J. P. T. and Green, S. (eds) *Cochrane Handbook for Systematic Reviews of Interventions (version 5.1.0)*, The Cochrane Collaboration. http://handbook-5-1.cochrane.org

Lim, J. K., Han, J. Y., Lee, H. C., Lee, J., Chung, H., Kim, J. M. and Kim, S. K. (2013) Analysis of Publication Status of Abstracts Presented at the Annual Meeting of the Korean Academy of Rehabilitation Medicine, *Annals of Rehabilitation Medicine*, **37** (3), 413-419.

Mahood, Q., Van Eerd, D. and Irvin, E. (2014) Searching for Grey Literature for Systematic Reviews: challenges and benefits, *Research Synthesis Methods*, **5** (3), 221-234.

McPheeters, M., Davis, A. M., Taylor, J. L. and Epstein, R. A. (2014) *AHRQ Comparative Effectiveness Technical Briefs. Transition Care for Children with Special Health Needs*, Agency for Healthcare Research and Quality (USA). www.ncbi.nlm.nih.gov/books/NBK222123

Moher, D., Hopewell, S., Schulz, K. F., Montori, V., Gøtzsche, P. C., Devereaux, P. J., Elbourne, D., Egger, M. and Altman, D. G. (2010) CONSORT 2010 Explanation and Elaboration: updated guidelines for reporting parallel group randomized trials, *Journal of Clinical Epidemiology*, **63** (8), e1-37.

National Institute for Health and Care Excellence (2013) *NICE Process and Methods Guides. Guide to the Methods of Technology Appraisal*, National Institute for Health and Care Excellence (NICE). www.nice.org.uk/process/pmg9/chapter/foreword

Nock, M. K., Borges, G., Bromet, E. J., Cha, C. B., Kessler, R. C. and Lee, S. (2008) Suicide and Suicidal Behavior, *Epidemiologic Reviews*, **30** (1), 133-154.

Olivo, S. A., Macedo, L. G., Gadotti, I. C., Fuentes, J., Stanton, T. and Magee, D. J. (2008) Scales to Assess the Quality of Randomized Controlled Trials: a systematic review, *Physical Therapy*, **88** (2), 156-175.

Poulin, C., Shiner, B., Thompson, P., Vepstas, L., Young-Xu, Y., Goertzel, B., Watts, B., Flashman, L. and McAllister, T. (2014) Predicting the Risk of Suicide by Analyzing the Text of Clinical Notes, *PLOS ONE*, **9** (1), e85733.

Prohaska, E., Generali, J., Zak, K. and Grauer, D. (2013) Publication Rates of Abstracts Presented at Five National Pharmacy Association Meetings, *Hospital Pharmacy*, **48** (3), 219-226.

Quigley, J. M., Halfpenny, N. J., Thompson, J. C. and Scott, D. A. (2015) Data Extraction for Systematic Review - Where to Look for Data Outside the Primary Publication, *Value in Health*, **18** (3), A12.

Relevo, R. and Balshem, H. (2011) Finding Evidence for Comparing Medical Interventions: AHRQ and the Effective Health Care Program, *Journal of Clinical Epidemiology*, **64** (11), 1168-1177.

Rivero, E. M., Cimini, M. D., Bernier, J. E., Stanley J. A., Murray, A. D., Anderson, D. A. and Wright, H. R. (2014) Implementing an Early Intervention Program for Residential Students Who Present with Suicide Risk: a case study, *Journal of American College Health*, **62** (4), 285-291.

Riveros, C., Dechartres, A., Perrodeau, E., Haneef, R., Boutron, I. and Ravaud, P. (2013) Timing and Completeness of Trial Results Posted at ClinicalTrials.gov and Published in Journals, *PLOS Medicine*, **10** (12), e1001566.

Rosenthal, R. (1979) The File Drawer Problem and Tolerance for Null Results, *Psychological Bulletin*, **86** (3), 638-641.

Rutter, D., Francis, J., Coren, E. and Fisher, M. (2010) *SCIE Systematic Research Reviews: guidelines*, 2nd edn, Social Care Institute for Excellence. www.scie.org.uk/publications/researchresources/rr01.asp

Saleh, A. A., Ratajeski, M. A. and Bertolet, M. (2014) Grey Literature Searching for Health Sciences Systematic Reviews: a prospective study of time spent and resources utilized, *Evidence Based Library and Information Practice*, **9** (3), 28-50.

Santillana, M., Nguyen, A. T., Dredze, M., Paul, M. J., Nsoesie, E. O. and Brownstein, J. S. (2015) Combining Search, Social Media, and Traditional Data Sources to Improve Influenza Surveillance, *PLOS Computational Biology*, **11** (10), e1004513.

Savić, D., Farace, D., Frantzen, J. and Stock, C. (2017) Policy Development for Grey Literature Resources: an assessment of the Pisa Declaration, *The Grey Journal (TGJ)*, **13** (3), 167-177.

Schardt, C., Adams, M. B., Owens, T., Keitz, S. and Fontelo, P. (2007) Utilization of the PICO Framework to Improve Searching PubMed for Clinical Questions, *BMC Medical Informatics and Decision Making*, **7** (1), 16.

Scherer, R. W., Langenberg, P. and von Elm, E. (2007) Full Publication of Results Initially Presented in Abstracts, *Cochrane Database of Systematic Reviews*, **2**, MR000005.

Schöpfel, J. (2011) Towards a Prague Definition of Grey Literature, *The Grey Journal (TGJ)*, **7** (1), 5.

Schroll, J. B., Penninga, E. I. and Gøtzsche, P. C. (2016) Assessment of Adverse Events in Protocols, Clinical Study Reports, and Published Papers of Trials of Orlistat: a document analysis, *PLOS Medicine*, **13** (8), e1002101.

Scott, K. R., Nelson, L., Meisel, Z. and Perrone, J. (2015) Opportunities for Exploring and Reducing Prescription Drug Abuse Through Social Media, *Journal of Addictive Diseases*, **34** (2-3), 178-184.

Shamseer, L., Hopewell, S., Altman, D. G., Moher, D. and Schulz, K. F. (2016) Update on the Endorsement of CONSORT by High Impact Factor Journals: a survey of journal 'instructions to authors' in 2014, *Trials*, **17** (1), 301.

Shea, B. J., Hamel, C., Wells, G. A., Bouter, L. M., Kristjansson, E., Grimshaw, J., Henry, D. A. and Boers, M. (2009) AMSTAR is a Reliable and Valid Measurement Tool to Assess the Methodological Quality of Systematic Reviews, *Journal of Clinical Epidemiology*, **62** (10), 1013-1020.

Sofean, M. and Smith, M. (2013) Sentiment Analysis on Smoking in Social Networks, *Studies in Health Technology and Informatics*, **192**, 1118.

Sollaci, L. B. and Pereira, M. G. (2004) The Introduction, Methods, Results, and Discussion (IMRAD) Structure: a fifty-year survey, *Journal of the Medical Library Association*, **92** (3), 364-371.

Song, F., Parekh-Bhurke, S., Hooper, L., Loke, Y. K., Ryder, J. J., Sutton, A. J., Hing, C. B. and Harvey, I. (2009) Extent of Publication Bias in Different Categories of Research Cohorts: a meta-analysis of empirical studies,

BMC Medical Research Methodology, **9**, 79.

Song, F., Parekh, S., Hooper, L., Loke Y. K., Ryder, J., Sutton, A. J., Hing, C., Kwok, C. S., Pang, C. and Harvey, I. (2010) Dissemination and Publication of Research Findings: an updated review of related biases, *Health Technology Assessment (Winchester, England)*, **14** (8), iii, ix-xi, 1-193.

Sterne, J. A., Hernan, M. A., Reeves, B. C., Savović, J., Berkman, N. D., Viswanathan, M., Henry, D., Altman, D. G., Ansari, M. T., Boutron, I., Carpenter, J. R., Chan, A. W., Churchill, R., Deeks, J. J., Hróbjartsson, A., Kirkham, J., Jüni, P., Loke, Y. K., Pigott, T. D., Ramsay, C. R., Regidor, D., Rothstein, H. R., Sandhu, L., Santaguida, P. L., Schünemann, H. J., Shea, B., Shrier, I., Tugwell, P., Turner, L., Valentine, J. C., Waddington, H., Waters, E., Wells, G. A., Whiting, P. F. and Higgins, J. P. (2016) ROBINS-I: a tool for assessing risk of bias in non-randomized studies of interventions, *BMJ*, **355**, i4919.

Turner, E. H., Knoepflmacher, D. and Shapley, L. (2012) Publication Bias in Antipsychotic Trials: an analysis of efficacy comparing the published literature to the US Food and Drug Administration database, *PLOS Medicine*, **9** (3), e1001189.

Vedula, S. S., Li, T. and Dickersin, K. (2013) Differences in Reporting of Analyses in Internal Company Documents Versus Published Trial reports: comparisons in industry-sponsored trials in off-label uses of gabapentin, *PLOS Medicine*, **10** (1), e1001378.

Walsh, C. G., Ribeiro, J. D. and Franklin, J. C. (2017) Predicting Risk of Suicide Attempts Over Time Through Machine Learning, *Clinical Psychological Science*, **5** (3), 457-469.

Whiting, P., Savovic, J., Higgins, J. P., Caldwell, D. M., Reeves, B. C., Shea, B., Davies, P., Kleijnen, J., Churchill, R. and ROBIS Group (2016) ROBIS: a new tool to assess risk of bias in systematic reviews was developed, *Journal of Clinical Epidemiology*, **69**, 225-234.

Whiting, P. F., Weswood, M. E., Rutjes, A. W., Reitsma, J. B., Bossuyt, P. N. and Kleijnen, J. (2006) Evaluation of QUADAS, a Tool for the Quality Assessment of Diagnostic Accuracy Studies, *BMC Medical Research Methodology*, **6**, 9.

Wieland, L. S., Rutkow, L., Vedula, S. S., Kaufmann, C. N., Rosman, L. M., Twose, C., Mahendraratnam, N. and Dickersin, K. (2014) Who Has Used Internal Company Documents for Biomedical and Public Health Research and Where Did they Find Them?, *PLOS ONE*, **9** (5), e94709.

Woo, H., Cho, Y., Shim, E., Lee, J. K., Lee, C. G. and Kim, S. H. (2016)

Estimating Influenza Outbreaks Using Both Search Engine Query Data and Social Media Data in South Korea, *Journal of Medical Internet Research*, **18** (7), e177.

World Health Organization (2014) *Preventing Suicide: a global imperative*, World Health Organization. www.who.int/mental_health/suicide-prevention/world_report_2014/en

Wright, J. M., Cottrell, D. J. and Mir, G. (2014) Searching for Religion and Mental Health Studies Required Health, Social Science, and Grey Literature Databases, *Journal of Clinical Epidemiology*, **67** (7), 800-810.

Yang, Y. T., Horneffer, M. and DiLisio, N. (2013) Mining Social Media and Web Searches for Disease Detection, *Journal of Public Health Research*, **2** (1), 17-21.

Young, T. and Hopewell, S. (2011) Methods for Obtaining Unpublished Data, *Cochrane Database of Systematic Reviews*, **11**, MR000027.

Zuccon, G., Khanna, S., Nguyen, A., Boyle, J., Hamlet, M. and Cameron, M. (2015) Automatic Detection of Tweets Reporting Cases of Influenza Like Illnesses in Australia, *Health Information Science and Systems*, **3** (Suppl 1), S4.

6

Social media as a source of evidence

Su Golder

Introduction

The internet has transformed the way in which we search for information and interactive Web 2.0 internet-based applications, such as social media, have advanced the way we use the internet. So, what do we mean by social media? A commonly used definition is that social media are any web-based computer-mediated tools to co-create, share or exchange information, ideas, pictures or videos in virtual communities and networks (such as message boards, social networks, patient forums, Twitter, blogs and Facebook) (Obar and Wildman, 2015). Estimates indicate that there are 3.58 billion internet users (Statista, 2018a) and 2.46 billion social media users worldwide (Statista, 2018b). In 2017, 66% of adults aged 16 and over in Great Britain and 69% of the public in the USA used the internet for some type of social media (such as Facebook or Twitter) and the trend is for the proportion of social network users to increase further (Office for National Statistics, 2017; Pew Research Center, 2018).

Facebook and Twitter may be the most widely known but there are a multitude of other social media networks, each with a different focus. For instance, while some sites aim to connect people (professionally or socially), others are platforms to share news, ideas or information (either with generic or a topic-specific focus to the site). Some social media sites are completely open to the public, others require logins or have privacy restrictions and some social media sites allow both private and public information (for instance through changing the settings). The format of posts also varies from text, images or videos and in some instances may be limited by size (either by characters or file size).

Social media are used to discuss a wide range of issues and views from hobbies and interests to trivia and politics. An increasingly common use of social media, however, is to discuss health issues. Patients often now use social media as a source for information on their health condition, to share their experiences and to find social support. In 2015, 80% of internet users in the USA searched online for health information and 34% read someone else's commentary about health or medical issues (Fox, 2011). In Great Britain, 53% of adults aged 16 and over used the internet for looking for health-related information within the last three months (Office for National Statistics, 2017).

Given these figures, it is unsurprising that social media have been discovered as a research tool across an array of disciplines and an information source for researchers, particularly for topics in the social sciences and, more recently, health-related subjects. Although primarily still used for social networking and often for social support and dissemination, data on social media platforms are now being used to facilitate research or to provide useful information for researchers.

Social media and research

Social scientists were quick to begin to use social media for research (Jones, 1999; Woodfield, 2014) and researchers in the health sciences are now realising its value (Golder, Norman and Loke, 2015; Sinnenberg et al., 2017). Researchers undertaking clinical trials and other forms of research are increasingly using social media to recruit and retain participants. Social media is also being used to distribute online surveys and questionnaires or conduct interviews (Eysenbach and Wyatt, 2002; Sinnenberg et al., 2017). There has been a surge in social media analytics, whereby posts or chats are analysed via qualitative methodologies or aggregate numerical data collection (Sinnenberg et al., 2017). The order of magnitude of data and the speed with which it is made available (approaching real time) make social media a useful tool in research. Topics studied have been far-reaching and include political, economic, cultural, social and health (see Table 6.1). Health-related social media research has also taken many forms, as illustrated in Table 6.2.

Table 6.1 *Examples of research that has used social media*

Topic	References
Predicting general elections	Elson et al., 2012 Sloan, 2016
Monitoring opinions on the Commonwealth Games	Sloan, 2016 Social Media Research Group, 2016
Stock market predictions	Bollen, Mao and Zeng, 2011

Table 6.2 *Examples of health-related social media research*

Topic	References
Drug or product surveillance, such as pharmacovigilance	Coloma et al., 2014 Golder, Norman and Loke, 2015 Kalf et al., 2018 Sarker et al., 2015
Monitoring diseases, such as flu or cholera	Aramaki, Maskawa and Morita, 2011 Broniatowski, Paul and Dredze, 2013 Carneiro and Mylonakis, 2009 Chew and Eysenbach, 2010 Chunara, Andrews and Brownstein, 2012 Culotta, 2010a Culotta, 2010b Denecke et al., 2013 Gesualdo et al., 2013 Lamb, Paul and Dredze, 2013 Lampos and Cristianini, 2010 Signorini, Segre and Polgreen, 2011 St Louis and Zorlu, 2012
Establishing health patterns or behaviours	Goh and Huang, 2009 Prier et al., 2011
Establishing suicide patterns	Jashinsky et al., 2014
Establishing patterns of Ilicit drug use	Hanson et al., 2013 Yakushev and Mityagin, 2014 Young et al., 2014
Health service quality	Huesch, Currid-Halkett and Doctor, 2012 Nakhasi et al., 2012
Experiences of patients	Ahlwardt et al., 2014 Bosley et al., 2013 Golder, Norman and Loke, 2015 Heaivilin et al., 2011 Mishra et al., 2013
Ascertaining patients' views, such as about vaccinations	Keelan et al., 2010 Larson et al., 2013 Nicholson and Leask, 2012 Penţa and Băban, 2014 Seeman, Ing and Rizo, 2010 Skea et al., 2008 Witteman and Zikmund-Fisher, 2012

Social media and systematic reviews

Information collected from social media is not only useful for primary research, such as data monitoring studies or qualitative research studies, but also for secondary research, such as systematic reviews. Systematic reviewers have become increasingly good at promoting and sharing their results or findings to a wide audience via social media. This has become increasingly important as researchers, including systematic reviewers, are valued on their research impact. For instance, academics are expected to demonstrate their impact outside of academia and many research councils require funding recipients to demonstrate impact, particularly in the UK. Measurements (such as Altmetrics) have also become available to help researchers track the reach and influence of their work on a broad range of sources including social media (www.altmetric.com/audience/researchers). Librarians and information specialists, in particular, have adopted the role of providing support for social media use (Crum and Cooper, 2013). This may be in providing training, advice or helping disseminate or promote studies.

However, social media can be more than just a dissemination tool for reviewers and information specialists. Much of the data posted on social media are publicly available and retrievable by searching the internet. This is even the case for deleted posts which by the time of deletion may already have been shared or had a screenshot taken. The availability of social media opens up new avenues for information specialists and systematic reviewers to identify or collect data, especially from sources that may have previously been difficult to access.

There are six main ways in which social media can be useful to systematic reviewers, as described below.

To identify new or forthcoming studies

The first and probably most obvious way in which social media can be useful to systematic reviewers and information specialists is as a supplementary method to identify research or studies to include in a review. This can most feasibly be carried out by following key leaders, groups or organizations in the research field. Many researchers or authors will post links to new or forthcoming publications, reports or presentations on social media sites such as Twitter or on blogs, or post their research on professional sites such as LinkedIn (www.linkedin.com), ResearchGate (www.researchgate.net) or Academia (www.academia.edu). This is a useful and timely addition to other approaches (such as e-mail alerts). Even the most proficient social media user may not be able to identify all new studies this way due to its serendipitous nature.

To retrieve the full-text publication

Some social media sites, such as ResearchGate or Academia, have links to PDFs of the full-text manuscripts and scholarly works by authors or a 'request the full-text' option. Scientists have been found to be keen on making their work available as this helps disseminate their research findings and has the potential to increase citations to their work. However, many of the articles have been posted by authors without regard to embargoes, licensing or other restrictions set by their publisher. Thus, any researcher who downloads or prints an article from such websites may be in breach of copyright legislation. Around 40% of articles have been estimated as infringing copyright law (Van Noorden, 2017). Whether these sites will continue to give full access in the future is debatable (Times Higher Education, 2017; Van Noorden, 2017).

Social media can also be utilised to retrieve full conference presentations either through videos posted on sites such as YouTube (www.youtube.co.uk) or through the posting of slides on sites such as SlideShare (www.slideshare.net), SlideBoom (www.slideboom.com) and Speaker Deck (www.speakerdeck.com).

To contact authors or key researchers in the area

Published articles often do not contain all the information required for inclusion in a systematic review or have ambiguous information making data extraction and quality assessment difficult (Maund et al., 2014; Golder et al., 2016a; Schroll, Penninga and Gøtzsche, 2016). One way to potentially gain more complete information is to contact the authors (Golder et al., 2016b; Schroll, Bero and Gøtzsche 2013), as discussed in Chapter 5. Researchers by their very nature, however, are prone to move or change jobs. A good way in which to track their current whereabouts is to use social media sites, particularly professional sites such as LinkedIn (www.linkedin.com), Academia (www.academia.edu) and ResearchGate (www.researchgate.net) to contact authors for more information or related articles or reports.

To help formulate the research question

Social media can be used to identify unanswered questions and thus prioritise areas for further research, such as exploring how patients feel about their medical interventions (Giles and Adams, 2015). Social media may be used to provide information on relevant and important outcomes in order to help formulate or focus a systematic review question. This potential use has been underused but research into adverse effects has shown the potential benefit of searching social media, particularly for symptomatic and non-serious harms from drugs (Golder, Norman and Loke, 2015). These reports of adverse events can then be used to generate hypotheses to test in a systematic review by indicating which potential adverse effects may be associated with an intervention, or which adverse effects terms should be searched in a safety profile review containing all adverse effects.

Other research has indicated the value of using social media data to identify where patients have posted about the benefits of their treatment and potential new indications for existing drugs (Rastegar-Mojarad, Liu and Nambisan, 2016). In addition, surveys have been distributed via social media to ascertain the most important outcomes for systematic reviews (Hopkins et al., 2016).

It is important to note that the number of posts expressing particular opinions or experiences may not represent the amount of people holding these attitudes or having these experiences. Some individuals post on multiple social media sites and the motivations to post can be complex. For instance, frequency data on health care outcomes show which symptoms may be the most salient to patients on a day-to-day basis, rather than indicating overall prevalence (Mao et al., 2013). The number of comments on a topic may simply indicate the strength of feeling toward an issue (Henrich and Holmes, 2011).

To recruit the review team

A balanced and well-thought out team to conduct a systematic review is important. A good review team should include patient and public representatives and subject and methodological experts. One way to recruit patient and public representatives is to advertise on relevant discussion forums or sites. Social media are already successfully used to recruit study participants for research (Burton-Chase et al., 2017; Whitaker, Stevelink and Fear, 2017). Academics or experts could be identified and their interests researched via professional communication sites.

To help provide a public perspective

The sixth way in which social media can be useful is in providing the public's perspective on an issue. The importance of this within systematic reviews is now commonly accepted, particularly with regard to disease and treatment impact (Beusterien et al., 2012; 2013). This is because systematic reviewers need to evaluate the most important outcomes (either beneficial or harmful) and consider aspects such as the acceptability, social impact, adherence and potential uptake of an intervention (Street et al., 2008). In health care, data collection about patient experiences is typically limited to controlled clinical trials where researchers may not ask the right questions in the right way or where patients when asked may not be as forthcoming with this information or may not recall the information asked of them. Studies have already acknowledged the value of social media in ascertaining a public perspective (Pestello and Davis-Berman, 2008; Rizo et al., 2011; Sarrazin et al., 2014; Sillence and Mo, 2014; Tan et al., 2012; Wicks, Sulham and Gnanasakthy, 2014; Yanagisawa and Zimmen, 2012).

Social media provides a unique opportunity for patients to post their experiences and thoughts about their treatments or condition spontaneously. People are more inclined to disclose information in an online environment than in interviews or surveys (Beusterien et al., 2013). Social media are therefore a great source of real-word data in a real-world setting (Beusterien et al., 2013). By assessing the content generated by patients via social media, a considerable amount of information on patient perspectives and experiences can be gathered. Social media can thus 'help explain' experiences of living with a disease or condition and uncover a richer explanation of the issues involved with interventions to inform systematic reviews (Street et al., 2008).

Certainly, a number of pharmaceutical companies have explored the use of social media to gain insight into patient perspectives on adverse effects and to assess their behaviour in regard to switching between treatments and adherence to their treatment (Davies, 2008; Pages et al., 2014a; Pages et al., 2014b; Powell et al., 2016; Risson et al., 2016; Sukkar, 2015; Visible Technologies, 2011). The Food and Drug Administration (FDA) in the USA is also increasingly looking to social media to gain insight into patient perspectives on adverse effects (Hill, 2015; PatientsLikeMe, 2015), as indeed are other regulatory authorities (Freifeld et al., 2014). Social media could, therefore, be used to supplement patient public involvement within a systematic review.

Challenges of using social media as an information source

Social media presents great opportunities for internet searchers and information specialists but also many challenges. Although social media provide huge amounts of near-time data, the quality of the data and the retrieval of the data are problematic.

We need to consider the validity of the information posted on social media and apply critical thinking more than ever before. Information posted on social media may not just be biased but may be false or inaccurate. Robots (or 'bots') that are programmed to appear as real people are common on social media. Validating authenticity (posts may not be genuine) and verifying the accuracy of information is problematic for social media data. E-mailing individuals is not only time consuming but also has ethical issues and is prone to a lack of response. Caution must also be applied when using social media as a data source because people who post on social media may not be representative of the general population, for example, less vocal or older adults may be under-represented.

Social media has been used successfully as a source of data. A study on attitudes towards breastfeeding found that comparing information from traditional sources and user-generated online content in systematic reviews led to a similar set of opinions (Giles and Adams, 2015).

Searching social media

Searching social media sites is challenging due to the lack of structure and formal indexing that is available with bibliographic databases. The language used by people posting on social media is prone to spelling mistakes, typos, sarcasm, abbreviations and slang. Not only is the search process difficult to execute but, as with all internet searching, it is difficult to adopt a transparent, reproducible or systematic approach to searching social media. This makes the reporting and updating of any searches in a systematic review challenging.

The huge and unimaginable amount of data in social media can cause problems for the searcher with a dramatic increase in the amount of data published via these resources (Bradley, 2017). In one minute in 2017 it was estimated that, on average, 452,000 tweets were sent, 300,000 logins were made on Facebook, and 120 new accounts on LinkedIn were set up (www.visualcapitalist.com/happens-internet-minute-2017).

Publishing has gone from months to literally seconds. This real-time data needs real-time searches. Traditional search engines, however, cannot keep pace with social media content. This gap has seen a rise in specialist search engines which focus on social media sites and networks. Socialmention* (www.socialmention.com), Social Searcher (www.social-searcher.com) and Qwant (www.qwant.com) are three examples of such social media search engines. Others are focused on a particular type of social media, for example, Twitter and Facebook themselves provide users with search functionality. It is useful to combine several searches; a researcher wanting to know more about how the public use ibuprofen when their children have chicken pox might use Socialmention* to get an overview of the top blogs, Qwant to see the latest news and then Twitter to collect positive and negative experiences.

Socialmention* focuses on posts from around 100 social media sites in the last month and has a simple search interface. It is useful to give a quick insight into what is currently being said as it presents information on the sentiment of the posts and the top keywords associated with the search terms. It also allows RSS feeds and e-mail alerts to be set up and data can be downloaded.

Social Searcher is another free social media search engine (but there is a limited number of requests per day allowed). Social Searcher allows real-time searching of ten sources without having to log into any of the platforms. The results can be sorted by date or popularity as illustrated in Figure 6.1.

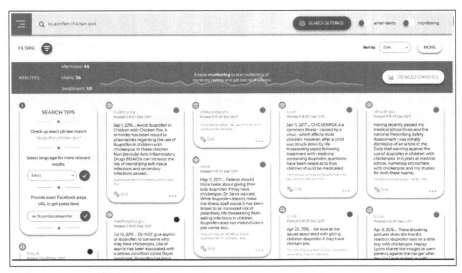

Figure 6.1 *Social Searcher screen-shot*
Reproduced with permission (https://www.social-searcher.com)

Qwant also allows real-time searching of Twitter at the same time as a web search and news search. There are many other social media search engines that have come and gone and they continue to do so (Bradley, 2017).

Searching Twitter is particularly useful for news updates and information on conferences. Twitter itself provides a basic and an advanced search facility (www.twitter.com/search-advanced). Another good way of following what is happening at conferences is to search using hashtags as attendees are often encouraged to use a specific hashtag when they tweet about the event.

Facebook has a very simple search engine at the top of every page on its site and it can also be searched via Google with the search 'site:facebook.com', for example, 'ibuprofen site:facebook.com'. To conduct a search of blogs or specialist discussion forums, there are search directories available to help, such as Blogspot Search (www. searchblogspot.com) or Find a Forum (www.findaforum.net). Charity websites, such as Parkinson's UK and the British Heart Foundation, often provide online community forums too, or umbrella sites such as

DailyStrength (www.dailystrength.org) can be searched. For some discussion forums, such as PatientsLikeMe (www.patientslikeme. com), permission needs to be obtained from the owners or moderators for researchers to view or use data.

Finding people can sometimes be more successful on social media than through a general search. Twitter (www.twitter.com/search-advanced) has an option for searching for people which can be useful for tracking a particular individual or an expert in a particular field. ResearchGate (www.researchgate.net) allows searching for particular individuals, projects, publications, institutions and departments. Details on individuals can help verify someone's expertise and skills when trying to identify people to join a review or advisory team. Academia (www.academia.edu) allows people and publications searches, as does Mendeley, a social networking site for scientists as well as a research tool (www.mendeley.com/research-network/ community), and ResearcherID (www.researcherid.com), which helps find researchers based on area of interest.

Examples of systematic reviews

There are few examples of systematic reviewers using social media as a data source (Golder et al., 2016b). A search on MEDLINE for systematic reviews mentioning Twitter or Facebook in the abstract identified only 28 records in March 2018 and in most of these they were used as an intervention rather than as systematic review tools for gathering data. In contrast, a search on MEDLINE for systematic review in the title, MEDLINE in the title and MEDLINE in the abstract identified 27,518 records. Social media have been used occasionally in systematic reviews, as Case studies 6.1 and 6.2 illustrate further.

Case study 6.1: Antenatal magnesium sulphate regimens
In a systematic review on the adverse effects of different antenatal magnesium sulphate regimens for improving maternal and infant outcomes, the authors searched both blogs and discussion forum threads in addition to traditional sources such as MEDLINE, Embase and ClinicalTrials.gov (Bain, Middleton and Crowther, 2013). The nature of searching personal blogs and forums meant that the authors could not search in the way commonly prescribed for systematic reviews. Instead, the authors sensibly pre-specified that sampling would cease at 20 relevant blogs and ten relevant discussion forum threads identified (with a maximum of five relevant threads from any

individual forum) (Bain, Middleton and Crowther, 2013). From the social media sites, the systematic review authors were able to identify information on the perceived purpose or benefits of the treatment and women's experiences, particularly with respect to adverse effects.

Case study 6.2: Retinal photography
A Health Technology Assessment (HTA) review on retinal photography for detection of diabetic retinopathy searched personal blogs and discussion forums in addition to traditional sources. In this review, the authors found that blogs provided insight into problems with screening and treatment compliance and the fear and distress associated with the intervention. These sources therefore enhanced the evidence offered by journal articles and provided a richer explanation of the issues (Street et al., 2008).

Future directions

The ways in which data from social media can help to inform secondary research (such as systematic reviews) have not been well developed and little has been published on the subject. The next step for researchers may be to conduct prospective evaluations on the added value of using social media when conducting systematic reviews. Evaluations could be undertaken using a wide variety of systematic review topics, such as reviews of adverse effects of drugs, complex interventions, public health, crime and justice, education and social policy. It is also worth investigating what impact social media could have on reviews of qualitative evidence in a range of topics.

Thoughtful consideration is needed on the ethics of using social media as a data source in systematic reviews (Golder et al., 2017). Researchers should consider any potential for harm to the people posting on the social media sites. Even if the primary research has directly quoted posts or presented information so that the person posting is traceable, it does not necessarily mean that any systematic reviews or other secondary research should reproduce this information. The points to consider before using the data (Golder et al., 2017) are:

- What was the original intention of the post?
- Is the information public or private?
- Is the individual identifiable or vulnerable?
- Is the information of a sensitive nature?
- Should consent be sought?

There are some helpful guidelines and recommendations published on the ethics of using social media in research (British Psychological Society, 2017; Im and Chee, 2012; Liberty University Institutional Review Board, 2012; Markham and Buchanan, 2012; Norwegian National Research Ethics Committees, 2014; Townsend and Wallace, 2017).

Conclusion

The use of social media as a data source for systematic searching is still in its infancy. It is unlikely that social media will replace other data sources as a port of call for information, but it has a number of potential advantages that make it worth exploring further and tackling the challenges it poses. This chapter has identified some of the issues and provided advice on some useful tools for information specialists to explore further.

Suggestions for further reading

Bradley, P. (2017) Social Media Search Engines. In Bradley, P., *Expert Internet Searching*, 5th edn, Facet Publishing.

Sloan, L. and Quan-Haase, A. (eds) (2017) *The SAGE Handbook of Social Media Research Methods*, SAGE Publishing.

Street, J. M., Braunack-Mayer, A. J., Facey, K., Ashcroft, R. E. and Hiller, J. E. (2008) Virtual Community Consultation? Using the Literature and Weblogs to Link Community Perspectives and Health Technology Assessment, *Health Expectations*, **11** (2), 189-200.

References

Ahlwardt, K., Heaivilin, N., Gibbs, J., Page, J., Gerbert, B. and Tsoh, J. Y. (2014) Tweeting about Pain: comparing self-reported toothache experiences with those of backaches, earaches and headaches, *Journal of the American Dental Association*, **145** (7), 737-743.

Aramaki, E., Maskawa, S. and Morita, M. (2011) Twitter Catches the Flu: detecting influenza epidemics using Twitter, *Proceedings of the 2011 Conference on Empirical Methods in Natural Language Processing, Edinburgh*, 27-31 July 2011, 1568-1576.

Bain, E. S., Middleton, P. F. and Crowther, C. A. (2013) Maternal Adverse Effects of Different Antenatal Magnesium Sulphate Regimens for Improving Maternal and Infant Outcomes: a systematic review, *BMC Pregnancy and Childbirth*, **13**, 195.

Beusterien, K., Tsay, S., Gholizadeh, S. and Su, Y. (2013) Real-world Experience with Colorectal Cancer Chemotherapies: patient web forum analysis, *ecancermedicalscience*, **7**, 361.

Beusterien, K., Tsay, S., Su, Y., Corral, M., Gholizadeh, S. and Wagner, S. (2012) Experience with Colorectal Cancer: analysis of patient web forums, *Journal of Clinical Oncology*, **30** (S4), 496.

Bollen, J., Mao, H. and Zeng, X. (2011) Twitter Mood Predicts the Stock Market, *Journal of Computational Science*, **2** (1), 1-8.

Bosley, J. C., Zhao, N. W., Hill, S., Shofer, F. S., Asch, D. A., Becker, L. B. and Merchant, R. M. (2013) Decoding Twitter: surveillance and trends for cardiac arrest and resuscitation communication, *Resuscitation*, **84** (2), 206-212.

Bradley, P. (2017) Social Media Search Engines. In Bradley, P., *Expert Internet Searching*, 5th edn, Facet Publishing.

British Psychological Society (2017) *Ethics Guidelines for Internet-mediated Research*, The British Psychological Society. www.bps.org.uk/news-and-policy/ethics-guidelines-internet-mediated-research-2017

Broniatowski, D. A., Paul, M. J. and Dredze, M. (2013) National and local Influenza Surveillance Through Twitter: an analysis of the 2012–2013 influenza epidemic, *PLOS ONE*, **8** (12), e83672.

Burton-Chase, A. M., Parker, W. M., Hennig, K., Sisson, F. and Bruzzone, L. L. (2017) The Use of Social Media to Recruit Participants with Rare Conditions: Lynch Syndrome as an example, *JMIR Research Protocols*, **6** (1), e12.

Carneiro, H. A. and Mylonakis, E. (2009) Google Trends: A web-based tool for real-time surveillance of disease outbreaks, *Clinical Infectious Diseases*, **49** (10), 1557-1564.

Chew, C. and Eysenbach, G. (2010) Pandemics in the Age of Twitter: content analysis of tweets during the 2009 H1N1 outbreak, *PLOS ONE*, **5** (11), e14118.

Chunara, R., Andrews, J. R. and Brownstein, J. S. (2012) Social and News Media Enable Estimation of Epidemiological Patterns Early in the 2010 Haitian Cholera Outbreak, *American Journal of Tropical Medicine and Hygiene*, **86** (1), 39-45.

Coloma, P., Becker, B., van Mulligen, E. and Kors, J. (2014) Use of Social

Media in Pharmacovigilance: testing the waters, *Pharmacoepidemiology and Drug Safety*, **23** (Suppl. 1), 290.

Crum, J. A. and Cooper, I. D. (2013) Emerging Roles for Biomedical Librarians: a survey of current practice, challenges, and changes, *Journal of the Medical Library Association*, **101** (4), 278-286.

Culotta, A. (2010a) Detecting in Influenza Outbreaks by Analyzing Twitter Messages, cited 8 August 2015. http://arxiv.org/pdf/1007.4748v1.pdf

Culotta, A. (ed.) (2010b) Towards Detecting Influenza Epidemics by Analyzing Twitter Messages, *1st Workshop on Social Media Analytics (SOMA'10)*, 25 July 2010, Washington, D. C., USA.

Davies, M. (2008) *Listening to Consumers in a Highly Regulated Environment. How Pharmaceutical Manufacturers Can Leverage Consumer-generated Media*, The Nielsen Company.
https://www.nielsen.com/us/en/insights/reports/2008/Pharma-Health-Listening-to-Consumers-in-a-Highly-Regulated-Environment.html

Denecke, K., Krieck, M., Otrusina, L., Smrz, P., Dolog, P., Nejdl, W. and Velasco, E. (2013) How to Exploit Twitter for Public Health Monitoring?, *Methods of Information in Medicine*, **52** (4), 326-339.

Elson, S. B., Yeung, D., Roshan, P., Bohandy, S. R. and Nader, A. (2012) *Using Social Media to Gauge Iranian Public Opinion and Mood after the 2009 Election*, Rand Corporation.
www.rand.org/pubs/technical_reports/TR1161.html

Eysenbach, G. and Wyatt, J. (2002) Using the Internet for Surveys and Health Research, *Journal of Medical Internet Research*, **4** (2), e13.

Fox, S. (2011) *The Social Life of Health Information, 2011*, Pew Research Center.
www.pewinternet.org/2011/05/12/the-social-life-of-health-information-2011

Freifeld, C. C., Brownstein, J. S., Menone, C. M., Bao, W., Filice, R., Kass-Hout, T. and Dasgupta, N. (2014) Digital Drug Safety Surveillance: monitoring pharmaceutical products in Twitter, *Drug Safety*, **37** (5), 343-350.

Gesualdo, F., Stilo, G., Agricola, E., Gonfiantini, M. V., Pandolfi, E., Velardi, P. and Tozzi, A. E. (2013) Influenza-like Illness Surveillance on Twitter Through Automated Learning of Naive Language, *PLOS ONE*, **8** (12), e82489.

Giles, E. L. and Adams, J. M. (2015) Capturing Public Opinion on Public Health Topics: a comparison of experiences from a systematic review, focus group study, and analysis of online, user-generated content,

Frontiers in Public Health, **3**, 200.

Goh, T. and Huang, Y. (2009) Monitoring Youth Depression Risk in Web 2.0., *VINE Journal of Information and Knowledge Management Systems*, **39** (3), 192-202.

Golder, S., Loke, Y. K., Wright, K. and Norman, G. (2016a) Reporting of Adverse Events in Published and Unpublished Studies of Health Care Interventions: a systematic review, *PLOS Medicine*, **13** (9), e1002127.

Golder, S., Loke, Y. K., Wright, K. and Sterrantino, C. (2016b) Most Systematic Reviews of Adverse Effects Did Not Include Unpublished Data, *Journal of Clinical Epidemiology*, **77**, 125-133.

Golder, S., Norman, G. and Loke, Y. K. (2015) Systematic Review on the Prevalence, Frequency and Comparative Value of Adverse Events Data in Social Media, *British Journal of Clinical Pharmacology*, **80** (4), 878-888.

Golder, S., Shahd, A., Norman, G. and Booth, A. (2017) Attitudes Towards the Ethics of Research Using Social Media: a systematic review, *Journal of Medical Internet Research*, **19** (6), e195.

Hanson, C. L., Burton, S. H., Giraud-Carrier, C., West, J. H., Barnes, M. D. and Hansen, B. (2013) Tweaking and Tweeting: exploring Twitter for nonmedical use of a psychostimulant drug (Adderall) among college students, *Journal of Medical Internet Research*, **15** (4), e62.

Heaivilin, N., Gerbert, B., Page, J. E., Gibbs, J. L. (2011) Public Health Surveillance of Dental Pain via Twitter, *Journal of Dental Research*, **90** (9), 1047-1051.

Henrich, N. and Holmes, B. (2011) What the Public Was Saying About the H1N1 Vaccine: perceptions and issues discussed in on-line comments during the 2009 H1N1 pandemic, *PLOS ONE*, **6** (4), e62.

Hill, A. (2015) *FDA Links with PatientsLikeMe*, 16 June 2015. www.pharmafile.com/news/497222/fda-links-patientslikeme

Hopkins, C., Philpott, C., Crowe, S., Regan, S., Degun, A., Papachristou, I. and Schilder, A. G. (2016) Identifying the Most Important Outcomes for Systematic Reviews of Interventions for Rhinosinusitis in Adults: working with patients, public and practitioners, *Rhinology*, **54** (1), 20-26.

Huesch, M. D., Currid-Halkett, E. and Doctor, J. N. (2012) Public Hospital Quality Report Awareness: evidence from national and Californian internet searches and social media mentions, *BMJ Open*, **4** (3), e004417.

Im, E. and Chee, W. (2012) Practical Guidelines for Qualitative Research Using Online Forums, *Computers, Informatics, Nursing*, **30** (11), 604-611.

Jashinsky, J., Burton, S. H., Hanson, C. L., West, J., Giraud-Carrier, C.,

Barnes, M. D. and Argyle, T. (2014) Tracking Suicide Risk Factors Through Twitter in the US, *Crisis*, **35** (1), 51-59.

Jones, S. (ed.) (1999) *Doing Internet Research: critical issues and methods for examining the net*, SAGE Publishing.

Kalf, R., Makady, A., Ten Ham, R., Meijboom, K. and Goettsch, W. (2018) Use of Social Media in the Assessment of Relative Effectiveness: an explorative review with examples from oncology, *JMIR Cancer*, **4** (1), e11.

Keelan, J., Pavri, V., Balakrishnan, R. and Wilson, K. (2010) An Analysis of the Human Papilloma Virus Vaccine Debate on MySpace Blogs, *Vaccine*, **28** (6), 1535-1540.

Lamb, A., Paul, M. and Dredze, M. (2013) Separating Fact from Fear: tracking flu infections on Twitter, *Proceedings of the 2013 Conference of the North American Chapter of the Association for Computational Linguistics: Human Language Technologies (NAACL-HLT)*, 789-795.

Lampos, V. and Cristianini, N. (2010) Tracking the Flu Pandemic by Monitoring the Social Web, *2nd International Workshop on Cognitive Information Processing*.

Larson, H. J., Smith, D. M., Paterson, P., Cumming, M., Eckersberger, E., Freifeld, C. C., Ghinai, I., Jarrett, C., Paushter, L., Brownstein, J. S. and Madoff, L. C. (2013) Measuring Vaccine Confidence: analysis of data obtained by a media surveillance system used to analyse public concerns about vaccines, *Lancet Infectious Diseases*, **13** (7), 606-613.

Liberty University Institutional Review Board (2012) *Guidelines for Internet Research with Human Subjects*, Liberty University.
www.liberty.edu/media/9997/Internet_Research.pdf

Mao, J. J., Chung, A., Benton, A., Hill, S., Ungar, L., Leonard, C. E., Hennessy, S. and Holmes, J. H. (2013) Online Discussion of Drug Side Effects and Discontinuation Among Breast Cancer Survivors, *Pharmacoepidemiology and Drug Safety*, **22** (3), 256-262.

Markham, A. and Buchanan, E. (2012) *Ethical Decision-Making and Internet Research: recommendations from the AoIR Ethics Working Committee (version 2.0)*, Association of Internet Researchers (AoIR).
http://aoir.org/reports/ethics2.pdf

Maund, E., Tendal, B., Hróbjartsson, A., Jørgensen, K. J., Lundh, A., Schroll, J. and Gøtzsche, P. C. (2014) Benefits and Harms in Clinical Trials of Duloxetine for Treatment of Major Depressive disorder: comparison of clinical study reports, trial registries, and publications, *BMJ*, **348**, g3510.

Mishra, M. V., Bennett, M., Vincent, A., Lee, O. T., Lallas, C. D., Trabulsi, E.

J., Gomella, L. G., Dicker, A. P. and Showalter, T. N. (2013) Identifying Barriers to Patient Acceptance of Active Surveillance: content analysis of online patient communications, *PLOS ONE*, **8** (9), e68563.

Nakhasi, A., Passarella, R., Bell, S., Paul, M., Dredze, M. and Pronovost, P. (2012) *Malpractice and Malcontent: analyzing medical complaints in Twitter*, AAAI Fall Symposium Series.

Nicholson, M. S. and Leask, J. (2012) Lessons from an Online Debate About Measles-mumps-rubella (MMR) Immunization, *Vaccine*, **30** (25), 3806-3812.

Norwegian National Research Ethics Committees (2014) *Ethical Guidelines for Internet Research*, The National Committee for Research Ethics in the Social Sciences and the Humanities (NESH).
www.etikkom.no/en/ethical-guidelines-for-research/
ethical-guidelines-for-internet-research

Obar, J. A. and Wildman, S. S. (2015) Social Media Definition and the Governance Challenge: an introduction to the special issue, *SSRN Electronic Journal*.
https://papers.ssrn.com/sol3/papers.cfm?abstract_id=2647377

Office for National Statistics (2017) *Statistical Bulletin: internet access – households and individuals: 2017*.
www.ons.gov.uk/peoplepopulationandcommunity

Pages, A., Bondon-Guitton, E., Montastruc, J. L. and Bagheri, H. (2014a) Undesirable Effects Related to Oral Antineoplastic Drugs: comparison between patients' internet narratives and a national pharmacovigilance database, *Drug Safety*, **37** (8), 629-637.

Pages, A., Bondon-Guitton, E., Montastruc, J. L. and Bagheri, H. (2014b) Adverse Drug Reactions Related to Oral Chemotherapy Drugs: patients' internet narratives vs. Pharmacovigilance Database, *Fundamental and Clinical Pharmacology*, **28** (Suppl. 1), 52.

PatientsLikeMe (2015) PatientsLikeMe and the FDA Sign Research Collaboration Agreement, 15 June 2015.
http://news.patientslikeme.com/press-release/patientslikeme-and-fda-sign-research-collaboration-agreement

Penţa, M. A. and Băban, A. (2014) Dangerous Agent or Saviour? HPV Vaccine Representations on Online Discussion Forums in Romania, *International Journal of Behavioral Medicine*, **21** (1), 20-28.

Pestello, F. G. and Davis-Berman, J. (2008) Taking Anti-depressant Medication: a qualitative examination of internet postings, *Journal of*

Mental Health, **17** (4), 349-360.

Pew Research Center (2018) *Social Media Fact Sheet.*
www.pewinternet.org/fact-sheet/social-media

Powell, G. E., Seifert, H. A., Reblin, T., Burstein, P. J., Blowers, J., Menius, J. A., Painter, J. L., Thomas, M., Pierce, C. E., Rodriguez, H. W., Brownstein, J. S., Freifeld, C., Bell, H. G. and Dasgupta, N. (2016) Social Media Listening for Routine Post-Marketing Safety Surveillance, *Drug Safety,* **39** (5), 443-454.

Prier, K., Smith, M., Giraud-Carrier, C. and Hanson, C. L. (2011) Identifying Health-related Topics on Twitter: an exploration of tobacco-related tweets as a test topic. In Salerno J., Yang S. J., Nau, D. and Chai, S. K. (eds), *Social Computing, Behavioral-Cultural Modeling and Prediction. SBP 2011. Lecture Notes in Computer Science,* volume 6589, Springer.

Rastegar-Mojarad, M., Liu, H. and Nambisan, P. (2016) Using Social Media Data to Identify Potential Candidates for Drug Repurposing: a feasibility study, *JMIR Research Protocols,* **5** (2), e121.

Risson, V., Saini, D., Bonzani, I., Huisman, A. and Olson, M. (2016) Patterns of Treatment Switching in Multiple Sclerosis Therapies in US Patients Active on Social Media: application of social media content analysis to health outcomes research, *Journal of Medical Internet Research,* **18** (3), e62.

Rizo, C., Deshpande, A., Ing, A. and Seeman, N. A. (2011) Rapid, Web-based Method for Obtaining Patient Views on Effects and Side-effects of Antidepressants, *Journal of Affective Disorders,* **130** (1-2), 290-293.

Sarker, A., Ginn, R., Nikfarjam, A., O'Connor, K., Smith, K., Jayaraman, S., Upadhaya, T. and Gonzalez, G. (2015) Utilizing Social Media Data for Pharmacovigilance: a review, *Journal of Biomedical Informatics,* **54**, 202-212.

Sarrazin, M. S., Cram, P., Mazur, A., Ward, M. and Reisinger, H. S. (2014) Patient Perspectives of Dabigatran: analysis of online discussion forums, *The Patient: Patient-Centered Outcomes Research,* **7** (1), 47-54.

Schroll, J. B., Bero, L. and Gøtzsche, P. C. (2013) Searching for Unpublished Data for Cochrane Reviews: cross sectional study, *BMJ,* **346**, f2231.

Schroll, J. B., Penninga, E. I. and Gøtzsche, P. C. (2016) Assessment of Adverse Events in Protocols, Clinical Study Reports, and Published Papers of Trials of Orlistat: a document analysis, *PLOS Medicine,* **13** (8), e1002101.

Seeman, N., Ing, A. and Rizo, C. (2010) Assessing and Responding in Real Time to Online Anti-vaccine Sentiment During a Flu Pandemic, *Healthcare Quarterly,* **13**, Spec No. 8-15.

Signorini, A., Segre, A. M. and Polgreen, P. M. (2011) The Use of Twitter to Track Levels of Disease Activity and Public Concern in the U.S. During the Influenza A H1N1 Pandemic, *PLOS ONE*, **6** (5), e19467.

Sillence, E. and Mo, P. K. (2014) Communicating Health Decisions: an analysis of messages posted to online prostate cancer forums, *Health Expectations*, **17** (2), 244-253.

Sinnenberg, L., Buttenheim, A. M., Padrez, K., Mancheno, C., Ungar, L. and Merchant, R. M. (2017) Twitter as a Tool for Health Research: a systematic review, *American Journal of Public Health*, **107** (1), e1-e8.

Skea, Z. C., Entwistle, V. A., Watt, I. and Russell, E. (2008) 'Avoiding Harm to Others' Considerations in Relation to Parental Measles, Mumps and Rubella (MMR) Vaccination Discussions – An Analysis of an Online Chat Forum, *Social Science & Medicine*, **67** (9), 1382-1390.

Sloan, L. (2016) *Using Twitter in Social Science Research*, SAGE Publishing.

Social Media Research Group (2016) *Using Social Media for Social Research: an introduction*, Social Media Research Group.

St Louis, C. and Zorlu, G. (2012) Can Twitter Predict Disease Outbreaks?, *BMJ*, **344**, e2353.

Statista: The Statistics Portal (2018a) *Number of internet users worldwide from 2005 to 2017 (in millions)*. www.statista.com/statistics/273018/number-of-internet-users-worldwide

Statista: The Statistics Portal (2018b) *Social Media Statistics and Facts*. www.statista.com/topics/1164/social-networks

Street, J. M., Braunack-Mayer, A. J., Facey, K., Ashcroft, R. E. and Hiller, J. E. (2008) Virtual Community Consultation? Using the Literature and Weblogs to Link Community Perspectives and Health Technology Assessment, *Health Expectations*, **11** (2), 189-200.

Sukkar, E. (2015) Searching Social Networks to Detect Adverse Reactions, *Pharmaceutical Journal*, 22 January 2015. www.pharmaceutical-journal.com/news-and-analysis/features/searching-social-networks-to-detect-adverse-reactions/20067624.article

Tan, M. L. H., Kok, K. L. M., Ganesh, V. and Thomas, S. (2012) Content Analysis on Breast Reconstruction in the Era of Internet Video-sharing Community, *European Journal of Surgical Oncology*, **38**, 455.

Times Higher Education (2017) Publishers Seek Removal of Millions of Papers from ResearchGate, 5 October 2017. www.timeshighereducation.com/news/publishers-seek-removal-millions-papers-researchgate

Townsend, L. and Wallace, C. (2017) *Social Media Research: a guide to ethics*, Dotrural, The University of Aberdeen.
www.dotrural.ac.uk/socialmediaresearchethics.pdf

Van Noorden, R. (2017) Publishers Threaten to Remove Millions of Papers from ResearchGate, *Nature*, 17 October 2017.
www.nature.com/news/publishers-threaten-to-remove-millions-of-papers-from-researchgate-1.22793

Visible Technologies (2011) *Pharmaceutical Industry Special Report: adverse event reporting in social media*, Visible Technologies.

Whitaker, C., Stevelink, S. and Fear, N. (2017) The Use of Facebook in Recruiting Participants for Health Research Purposes: a systematic review, *Journal of Medical Internet Research*, **19** (8), e290.

Wicks, P., Sulham, K. A. and Gnanasakthy, A. (2014) Quality of Life in Organ Transplant Recipients Participating in an Online Transplant Community, *The Patient: Patient-Centered Outcomes Research*, **7** (1), 73-84.

Witteman, H. O. and Zikmund-Fisher, B. J. (2012) The Defining Characteristics of Web 2.0 and Their Potential Influence in the Online Vaccination Debate, *Vaccine*, **30** (25), 3734-3740.

Woodfield K. (ed.) (2014) *Social Media in Social Research: blogs on blurring the boundaries*, NatCen Social Research.

Yakushev, A. and Mityagin, S. (2014) Social Networks Mining for Analysis and Modeling Drugs Usage, *Procedia Computer Science*, **29**, 2462-2471.

Yanagisawa, M. and Zimmen, P. (2012) Topix Discussion Board: a qualitative insight into the lives of women affected by tape complications, *Neurourology and Urodynamics*, **31**, 274-275.

Young, A. M., DiClemente, R. J., Halgin, D. S., Sterk, C. E. and Havens, J. R. (2014) Drug Users' Willingness to Encourage Social, Sexual, and Drug Network Members to Receive an HIV Vaccine: a social network analysis, *AIDS and Behavior*, **18** (9), 1753-1763.

7

Text mining for information specialists

Julie Glanville

Introduction

Information specialists search resources to identify information to answer research questions. Typically, we investigate the questions, identify relevant sources of information that might answer those questions, search those sources and retrieve documents. We may also be involved in managing retrieved records and documents and sometimes we also select information from the records or documents that may be most relevant to the questions being asked. Sometimes information specialists produce summaries of the most relevant information.

Information specialists have been undertaking these tasks for decades and many textbooks and guidance documents are available to support them. New techniques are constantly developing which can help with information retrieval and it is important to assess and appreciate what they may offer. New text mining tools, which analyse the frequency and relationship of words in texts, are growing in number and availability. These tools may be particularly relevant and attractive to information specialists developing searches for systematic reviews since text mining can assist with developing searches for broad-based and hard to define topics. It can also provide opportunities to manage and process large volumes of records, which can be a challenge for some research questions.

The use of text mining is not yet standard practice in systematic review searching and indeed is not necessary for many non-complex topics. However, its potential is being recognised and explored and it has been subject to several recent scoping reviews in the health sector. In disciplines where systematic reviews are not yet a common method, an awareness of the potential value of text mining is likely to be similarly low. Outside of the systematic review context, information specialists should also find that text mining is useful for many tasks needing textual analysis, including assessing terminology in complex topics, for appreciating the concepts being covered within a specific literature and for undertaking a variety of citation analyses.

This chapter presents an overview of what text mining tools have to offer for all disciplines and their potential value to information specialists. Table 7.1 (pages 165–7) contains the names and website addresses of all the text mining tools referred to in this chapter.

What is text mining?

Text mining is an umbrella term that covers a wide variety of techniques involving the computer analysis of words within documents and their relationships to each other within a document. Text mining can range from simple counts of the number of times that words appear in documents (frequency analysis), to distinguishing relevant from irrelevant texts (machine learning). Another aspect of text mining is semantic analysis, where the role of words within sentences can be specified and hence the context of words can be identified, creating possibilities to make searches more precise and meaningful.

The UK's National Centre for Text Mining (NaCTeM) defines text mining as 'the process of discovering and extracting knowledge from unstructured data' through identifying relevant texts, identifying and extracting from the texts 'entities, facts and relationships between them' and 'data mining to find associations among the pieces of information extracted from many different texts' (www.nactem.ac.uk/faq.php?faq=1). Other text mining centres are working across the world in academic departments and national institutes. Identifying experts in your local university computer science department might be a useful first step in building text mining knowledge. Cross-disciplinary text mining initiatives are also being funded internationally, including FutureTDM (http://project.futuretdm.eu), which is trying to increase the update of text and data mining in the European Union, and OpenMinTed (www.openminted.eu) which offers a gateway to text mining tools.

Text mining tools come in many forms:

- interfaces to individual databases, such as PubReMiner for PubMed
- standalone packages or web-based software into which we can load sets of database records or other text for analysis (e.g. Voyant)
- modules integrated into larger software packages (e.g. EPPI-Reviewer).

They may be simple one-task tools or sophisticated function packages with many programmable options.

Text mining tools usually accept any form of text. This means that they can analyse detailed text contained in books or journal articles or structured bibliographic records (singly or in batches). Some tools will analyse database records one by one and others will analyse a batch of records as if they were a single document. Information specialists may experience a shift in perspective because text mining tools are not always designed to analyse text in the ways we might expect. Our search strategies are often geared to find database records, but text mining tools analyse documents. This means that many text mining tools may not be able to distinguish between words in the titles and abstracts from those in subject heading fields. Many tools may not recognise bibliographic database record structures that help us with search efficiency, such as fields capturing publication types or language codes. It is important to remember this key difference when assessing how and when to use text mining.

Information specialists typically work in a Boolean world. Search construction in database interfaces such as Ovid, EBSCOhost and ProQuest has historically used Boolean logic and proximity operators. This approach retrieves records based on the presence or absence of terms. In contrast, document retrieval using text mining is determined by formulae informed by the frequency of occurrence of words within documents and their collocation with other words. Collocation is a sequence of words or terms that occur often together more than would be expected by chance.

Text mining software may offer threshold or cut-off values which need to be selected to determine at what level of occurrence terms need to be found within documents in order to contribute to the search. Relevance, and hence retrieval, is often determined by probability calculations or, in semantic analysis, by the role that words play within sentences. For example, semantic analysis might be able to recognise the different meanings suggested by the phrases 'children support parents' and 'parents support children' based on the subject-verb-object relationship. On the other hand, a Boolean search can only recognise that the terms 'children' and 'parents' are both present in a record, while with proximity operators the relationship of the terms is that they are near to each other (perhaps in the same sentence).

Since most text mining software is not designed with information specialists in mind, it may not be optimised to help us in the ways to which we have become accustomed. This means we may need to explore how a particular text mining tool can be most useful to us and sometimes, to get the best out of the software, we may need help from experts in software, linguistics or statistics.

Information specialists achieve effective and efficient information retrieval from bibliographic databases by gaining a detailed knowledge of database structure, the content of databases and search interface options. We implement this knowledge to build search strategies by selecting options such as limits, truncation lengths and operators, as well as choosing search terms and deciding how to combine them into a strategy. Text mining tools also require a similar degree of expertise in terms of learning what the tools have to offer so that the choice of settings for the text analyses are made effectively. The settings might include choices about how to analyse the text, how often or how closely specific terms need to be found near to other terms and whether to analyse terms by their role within sentences. The more sophisticated the text analysis tool, the more extensive the requirement for learning, coding and testing to achieve useful results.

Many users value the fact that text mining is an automated process allowing the analysis of large volumes of text in a rapid and consistent way, minimising human factors, such as inconsistency and lack of concentration. It has also been suggested that text mining is less subjective than record processing by human beings. However, the range of coding choices required in text mining means that text mining is not necessarily totally objective and the use of algorithms, some of which may not be reported in detail, means that the processing may not be transparent.

Major developments in the last 10 years

Text mining techniques, such as concordances (which list the words in a text with a reference to the pages where they occur), frequency analysis (which list words by frequency of occurrence) and word clustering (which list words which occur frequently near to other words) have long been available in statistical packages, such as Excel, and in qualitative research tools, such as Nudist. Simple text frequency analysis has been available in EndNote bibliographic software and concordance software for many years. However, it is only in the last decade that information specialists have been able to use free to access and easy to use interfaces to analyse records within publicly available databases such as PubMed or to use tools to analyse documents from a range of sources. Search filters to find records for specific study designs began to be developed using text mining techniques in the late 1990s and text mining is now routinely used by some health technology assessment agencies to develop search strategies (Hausner, et al., 2012; White, et al., 2001). Since 2000, tools that interface to PubMed, such as PubMed PubReMiner, have become available, offering a range of ways to explore this major free resource. Many other tools have been published that are database and discipline independent (for example, TerMine). Database publishers, such as Embase.com, are increasingly offering text mining options such as listings of related terms identified from a batch of search results.

The results of text analysis are often shown in tables but can also be shown visually. Simple free to access word or tag cloud software, such as Wordle, have been available for decades. More recently, free sophisticated text visualisation packages, such as VOSviewer and Voyant, have been developed that offer a variety of views on the relationships between words within texts.

For systematic reviewers, text mining is increasingly available as a module within systematic review management software (for example, EPPI-Reviewer, SWIFT-Review). These developments offer opportunities to streamline study identification and record management processes and to minimise the amount of time-consuming data transfer between different packages at different stages of the review process.

Text mining software is a fast-moving area with many well established and maintained tools but it is also a field that is prone to short-lived demonstration programs which may not be maintained or kept updated by their authors. It is important for information specialists to research the latest developments when they need to use a new text mining tool. Text mining is an active field of research and discovery and the SR Toolbox (www.systematicreviewtools.com) offers a database of systematic review software tools, including those using text mining techniques.

Discussion

How can text mining help reviewers?

A recent review by Paynter et al. (2016) explored ways that systematic reviews are using text mining. It is used to identify words to include in search strategies and, most frequently, to assist with search filter development (Paynter et al., 2016). It is also used beyond searching to screen retrieved studies, to help with data extraction and risk of bias assessment and to determine when reviews should be updated. Paynter et al. (2016) suggest that despite researchers' enthusiasm for text mining, it is not yet widely adopted and, where it is adopted, the tools are used in addition to existing tools and processes, rather than as replacements (Paynter et al., 2016). The review suggests that reviewers will use text mining more and more but it will continue to be an additional tool, rather than replacing current processes.

Reviewers will need to identify the review tasks and questions where text mining might be most useful. A particular barrier to more widespread adoption or integration of text mining within systematic review practice is the lack of standardisation in the 'underlying rules, ontologies, and algorithms' within the tools (Paynter et al., 2016). This is important since systematic review methods emphasise transparency and replicability, but it also illustrates the fact that sophisticated text mining tools may be complex and are likely to require expert users. Adding text mining skills to a review team may not be trivial. Researchers may also be hesitant to use text mining because of the absence of evaluation and replication studies.

How can information specialists use text mining for search strategy development?

Information specialists can use text mining for various aspects of search development and results analysis:

- understanding a topic before beginning a search
- term and phrase identification to build search strategies
- developing search filters
- identifying relevant papers to develop or validate search strategies
- identifying concepts or themes within sets of records
- screening results.

The next section explains each of these roles in turn and then Case study 7.1 provides an in-depth look at how they can be put into practice in a systematic review.

Understanding a topic

When you are beginning a search, text mining software can help to identify background material in order to understand topics and their complexities better. It can help with identifying whether a topic is vague or complex, whether it involves terms with many meanings, whether it involves many concepts or is defined in many different ways. Text mining may also help to identify terminology in emerging topics where definitions and terms are still evolving. Document clustering tools such as Carrot[2] or Ultimate Research Assistant can identify highly relevant documents (rather than bibliographic records), which can then be scanned for relevant terms. These tools have added value in that they access grey literature. Searching Ultimate Research Assistant with a search phrase produces a topic summary, a list of key themes taken from the result documents and a list of frequent words and phrases. These can help to scope topics and to identify relevant and irrelevant search terms and concepts. The program also offers a 'taxonomy' which presents the concepts in a hierarchy and a mind map of the taxonomy, which can help to show the extent of a topic and its boundaries.

Term and phrase identification

Although many text mining tools do not recognise the structure of bibliographic database records, some tools can analyse the individual fields within records to identify the frequency with which search terms appear in titles, abstracts and subject index fields. This can help to identify search terms to test out within search strategies and can also help us to choose where to truncate terms. Frequency analysis can also reveal terms which are introducing irrelevant records into results, which may help us to design strategies to exclude those terms or minimise their retrieval. The analysis of hundreds of records can take only a matter of minutes and provides a more detailed and reliable approach than information specialists' traditional methods of developing searches by screening search results for new terms by eye. The analyses are usually presented as a table of results, which could be used to guide discussions with team members on eligible search terms and can also act as a record of terms that have been reviewed and/or selected.

For MEDLINE searchers, there are text mining tools, such as MeSH on Demand, which, if provided with some sample text or abstracts, can suggest Medical Subject Headings (MeSH) that reflect the subjects within the sample.

Many frequency analysis packages are database and topic independent. To make best use of these packages it is best to carry out searches in one or more databases, load the database results into bibliographic management software and then export into a file only the fields that you would like to analyse. This file can then be loaded into the text analysis package. Antconc is one example of a tool that offers frequency analyses. Results can typically be saved to a text file.

Antconc looks and feels like spreadsheet software. Other software, such as Voyant and VOSviewer, provide visual analyses of documents or sets of records and present the results as coloured charts, heat maps or networks. These visual presentations can help to identify the concepts or themes within a set of records.

Some text mining software (for example, Antconc, WriteWords, TerMine) identifies phrases and words in proximity to each other. This can help to identify ways to improve search strategy precision by suggesting terms that could be searched using proximity operators.

Information specialists will want to minimise file transfers between databases, bibliographic software and text mining software and ideally achieve search result analysis, record management and record selection within a single program. Usually, this type of integration is more likely to be available in priced software. EPPI-Reviewer is a subscription web-based software program that is designed to support all stages of the systematic review process from record management through to synthesis and includes text mining modules. It accepts large volumes of records in RIS format, meaning that text mining analysis can be used against the combined outputs from many bibliographic databases. One option within EPPI-Reviewer is TF*IDF (Term Frequency–Inverse Document Frequency). TF*IDF is a statistic which reflects how important a word is to a document in a collection. The value increases proportionally to the number of times a word appears in the document but is offset by the frequency of the word in the collection. TF*IDF may be applied to records to identify and extract the key terms within the records. This might reveal new relevant terms to include in search strategies and may also identify potentially 'noisy' terms that are found in a large proportion of the records.

Developing search filters

Search filters are sets of search terms which have been developed using research methods to find a topic with a high degree of consistency (Glanville et al., 2008). Search filters are widely used in health care to identify research designs, such as randomised controlled trials (RCTs). Search filter development is a time-consuming process which requires sets of known relevant records (a gold or reference standard) from which to select sets of records to both develop the filter and to test and validate filter performance.

Many of the text mining tools described in this chapter can be used to analyse gold standards to identify search terms for testing in search filters. Text mining will find candidate terms, but the next challenge is to choose which terms to test in the filter (Hausner et al., 2012; Kok et al., 2015; Li and Lu, 2013). Various publications have suggested ways to use text mining to identify and select terms (Li and Lu, 2013) and cut-offs to use when selecting terms, but as yet there is no generally agreed standard approach.

Identifying relevant papers

Sometimes we just want to find a few relevant papers to help us start strategy building. Text mining tools, such as HelioBLAST and many interfaces to bibliographic databases, can help with this task. HelioBLAST finds PubMed records that are similar to a highly relevant record we have already identified. As well as providing a list of the 50 best PubMed records and displaying a relevance score, it also provides a list of 'implicit' keywords, some of which may be new to us.

Semantic analysis tools, such as MEDIE and Semantic MEDLINE, can help to identify relevant studies. These tools interpret the meaning of words by their position or role within sentences. Free to use and off the shelf semantic analysis tools tend to focus on a specific task, such as identifying genes or proteins, and are not really designed for general use. MEDIE accepts queries structured as a 'subject-verb-object' and runs the search in PubMed. For example, to find records about parents caring for children, rather than children caring for parents, MEDIE could be searched for 'parents' 'care' 'children'. MEDIE identifies verb variants and similar or related verbs to enable it to provide relevant records.

The RCT Tagger identifies reports of RCTs in PubMed. The searcher uses a Population and Intervention search strategy, or even just the Intervention search terms, and the program presents the search results in order of the probability (on the right hand of the screen) that the record is a report of a RCT.

Some software, such as ProtAnt and WordStat, can identify terms which differentiate relevant records from irrelevant records when provided with a set of relevant records and a set of irrelevant records.

Identifying concepts

Many text mining tools help with concept identification, but visual tools, such as VOSviewer, may be the most helpful way to identify rapidly the concept groupings or themes in a batch of records retrieved by scoping searches. Easy to use tools that show the relative sizes of search concepts and the impacts of expanding concepts in PubMed include PubVenn and Search Workbench. In response to a query, CoreMine Medical or Anne O'Tate generate a breakdown of concepts in the PubMed records returned by the query.

More sophisticated software offers further features to help with concept identification. EPPI-Reviewer uses the Lingo3G clustering engine to automatically categorise records into clusters based on the terms used in the title and abstract. Significant terms are extracted and used to code the records by theme. Lingo3G arranges these codes in a tree structure allowing the relationship between them to be investigated. Clustering can show themes in a large or complex literature and might assist with identifying options to focus a search and help to prioritise groups of records for screening.

Screening results

Recent systematic reviews describe research that has been conducted using text mining and machine learning to assist in record selection (O'Mara-Eves et al., 2014; O'Mara-Eves et al., 2015; Paynter et al., 2016). Machine learning often involves 'teaching' the program about 'relevance' by indicating which records are relevant and which are not. At some point the software should be able to identify further relevant records automatically and present the most likely relevant records first to the reviewers.

The length of time to teach the software can vary. In some scenarios, the machine learning software is used as the second reviewer. O'Mara-Eves et al. (2014) note that only six systems were 'deployed' in 2015, so the number of usable 'off the shelf' systems is still limited but the authors are positive that efficiencies in workload can be achieved and that text mining is safe and ready to use to prioritise records for screening (O'Mara-Eves et al., 2015).

Information specialists involved in record selection could use text mining to provide their teams with pre-ordered results to make processing more efficient or might code the screening software with terms to indicate relevance or irrelevance, so that when reviewers are making selection decisions, the terms are already highlighted to make selection easier.

Medline Ranker is a simple to use but a seemingly highly effective prioritising tool. It requires a set of known relevant records with PubMed identifiers and a test set of records to prioritise. The latter could be search results from a highly sensitive search, comprising hundreds of records. Medline Ranker sorts the records in the test set and presents those that were most similar to the relevant records first. It also provides a list of discriminating terms which distinguish relevant records from non-relevant records.

Sciome Workbench for Interactive computer-Facilitated Text-mining (SWIFT) is a free to use systematic review package that includes a machine learning option which orders records by predicted relevance using reviewers' decisions on a sample of records. Currently, it only processes PubMed records.

Abstrackr is a record selection and screening program that can also semi-automate the screening process using active learning principles. It uses inclusion/exclusion decisions made by selectors to predict the likelihood of the remaining records being relevant. Once a selector has assessed 'enough' records, the remainder can be screened automatically by Abstrackr. An evaluation, using records from four systematic reviews with eligible studies comprising a range of study designs and publication types, found the record prediction algorithm correctly identified all the relevant references for two reviews (Rathbone, Hoffmann and Glasziou, 2015). In the remaining two reviews, it incorrectly predicted an included study was irrelevant but neither of these studies had an abstract. The precision varied depending on the size and complexity of the review (16% to 45%). Very large sets of records with very few relevant records proved problematic for record selection. The prediction function is still being developed and the number of records needed to screen before predictions are made is arbitrarily set at approximately 'a couple of hundred'.

EPPI-Reviewer contains a built-in machine learning classifier; the tool learns which records belong to a particular category as the selector classifies a sample and then applies this to the unscreened records. EPPI-Reviewer contains one pre-built machine learning model, the 'RCT model', which is designed to automatically identify RCTs and has been based on training from over 280,000 records screened by the Cochrane Crowd (see Chapter 9). Users can build models to find other types of record.

Researchers have also explored how text mining can help with data extraction and risk of bias assessment of eligible studies, as well as peer review (Blake and Lucic, 2015; Jonnalagadda, Goyal and Huffman, 2015; Marshall, Kuiper and Wallace, 2015; Millard, Flach and Higgins, 2015; Sarker, Mollá and Paris, 2015). These activities still seem to be at an early stage of development. Case study 7.1 opposite explores how text mining can be used for various aspects of search development.

Case study 7.1: Isoflavones and cancer in women
In this case study we show how text mining might help with developing a
specific search to find studies reporting on the link between the consumption
of isoflavones and the development of cancers in women. Isoflavones are
chemicals found in plants, and hence some foods, that resemble human
oestrogen. The resources chosen are just a selection of those available free of
charge on the internet and all but two could be used to explore topics in any
discipline following a search of any database that can provide output as text or
RIS files.

Resources such as Carrot[2] can highlight relevant background material to
help us to a better understanding of the issues. Entering a pragmatic search
such as 'isoflavones AND (breast or uterine or cervical) AND cancer' into
Carrot[2] produces a FoamTree picture (see Figure 7.1) that shows a range of
themes produced by this search along with dictionary, encyclopedia and
report information. These documents can give us a sense of additional words
that we could add to build into our search, such as 'soy', 'soybean' and
'soyfoods', as well as topics that might not be of interest, such as 'drought
stress' affecting soybean harvests.

Using the same pragmatic search phrase in an interface to PubMed such as
PubReMiner can also yield a table of the frequency with which words (including
MeSH terms) appear in the search results (see Figure 7.2). Hundreds of records
can be analysed in seconds and the list can be assessed for additional relevant
title and abstract terms such as 'dietary', 'genistein', 'daidzein' and
'phytoestrogen', as well as MeSH terms such as 'Phytoestrogens' and 'Soybeans'.

To explore records further, we can carry out searches in PubMed and
export the results to a file using the 'Send to' option and choosing the
Abstract format. The output file can be uploaded into Voyant Tools where a
range of analyses allow us to select phrases, words in collocation or words in
context (see Figure 7.3). Phrase identification can help with making searches
more precise and words in collocation can help to find words that can be
linked with proximity operators. The keywords in context display can assist
with identifying unhelpful phrases. Voyant Tools will function more clearly if
the PubMed records can be pruned, perhaps by importing into EndNote and
exporting only the PubMed identifier, title and abstract. This makes the text
being analysed more relevant and removes noisy information such as authors'
addresses. It is also possible to edit the stopword list in Voyant Tools to
remove the common but unhelpful terms such as 'a', 'the' and 'which'.

The concepts included within a collection of records can be seen by loading
a PubMed result file saved in the MEDLINE format into VOSviewer. Within
VOSviewer select 'Create' and then 'Create a map based on text data'. There is
a PubMed tab to allow the loading of PubMed files but there are also other
options to load Web of Science, Scopus or RIS files. There is a series of
settings to choose after this point which will determine which data are
analysed and how. The resulting visualisations (see Figure 7.4) show the

themes within the set of records. From this picture we can see that there is a literature around women on the right, a literature on cellular activity on the left and a third focus around animal research towards the middle of the picture. This presentation suggests that a strategy could be devised to minimise the recall of the animal and cellular studies. Using the arrow option in the top right of the screen it is possible to dive into the picture and see more and more textwords, which can then be used to develop the search.

In the situation where we have a few highly relevant studies, we can use text mining packages to help us identify further studies. Using Medline Ranker (see Figure 7.5) we can add the PubMed identifiers of the relevant studies (as examples of relevant records or 'seeds') and then ask the Ranker to select similar studies from a batch of studies retrieved by a broad search or a search of publications in the past few years. This might be used to bring highly relevant studies to the top of a set of search results or to just find some additional relevant studies to mine for search terms to build up a search strategy. In the results display, the 'seed' studies are shown at the top of the list and the most similar studies are shown below in order of probability that they are similar to the 'seeds'. Words that discriminate the isoflavone seed records (discriminative words) are shaded, for example 'phytoestrogens' and 'phytochemicals', and these are likely to be useful in a search strategy.

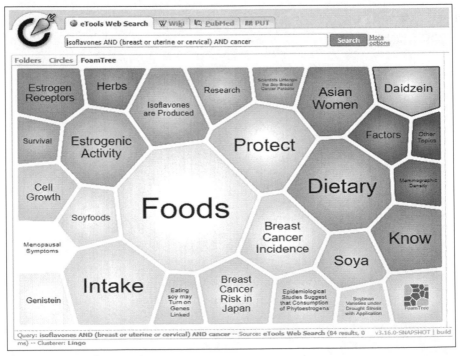

Figure 7.1 Carrot² screen-shot
Reproduced with permission of the Carrot² Project (www.carrot2.org)

Figure 7.2 *PubMed PubReMiner screen-shot*
Reproduced with permission of PubMed PubReMiner (http://hgserver2.amc.nl)

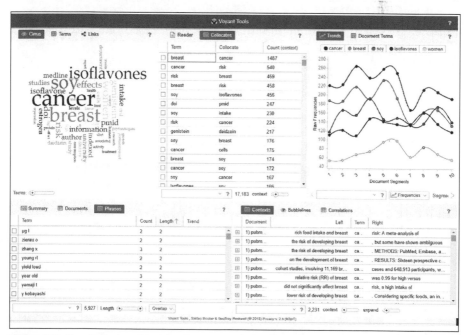

Figure 7.3 *Voyant Tools screen-shot* (https://voyant-tools.org)

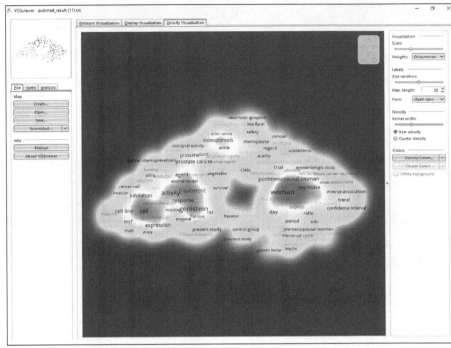

Figure 7.4 *VOSviewer density visualisation screen-shot*
Copyright © 2009-2018 Nees Jan van Eck and Ludo Waltman
(www.vosviewer.com)

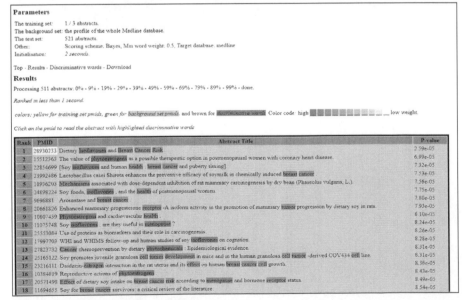

Figure 7.5 *Medline Ranker screen-shot*
Copyright © Fontaine 2012 (http://cbdm-01.zdv.uni-mainz.de/~jfontain/cms)

Sophisticated text mining packages

Information specialists may find the 'off the shelf' and easy to use text mining software discussed so far helpful for a range of tasks but we face many challenges that might be better approached using sophisticated 'fully featured' text mining software. This is particularly the case where search questions are complex and broad-based (see Chapter 3).

Free sophisticated text mining packages, such as GATE, can be tailored by experienced users to achieve sophisticated text processing and querying. There are also a range of commercial packages available, such as Simstat (and its add-on Wordstat) and EPPI-Reviewer. Option-rich programmable free and commercial packages require time to review, learn, explore and optimise to achieve informed outputs. Optimal use is likely to require training and a knowledge of statistics and the differences between algorithms, as well as a knowledge of linguistics. These types of text mining package could offer opportunities to build filters within the software. These filters could be used to distinguish records by subject or study design, for example it might be possible to develop a filter to identify qualitative research or a topic that is needed repeatedly. The disadvantage of this approach is that filters developed within specific software could only be shared with people who used the same software.

Text mining also offers opportunities to capture semantic relationships within texts so that records can be selected according to the meaning of words rather than just their presence within records. As described earlier, this might facilitate the identification of records where terms can be in a variety of relationships, such as 'parents' and 'children' or where terms are ambiguous unless their context is known, for example 'spades' are tools but they also appear on playing cards. Being able to code relationships and other meanings into text mining software requires an investment of time to identify the terminology and the typical expressions that suggest a specific word grouping is indicative of a particular relevant issue, and then to code the rules that will ensure that these concepts can be retrieved in the future. These rules may also rely on ontologies where the structure of a topic is captured in a series of formal definitions. The time and skills to develop and code such definitions, and then test them out, is not trivial. However, in situations where frequent similar searches are required then it might be worth the investment of time and effort to develop a set of rules that could be used repeatedly and used across records downloaded from any number of databases. The additional benefit of this approach is that the bibliographic database searches could be as sensitive as possible because the focusing activity would be carried out within the text mining software using filters, rules or machine learning.

Future directions

Despite great advances in the use of text mining in information retrieval and the availability of easy to use tools, there is still only limited uptake of text mining by information specialists (Paynter et al., 2016). Barriers to uptake are likely to include lack of awareness as well as the need to learn and exploit yet another software package. Having to pre-process and load information into some of the packages might be a barrier to uptake. Other barriers may include the fact that in text mining the perspective is document focused and non-Boolean. In addition, information specialists may be cautious about relying on tools with algorithms that may be hard to interpret and communicate to others and where there is no agreement on the best algorithm. It may also be difficult to persuade colleagues to use pioneering tools.

Information specialists need concrete examples of how text mining can offer practical help in their searching and selecting tasks. Uptake will follow the development of more formal guidance on what would be acceptable in the context of systematic reviews. Information specialists also need more text mining tools that are record-based and designed to assist with the tasks of the information specialist. Ideally, software developers will follow the lead of EPPI-Reviewer and will develop more text mining options within systematic review software. The trend for publishers to include text mining options within database interfaces is likely to continue.

Conclusion

There are many text mining packages available (see Table 7.1 opposite) and many of these are independent of specific disciplines. This means that they could be used to analyse texts from any database that offers structured output. Text mining has the potential to assist in systematic reviews in any topic, including education, social work, criminology and public health, and can help to interrogate, conceptualise and screen broad-based and complex topics.

Free text mining tools available via the internet are likely to be accessible by information specialists anywhere in the world. Commercial text mining packages may have licensing restrictions and may not be available for purchase worldwide.

Sophisticated text mining packages look likely to offer opportunities for information specialists to develop new approaches to gathering, grouping and interrogating large numbers of bibliographic records and other documents. Sensitive bibliographic database searches from a range of databases, as well as full documents, can be loaded into sophisticated text mining software, which can be programmed to search and identify relevant documents using a range of non-Boolean approaches, such as machine learning and rules-based techniques.

Other developments will see the increasing integration of text mining tools into database interfaces and systematic review software. Simple text mining options have recently been introduced into the Ovid interface and Embase.com. In that setting, more information specialists are likely to explore and use text mining tools. More case reports describing text mining research and the use of text mining in information retrieval practice will also enhance the uptake of tools, as will the inclusion of more formal guidance in methods handbooks.

Table 7.1 *Selected text mining tools*

Role	PubMed-specific (record by record)	Other databases (record by record analysis)
Identifying terms in the title and abstract	PubMed PubReMiner (http://hgserver2.amc.nl/cgi-bin/miner/miner2.cgi) SWIFT-review (Howard et al., 2016) HelioBLAST (http://helioblast.heliotext.com) Anne O'Tate (http://arrowsmith.psych.uic.edu/cgi-bin/arrowsmith_uic/AnneOTate.cgi)	Antconc (www.laurenceanthony.net/software.html#antconc) EndNote Voyant (https://voyant-tools. org) EPPI-Reviewer 4 (https://eppi.ioe.ac.uk/cms/er4) Wordle (www.wordle.net) Simstat and Wordstat (https://provalisresearch.com/products)

(Continued)

Table 7.1 *Continued*

Role	PubMed-specific (record by record)	Other databases (record by record analysis)
Identifying frequently occurring subject headings and subheadings	PubMed PubReMiner (http://hgserver2.amc.nl/cgi-bin/miner/miner2.cgi) Anne O'Tate (http://arrowsmith.psych.uic.edu/cgi-bin/arrowsmith_uic/AnneOTate.cgi)	EndNote Simstat and Wordstat (https://provalisresearch.com/products)
Identifying MeSH terms from relevant text such as a protocol	MeSH on Demand (https://meshb.nlm.nih.gov/MeSHonDemand)	
Identifying MeSH terms used to index relevant records	Yale MeSH Analyzer (http://mesh.med.yale.edu)	
Phrases in the title and abstract	Anne O'Tate (http://arrowsmith.psych.uic.edu/cgi-bin/arrowsmith_uic/AnneOTate.cgi)	Voyant (https://voyant-tools.org) Antconc (www.laurenceanthony.net/software.html#antconc) TerMine (www.nactem.ac.uk/software/termine) Simstat and Wordstat (https://provalisresearch.com/products)
Words in proximity in the title and abstract	Writewords (www.writewords.org.uk/phrase_count.asp) Antconc (www.laurenceanthony.net/software.html#antconc) Simstat and Wordstat (https://provalisresearch.com/products)	
Visual presentation of text analysis	Voyant (https://voyant-tools.org) VOSviewer (www.vosviewer.com) EPPI-Reviewer 4 (https://eppi.ioe.ac.uk/cms/er4) Search Workbench (https://searchworkbench.info) CoreMine Medical (https://www.coremine.com/medical) WordStat (https://provalisresearch.com/products/content-analysis-software) Wordle (www.wordle.net)	

(Continued)

Table 7.1 *Continued*

Role	PubMed-specific (record by record)	Other databases (record by record analysis)
Identifying similar records based on known relevant records	Medline Ranker (http://cbdm-01.zdv.uni-mainz.de/~jfontain/cms/?page_id=4) RCT Tagger (http://arrowsmith.psych.uic.edu/cgi-bin/arrowsmith_uic/RCT_Tagger.cgi) Sciome Workbench for Interactive computer-Facilitated Text-mining (SWIFT) (www.sciome.com/swift-review) Abstrackr (http://abstrackr.cebm.brown.edu)	ProtAnt (http://www.laurenceanthony.net/software/protant)
Scoping the size of concepts and identifying themes or concepts within a literature	PubVenn (https://pubvenn.appspot.com) Carrot^2 (http://search.carrot2.org/stable/search) Ultimate Research Assistant (www.ultimate-research-assistant.com/GenerateResearchReport.asp)	
Simple semantic analysis	MEDIE (www.nactem.ac.uk/medie) Semantic MEDLINE (https://skr3.nlm.nih.gov/SemMed)	
Developing rules, machine learning and semantic analysis	GATE (https://gate.ac.uk/overview.html) EPPI-Reviewer 4 (https://eppi.ioe.ac.uk/cms/er4) WordStat (https://provalisresearch.com/products/content-analysis-software)	

Suggestions for further reading

O'Mara-Eves, A., Thomas, J., McNaught, J., Miwa, M. and Ananiadou, S. (2015) Using Text Mining for Study Identification in Systematic Reviews: a systematic review of current approaches, *Systematic Reviews*, **4** (1), 5.

Paynter, R., Bañez, L. L., Berliner, E., Erinoff, E., Lege-Matsuura, J., Potter, S. and Uhl, S. (2016) EPC Methods: an exploration of the use of text-mining software in systematic reviews, Research White Paper, Agency for Healthcare Research and Quality (USA). https://www.ncbi.nlm.nih.gov/books/NBK362044

References

Blake, C. and Lucic, A. (2015) Automatic Endpoint Detection to Support the Systematic Review Process, *Journal of Biomedical Informatics*, **56**, 42-56.

Glanville, J., Bayliss, S., Booth, A., Dundar, Y., Fernandes, H., Fleeman, N. D., Foster, L., Fraser, C., Fry-Smith, A., Golder, S., Lefebvre, C., Miller, C., Paisley, S., Payne, L., Price, A. and Welch, K. (2008) So Many Filters, So Little Time: the development of a search filter appraisal checklist, *Journal of the Medical Library Association*, **96** (4), 356-361.

Hausner, E., Waffenschmidt, S., Kaiser, T. and Simon, M. (2012) Routine Development of Objectively Derived Search Strategies, *Systematic Reviews*, **1**, 19.

Howard, B. E., Phillips, J., Miller, K., Tandon, A., Mav, D., Shah, M. R., Holmgren, S., Pelch, K. E., Walker, V., Rooney, A. A., Macleod, M., Shah, R. R. and Thayer, K. (2016) SWIFT-Review: a text-mining workbench for systematic review, *Systematic Reviews*, **5**, 87.

Jonnalagadda, S. R., Goyal, P. and Huffman, M. D. (2015) Automating Data Extraction in Systematic Reviews: a systematic review, *Systematic Reviews*, **4**, 78.

Kok, R., Verbeek, J. A., Faber, B., van Dijk, F. J. and Hoving, J. L. (2015) A Search Strategy to Identify Studies on the Prognosis of Work Disability: a diagnostic test framework, *BMJ Open*, **5** (5), e006315.

Li, J. and Lu, Z. (2013) Developing Topic-specific Search Filters for PubMed with Click-through Data, *Methods of Information in Medicine*, **52** (5), 395-402.

Marshall, I. J., Kuiper, J. and Wallace B. C. (2015) Automating Risk of Bias Assessment for Clinical Trials, *IEEE Journal of Biomedical and Health Informatics*, **19** (4), 1406-1412.

Millard, L. A. C., Flach, P. A. and Higgins, J. P. T. (2015) Machine Learning to Assist Risk-of-bias Assessments in Systematic Reviews, *International Journal of Epidemiology*, **45** (1), 266-277.

O'Mara-Eves, A., Brunton, G., McDaid, D., Kavanagh, J., Oliver, S. and Thomas, J. (2014) Techniques for Identifying Cross-disciplinary and 'Hard-to-detect' Evidence for Systematic Review, *Research Synthesis Methods*, **5** (1), 50-59.

O'Mara-Eves, A., Thomas, J., McNaught, J., Miwa, M. and Ananiadou, S. (2015) Using Text Mining for Study Identification in Systematic Reviews: a systematic review of current approaches, *Systematic Reviews*, **4** (1), 5.

Paynter, R., Bañez, L. L., Berliner, E., Erinoff, E., Lege-Matsuura, J., Potter, S.

and Uhl, S. (2016) *EPC Methods: an exploration of the use of text-mining software in systematic reviews.* Research White Paper, Agency for Healthcare Research and Quality (USA).
https://www.ncbi.nlm.nih.gov/books/NBK362044

Rathbone, J., Hoffmann, T. and Glasziou, P. (2015) Faster Title and Abstract Screening? Evaluating Abstrackr, a Semi-automated Online Screening Program for Systematic Reviewers, *Systematic Reviews*, **4**, 80.

Sarker, A., Mollá, D. and Paris, C. (2015) Automatic Evidence Quality Prediction to Support Evidence-based Decision Making, *Artificial Intelligence in Medicine*, **64** (2), 89-103.

White, V. J., Glanville, J. M., Lefebvre, C. and Sheldon, T. A. (2001) A Statistical Approach to Designing Search Filters to Find Systematic Reviews: objectivity enhances accuracy, *Journal of Information Science*, **27** (6), 357-370.

8

Using linked data for evidence synthesis

Andy Mitchell and Chris Mavergames

Introduction

Information has long been captured and shared using documents. The success of the internet, and in particular the world wide web, in enabling the rapid and far-reaching sharing of information is undeniable and it has done this largely through sharing digital documents. Finding the right information in this ever-growing sea of documents has always been a challenge. The use of labels and categories to group documents by their subject matter offers some assistance. The use of search engines that can trawl through many of these documents on our behalf is also an important tool. However, where we have more and more information and less and less time to search and sift through it, we often do not have the luxury of reading through many books or documents to find the information we need. We need to identify with greater precision the relevant and trust-worthy knowledge and do it more quickly. This requires capturing our knowledge in a different way and so we need to go beyond documents and think more about the 'things' (such as concepts, ideas and knowledge) captured within the documents.

A common language is essential when sharing information, whether it is a spoken language between two people or a digital message sent between two computers. To make a language common then both parties must understand the structure of the sentences and the meaning of the words; the syntax and the semantics. When trying to arrive at a standard way of using language in the digital world we often make use of ontology (Uschold and Gruninger, 1996).

The field of ontology has its roots in philosophy, in the understanding and classification of all things. In this context, ontologies are often only judged true ontologies if they successfully describe unchanging aspects of the world. Fascinating as this may be, it is an enormous field in its own right and is therefore not the focus of this chapter. From an information management and computer science perspective, ontology development has taken on a more pragmatic purpose. Here, many of the same principles and methods are used to capture definitions of things by understanding their properties and how they relate to other things. Linked data is, in essence, Tim Berners-Lee's attempt to take these ideas and apply them pragmatically to the world's information to enable us to join up our knowledge in a more efficient manner than simply indexing and linking documents.

It is important to recognise of course that this approach is not a silver bullet to our information management needs and that there is an ongoing debate between those who argue for the merits of algorithms and semantics (for example, Natural Language Processing, semantic search) and those who argue for the merits of a more human touch (for example, bibliographic datastores and Boolean search). This chapter is not about fighting either corner but about accepting that every tool has its place and that we need to work constructively together in understanding, further developing and ultimately using the right tool for the job as effectively as possible. The amount of information we now have to manage means that using these newer approaches to best effect is becoming more important than ever.

Overview of the topic: what is linked data?

Linked data represents a move away from linking documents on the world wide web to exposing and linking the 'things' that the documents are about. This phase in the evolution of the web is often referred to as the 'semantic web' because the links are not handcrafted like hyperlinks, but simply by writing about the same thing in two different places a connection is made. The important thing here is that we need to tell the computer that these two things are actually the same and that they mean the same thing. This is done by using standard Uniform Resource Identifiers (URI) and definitions of these things. Definitions are being developed and shared at a rapidly increasing rate. Effectively it is linking things with a standardised set of metadata across the whole world wide web. The simple principles of linked data as outlined by Tim Berners-Lee are:

- Use URIs as names for things
- Use HTTP URIs (publish the identifier online) so that people can look up those names
- When someone looks up a URI, provide useful information, using standards
- Include links to other URIs so that they can discover more things.
                    (Berners-Lee, 2006; Bizer, Heath and Berners-Lee, 2011)

The notion of moving away from documents is quite disconcerting as many people have learned that a document is the way to group a collection of ideas that need to be read together to make sense; documents have a beginning, middle and end. People often have the image of breaking apart a document as being akin to smashing a pane of glass, concerned that in the process each fragment will have lost its meaning. In reality, linked data seeks to address the problem of people failing to read entire documents online by making more explicit the links between different things.

Linked data uses the idea of *resources* where a resource can be absolutely anything. Imagine we have a pet dog called Fido as an example! A photo of Fido may be a resource, there may be a newspaper article about him and this would also be a resource. Fido himself would actually be classed as a resource too! So, the foundation of linked data is this idea of resources that are then explicitly linked in some way. To manage these resources, linked data uses the Resource Description Framework or RDF (https://www.w3.org/RDF).

Now, of course, in reality things are not just defined by a text definition but by their properties and their relationship with other things. Let's continue with the simple example of our pet dog Fido. The general concept, the idea of a dog, would be a linked data resource. In terms of properties, a dog has legs and is a type of animal. 'Leg' and 'Animal' are separate concepts so these too could be treated as resources and links between these two concepts could be made. RDF allows many different kinds of links to be captured between resources. Here we could say that 'Dog - has a - Leg' and that 'Dog - is an - Animal' for example. These connections eventually build in to an interconnected network of information that is often referred to as a 'graph' or 'knowledge graph'. In our example, if we connected to a graph about animals we may be able to infer further information about dogs than we had captured in our own simple graph. For example, if the animal knowledge graph contained the fact that 'Animal - is a - Multi-cellular organism', then we would be able to infer that our dog Fido is a multi-cellular organism.

The impact of linked data on evidence

Even though the semantic web, as it was originally envisaged, has not yet fully taken hold, and maybe it never will, the fundamental principles continue to have an impact on the way we capture and organise information. These principles become more and more useful with the increasing rate and amount of data and information that is produced, coupled with the need to make sense of the varying quality of this information. Advances in areas broadly described as artificial intelligence and machine learning are increasing the demand for this kind of structured way of representing information as it allows these technologies and methods to be applied more effectively (Webber, 2018).

Clearly, any alternative way to store information will have an impact on those tasked with retrieving information. There may be many potential impacts on the information specialist but this chapter will focus on three broad areas of challenge: granularity, provenance and semantic search.

Granularity

Granularity is often used as a way to describe how many identifiable sub-components the information we are working with can be usefully separated into. What are the units of information we are working with? Is it the library as a whole? The topics that it covers? The individual books? The chapters within the books? Each of these levels of detail adds more granularity.

If we are no longer just thinking about documents and bibliographic databases or search engines that allow us to find documents, then what exactly are we working with? What are the more granular units of information that linked data enables us to think about?

A group based in the University of Manchester (www.researchobject. org/overview) is using linked data to enable research to be published as 'research objects', a more granular representation of information that includes data and other artefacts resulting from a specific research project (Bechhofer et al., 2013). Other initiatives such as *nanopub* (www.nanopub.org/wordpress/?page_id=65) have also made use of linked data to develop and promote this need to think about publishing not just an article but a much smaller single statement or fact and the associated data in an open, reusable and reproducible format. The idea of *micropublications* goes even further again, using linked data to capture statements linked to their underlying evidence, which can also be accompanied by additional rationale (Clark, Ciccarese and Goble, 2014). Crucially, all these initiatives are thinking about sharing information in a different way, moving away from traditional document-centric publishing and considering the importance of linking consistently to other data as well as reducing the size of the published resource.

There are many efforts relating to the creation of a more structured representation of knowledge in the health and care sector (ten Teije et al., 2006). This is often with the aim of supporting clinical decision-making or improving the sharing of information from electronic health records, rather than on the capture and sharing of research from, for example, clinical trials. However, these two areas are inextricably linked and so frameworks such as RDF are proving useful in bridging this gap.

There are also linked data models used to represent the more traditional world of publishing and the related bibliographic information. The FRBR-aligned Bibliographic Ontology, or FaBiO as it is known, is an ontology represented using RDF that can be used to describe bibliographic information, potentially offering a route to a more standardised representation of these datasets across different bibliographic database providers (https://sparontologies.github.io/fabio/current/fabio.html). FaBiO includes standard definitions for things such as *abstract* and *article* for example.

Provenance

Information or data provenance is the additional information needed to understand the origin of the data or information in question. Provenance information often includes details relating to the activities or events and agents (people or machines) that have produced or processed the data.

When talking about documents we perhaps do not think about provenance explicitly, we simply look for the publisher or the author of the document and consider how reputable they are as a mark of whether or not the information attributed to them will be accurate and trustworthy. Or we follow an existing process or agreement with a given, and therefore trusted, bibliographic database provider as a way of ensuring we find all the most valuable and reliable research: this may often be captured as part of a search protocol or search strategy. We need to consider these issues of provenance when we are considering alternative, more granular resources, which might not be accessed through well established and trusted organizations. These resources are being shared and updated more frequently, possibly via online collaborations, so we need to consider the impact on how we search for and trust the information we find, both in terms of accuracy and completeness.

The World Wide Web Consortium (W3C) is an international consortium founded by Tim Berners-Lee that develops standards for the web. They have started to address this challenge by releasing a standard linked data model for provenance (World Wide Web Consortium, 2013). This model can be used to capture provenance information relating to any resource by linking it to an activity and an *agent* (usually a person or organization but it could also be a robot or algorithm). Using this model, it is possible to also capture when and why changes have been made to a resource.

The health and care perspective is useful for illustrating the importance of provenance. The concept of a Learning Health System proposes a fully interconnected health and care system where continual learning and improvement, facilitated by the rapid sharing of feedback data and knowledge, is central (Powers, Grossman and McGinnis, 2011). The role of finding and connecting this valuable information or research to inform decision-making is fundamental to this kind of learning system. The TRANSFoRm project (Curcin, 2017) represents some early work into efficient ways to capture provenance information relating to scientific research and relay it across such a system.

Semantic search

In simple terms, semantic search is a label given to search technologies that seek to bring a better understanding of the information or knowledge being searched together with a better understanding of the context, and therefore intent, of the searcher. Linked data assists in this space by providing a framework to capture the conceptual under-standing of the knowledge and also by identifying smaller units of information to return to the searcher. The most prevalent example of semantic information being used to enhance search is perhaps the simple 'answer engine' feature provided by home assistants such as Amazon's Alexa and Google Home. This type of search is currently less appropriate for the work of an information specialist seeking resources to feed into a systematic review process, although it is important to recognise its significance for other types of search and the potential for the underlying technologies to enhance all types of searching in the future.

Most of the well known search engines, such as Google, also continue to develop linked data knowledge graphs across a variety of domains. As part of their efforts to improve their search products they have also formed Schema.org (https://schema.org) which seeks to build and promote standard schemas or data models for many domains of interest. These standard models, often implemented as RDF, make it easier for producers of content and information to improve their content structure and descriptions, with the ultimate aim of improving the accuracy of web search results and the usability of knowledge. Considering the web as the means to share information between organizations and not just as a consumer tool for personal use, these models are also very useful as a starting point for many organizations wishing to better structure and connect their infor-mation.

It is also possible to query linked data knowledge graphs directly using a query language called SPARQL. For those who are used to querying structured relational databases, such as Microsoft Access, using Structured Query Language (SQL) or performing bibliographic searches using Boolean search, who have a deeper understanding of the information they are looking for, then SPARQL may be an appropriate place to start. Complex filters and conditions can be expressed using SPARQL and similar query languages as a way of reducing the search in a specific way.

Natural language processing (NLP) is also an important part of the semantic search family. These technologies can be used to process both the information being searched and the search query when written in natural language. NLP can be applied in many ways, such as to identify key concepts and phrases improving the understanding of the searcher's intent. NLP offers the chance to improve the recall and precision of our searches where it has not been possible to create or enhance the structure of the underlying information. It can also offer the chance to improve the quality of searches carried out by non-search specialists who prefer to use natural language to interrogate data sources. MEDIE (www.nactem.ac.uk/medie) is an example of this approach developed by the National Centre for Text Mining (NaCTeM) in the UK. NaCTeM have produced a wider review of projects that develop and make use of NLP and semantic search (www.nactem.ac.uk/research.php).

Discussion

This section is intended to consider more specifically the possible practical implications for an information specialist or others involved in systematic reviews and it covers each of the three areas introduced previously.

Granularity

It is important for information specialists to understand that new types of databases holding different types of information are available. These sources will be capturing smaller artefacts of data and representing knowledge in richer formats.

The idea of increased granularity is aided by linked data but it has also been with us for some time due to the use of 'semi-structured' document formats such as Extensible Markup Language (XML). At first glance, the idea of increasingly granular content may therefore not have such a dramatic impact on the information specialist or systematic review process. Smaller publications such as nanopublications are also not yet commonplace and so perhaps less likely to have an immediate and direct impact on information specialists' practice.

Where linked data has an effect on granularity is enabling the more effective management of these smaller pieces of content and the complex relationships between them. In addition, the use of common ontologies to describe documents, identify concepts within documents and also describe highly-structured datasets (traditional databases typically containing tables of numeric data) enables information of different granularities to be brought together more effectively. This kind of analysis of data and information is arguably more pervasive already in the commercial sector to provide evidence or insight for decision-making relating to product sales. However, this identification and linking of different types of information may be something information specialists could actively support.

Considering just the highly-structured data element of this, research data usually has to be made publically available and increasingly many datasets are being published as 'open data'. This may not always be data that has come from a formal research project but may be a government dataset or social data freely available on the web, for example. Large amounts of data becoming available in this way provides additional sources of evidence that could be processed to enhance and complement systematic reviews. Searching for relevant data repositories and registers will require information specialists to perhaps support reviewers and data scientists in finding these appropriate data stores.

Beyond the technology there remain questions and challenges regarding the wider publishing ecosystem. How do you know which version of a knowledge graph and the information contained within it is being used? How do you know you have found everything related to your search query if it returns parts of documents? What are the implications for copyright and licensing? There may be many other questions and considerations or opportunities that you can see should also be explored. The future directions section below suggests several ways you might get involved and help to explore those ideas.

Provenance

Information specialists already implicitly filter based on provenance by selecting only certain sources for searching. Having a more granular and explicit representation of provenance against information resources may enable information specialists to filter their queries more accurately, including and excluding resources based on information relating to who, when and why information has been created or updated. For example, if assertions or data have been generated and published using an artificial intelligence algorithm rather than a person, this may not be seen as sufficiently trustworthy for certain projects.

It may also be valuable to capture in a more explicit and granular form the search strategy followed by an information specialist as part of the chain of provenance. Those next in line may value this when trying to understand what information has been found and what may have been excluded or missed. Why did you make these decisions when developing and refining your search strategy? Who did you involve in this process of refinement? What are your thoughts regarding the ability to reuse the outputs of your search for different purposes?

Presenting information that explains the trade offs made between recall and precision in relation to time and budget constraints when designing a search strategy may be important for others to understand when they are considering the level of uncertainty present and making decisions based on the evidence, as discussed in Chapter 4. Information specialists are already encouraged to record their decision-making process (Cooper et al., 2018) and the idea of provenance is taking this a step further.

Clearly, there is effort involved in recording this information and so work is required to understand just what kind of provenance is valuable to capture and the appropriate level at which it should be recorded. There is also a need to consider how technology can automate the capture of some of the provenance information, for example by understanding who is logged on to a database, information regarding the person or agent involved in executing a search strategy could be captured automatically. It is also important for information specialists to be involved in helping to understand the value of provenance and the right way to capture this information.

Semantic search

An information specialist with a good understanding of a domain will not only understand the structure of resources (for example, documents, books, data tables) and associated metadata (for example, title, author, abstract, date) used for describing the resources, but also have an understanding of concepts and vocabularies used in the subject of interest. Semantic search applied to more structured data sources, such as linked data knowledge graphs, or to those enhanced and tagged using NLP, will allow information specialists to retrieve information that uses language beyond their own understanding for describing the things of interest. This is because the search does not just look at the words and syntax, it connects words of similar meaning, which enables searching at a concept level. It remains important for an information specialist to not only understand the vocabularies but also how they have been used to tag or classify information. However, with semantic search it may be less important for the information specialist to have a broader vocabulary themselves and more important to understand the breadth of vocabularies used by the semantic search engine and underlying data sources.

There are limitations to semantic technologies relating to the accuracy and consistency of tagging, just as there are with searching bibliographic databases. The people or algorithms that have created the database and entered information may be constrained by time or technology, which could result in errors or incomplete metadata that affects the quality of the search results. These may never be fully removed and while these technologies may help in some areas, the issues here may simply take on a different form. It is valuable for information specialists to be involved in these areas to continue in helping to identify and resolve these issues of accuracy and consistency. As vocabularies continue to be developed and used to describe information, there is a role for the information specialist to help shape their use.

It is particularly crucial that vocabularies are applied consistently when used to tag the subject of an article for example. As we have seen, linked data allows us to go further and consider how the concepts within a controlled vocabulary link to the entities within a knowledge graph, for example a graph relating to health care may refer to 'Cancer' and this could be defined by using an appropriate code from the

SNOMED CT nomenclature. However, there are usually many different ways to link terms and concepts. With a greater understanding of the decisions that are taken when applying vocabularies in this way, an information specialist will have a greater ability to query and filter this kind of graph-structured, semantically-rich resource.

As approaches are developed to automatically identify concepts and vocabularies to help in annotating resources, the information specialist may offer significant insight into the specific issues relating to consistent tagging. Informing the needs of these automated systems early will allow their development in a way that aids the information specialist and that is congruent with trusted methods. Enabling these systems and ontologies to be developed, to effectively learn from the expertise of the information specialist, will ultimately result in better tools for the information specialist to then use.

There is a need for the information specialist to consider different approaches being applied to ranking search results. This has been explored in the context of priority screening (O'Mara-Eves et al., 2015), although it also applies more generally to search. Reinforcement learning methods that provide feedback and effectively train an algorithm to improve the precision of a set of search results have been applied in some contexts to enable more of the relevant information to be identified and processed more efficiently (www.nactem.ac.uk/robotanalyst). Once again this relies on structure and semantics being present within the information being searched. NLP can be applied effectively to attach retrospectively semantic meaning by linking to identifiable concepts with a URI, if they were not added at the point of authoring. However, linked data (perhaps in conjunction with NLP) offers the ability to apply structure and semantic meaning explicitly and with quality checking by a human during the authoring process (see Case study 8.1).

Case study 8.1: Linked data at Cochrane
Overview
Cochrane is the largest producer of systematic reviews of health care interventions. There are huge challenges in tackling 'data deluge' from published reports of clinical trials and synthesising this evidence into knowledge that can be used to inform health and care decision-making. The figures for new research are even higher now than back in 2010 when it was

estimated that 75 new trials and 11 systematic reviews were published every day (Bastian, Glasziou and Chalmers, 2010). New approaches to finding, managing, curating and re-using data are needed.

Beginning with its new *Strategy to 2020* in 2014 (www.community.cochrane.org/organizational-info/resources/strategy-2020), Cochrane has undertaken several initiatives to tackle this massive influx of new data. The Cochrane Linked Data Project (www.linkeddata.cochrane.org) aims to semantically enrich Cochrane's content using semantic technologies. The PICO (Population, Intervention, Comparison, Outcomes) ontology, using a Web Ontology Language (OWL), provides a computable framework for describing Cochrane evidence and the underlying data that contributes to the analyses.

This model is being populated with instance data from controlled vocabulary sets such as SNOMED CT (www.snomed.org/snomed-ct), RxNorm (www.nlm.nih.gov/research/umls/rxnorm), MedDRA (www.meddra.org), MeSH (https://meshb.nlm.nih.gov/search) and the Anatomical Therapeutic Chemical classification system (www.whocc.no). This creates an RDF triple store of PICO metadata linked to Cochrane Reviews, the studies included in them and related datasets. In parallel, via Project Transform (www.community.cochrane.org/help/tools-and-software/project-transform), Cochrane has invested in the use of machine learning and text mining technologies, along with a crowdsourcing platform (http://crowd.cochrane.org/index.html), to support tasks such as classifying evidence. Further phases are planned to tackle extracting data from published trial reports as well as semi-automating other tasks in the evidence synthesis process.

Granularity

Systematic reviews are large, complex documents representing the long and involved process of conducting them. This output format is far from ideal from a user experience standpoint. Users want more granular pieces of information and knowledge. The PICO metadata Cochrane is generating enables more granular descriptions of the evidence which can be linked across clinical areas. These links facilitate, for example, answering questions about clinical effectiveness across a range of interventions for a given disease or condition and sets of outcomes. These information and knowledge 'chunks' then become well-described research objects which can be more easily discovered, combined and contextualised.

Provenance

Having better metadata, combined with more structured numerical outcome and analysis data, facilitates dissemination but also reuse and provenance. The underlying datasets can be found, tracked and reused, which enhances transparency and reproducibility, which are key components in the way science is done in the 21st century. Tracking the provenance of data and information in systematic reviews is critical to driving efficiency and streamlining the audit and peer review processes.

Semantic search

Cochrane's linked data initiatives, combined with the use of machine learning and crowdsourcing, enables faster curation of evidence. The rich metadata generated through these technologies and processes, combined with the structured data behind Cochrane reviews, is being used to improve the discoverability of Cochrane evidence through the use of semantic search technologies and other user interfaces for both machines (using Application Programming Interfaces (APIs)) and people. PICO search on the Cochrane Library (www.cochranelibrary.com), as well as potential federated models of semantic, cross-platform and cross-data repository search and browse, are all being explored and will be implemented in the future. Chapter 9 looks in more depth at some of these applications.

There are always benefits and constraints to consider when working with different databases and search tools. It is important to choose the right tool for the job and to be able to document the rationale for the approach taken. It is the same with linked data. For example, some uses of NLP or other machine learning approaches to search may be deemed more accurate (more recall and higher precision) but less repeatable, as they could provide slightly different results each time. The trade offs being made, such as balancing accuracy and reproducibility, are important to the information specialist and it is important to understand how to work with semantic content and associated search methods to continue to improve and validate their suitability.

It is clear that for some time to come there needs to remain a human expert in the process of searching for high-quality information, especially within domains such as health and care. However, with an increase in the semantic identifiers embedded in the information and with computers being able to understand our natural language more accurately, the mix of human and artificially intelligent agents involved in information retrieval is shifting. This emerging partnership is helping to provide us with the appropriate tools we need to deal with the amount of information that now faces us.

Future directions

It is probably clear that this area of linked data and the ways in which it is being applied are still actively being developed. This means that there are many research groups working on developing and implementing the technologies presented in this chapter. It may be that you are interested in becoming more actively involved in some of this research. For example, the Research Objects group (www. researchobject.org/about) use linked data technologies and they are described as 'a community aimed at gathering together information, ideas, and interest around the topic of scholarly publication'. Why not visit them and join their community? There are many other research groups out there that may be focusing on your particular area of interest. Sharing your working experience of the systematic review world with these groups will always be appreciated!

The fundamentals of linked data are often difficult to grasp and perhaps even more difficult to explain, so the first thing to bear in mind is not to worry if this does not make sense straight away. It is not necessary for most people to understand the real detail of the subject, but for those who are interested a first step may be to read some of the suggested further reading listed at the end of this chapter. There are also courses, often being offered for free online, that you might consider joining to get an in-depth perspective on the subject.

It may be that your organization is already working on research projects or actively developing new ways that they can make use of these technologies and increase their understanding of the opportunities they offer to the information specialist and systematic reviewer. If that is the case, requesting to take part in this work and sharing your expertise would be enormously valuable. Most developments of this kind benefit from a multidisciplinary approach so do not be concerned if you do not feel confident with the technologies, others in the team will provide that expertise alongside your own.

And if you are working for an organization that is less aware of linked data and related semantic technologies, a good next step would be to start the conversation. Share this book and others from the references. Be the person to start the ball rolling!

Conclusion

There is an ever-growing, ever-changing amount of information that an information specialist is required to understand and process.

Linked data is just one area that requires attention to ensure it is appropriately understood and incorporated into the information specialist's toolkit. Linked data alone will not solve our information management needs, but it acts as an important enabler for change and for many of the other advances in technology that we now see in areas such as artificial intelligence.

Unless we start to capitalise on new and appropriate assistive tools demanded by the rising tide of information, humans using existing tools will have to accept the need to reduce the scope or quality of our information processing powers. To that end, it is important for the information specialist to understand the underlying principles and technologies that are being applied and to be involved as far as they are able in continuing to develop them.

Information specialists may be involved now in numerous ways, but here are just two that could be considered:

- To ensure effective and appropriate use of linked data and semantic technologies to improve the way we find information
- To act as proactive agents of change not as passive recipients of new technology: it cannot be developed effectively without you!

Suggestions for further reading

For a good introduction to linked data and a selection of useful case studies see:

Van Hooland, S. and Verbogh, R. (2014) *Linked Data for Libraries, Archives and Museums: how to clean, link and publish your metadata*, Facet Publishing.
The Educational Curriculum for the usage of Linked Data (EUCLID) project was set up to develop learning resources, which are available online www.euclid-project.eu/resources/learning-materials.html.

For more information about natural language processing, linked data and semantic search, two leading research groups based in the UK provide a wealth of resources and tools, as well as services for business: NaCTeM (www.nactem.ac.uk) and GATE (www.gate.ac.uk).

There are free online courses and, although often quite technical, they usually include high level overviews that can be useful even if you do not complete the whole course. This site provides a list of those that are currently available: www.mooc-list.com/tags/semantic-web.

References

Bastian, H., Glasziou, P. and Chalmers, I. (2010) Seventy-five Trials and Eleven Systematic Reviews a Day: how will we ever keep up?, *PLOS Medicine*, **7** (9), e1000326.

Bechhofer, S., Buchan, I., De Roure, D., Missier, P., Ainsworth, J., Bhagat, J., Couch, P., Cruickshank, D., Delderfield, M., Dunlop, I., Gamble, M., Michaelides, D., Owen, S., Newman, D., Sufi, S. and Goble, C. (2013) Why Linked Data is Not Enough for Scientists, *Future Generation Computer Systems*, **29** (2), 599-611.

Berners-Lee, T. (2006) Linked Data. www.w3.org/DesignIssues/LinkedData.html

Bizer, C., Heath, T. and Berners-Lee, T. (2011) Linked Data: the story so far. In Sheth, A. (ed), *Semantic Services, Interoperability and Web Applications: emerging concepts*, IGI Global.

Clark, T., Ciccarese, P. N. and Goble, C. A. (2014) Micropublications: a semantic model for claims, evidence, arguments and annotations in biomedical communications, *Journal of Biomedical Semantics*, **5**, 28.

Cooper, C., Dawson, S., Peters, J., Varley-Campbell, J., Cockcroft, E., Hendon, J. and Churchill, R. (2018) Revisiting the Need for a Literature Search Narrative: a brief methodological note, *Research Synthesis Methods*, **9** (3), 361-365.

Curcin, C. (2017) Embedding Data Provenance into the Learning Health System to Facilitate Reproducible Research, *Learning Health Systems*, **1** (2), e10019.

O'Mara-Eves, A., Thomas, J., McNaught, J., Miwa, M. and Ananiadou, S. (2015) Using Text Mining for Study Identification in Systematic Reviews: a systematic review of current approaches, *Systematic Reviews*, **4**, 5.

Powers, B., Grossman, C. and McGinnis, J. M. (2011) *Digital Infrastructure for the Learning Health System: the foundation for continuous improvement in health and health care*, Institute of Medicine. www.nap.edu/catalog/12912/digital-infrastructure-for-the-learning-health-system-the-foundation-for

ten Teije, A., Marcos, M., Balser, M., van Croonenborg, J., Duelli, C., van Harmelen, F., Lucas, P., Miksch, S., Reif, W., Rosenbrand, K. and

Seyfang, A. (2006) Improving Medical Protocols by Formal Methods, *Artificial Intelligence in Medicine*, **36** (3), 193-209.

Uschold, G. and Gruninger, M. (1996) Ontologies: principles methods and applications, *Knowledge Engineering Review*, **11** (2), 93-136.

Webber, J. (2018) Why Knowledge Graphs are Foundational to Artificial Intelligence, *Datanami*, 20 March 2018.
www.datanami.com/2018/03/20/why-knowledge-graphs-are-foundational-to-artificial-intelligence

World Wide Web Consortium (2013) *PROV-DM: The PROV Data Model: W3C recommendation, 30 April 2013.*
www.w3.org/TR/2013/REC-prov-dm-20130430

9

Evidence surveillance to keep up to date with new research

James Thomas, Anna Noel-Storr and Steve McDonald

Introduction

Research is being published at an ever-increasing rate and it is becoming more and more difficult for systematic reviewers to find research in a timely way and keep existing reviews updated as new studies are published (Bastian, Glasziou and Chalmers, 2010). This is a particular problem for organizations which maintain libraries of systematic reviews, such as Cochrane and the Campbell Collaboration, as the more systematic reviews they publish, the greater the burden of maintenance. It is also a challenge for guideline-producing organizations which, for pragmatic reasons, typically invest significant resources and effort in one-off periodic updates without knowing whether the evidence base has changed or has actually changed so rapidly that more frequent updating would have been warranted. Previous work has shown that systematic reviews can date very quickly, with some out of date as soon as they are published (Shojania et al., 2007). It is becoming clear that our current methods of research curation are wasteful of societal investment in research and risk resulting in suboptimal outcomes (MacLeod et al., 2014).

This chapter is concerned with this problem of 'data deluge' and the need to establish better surveillance of research in order to keep abreast of new developments. It is thus related to work on living systematic reviews (LSRs), and these are 'continually updated, incorporating relevant new evidence as it becomes available' (Elliott et al., 2014;

Elliott et al., 2017). The chapter outlines developments in automation technologies that are already making the systematic review process more efficient and then focuses on the way that global research curation systems are organised. The chapter suggests that new approaches are needed in order to support the production of evidence syntheses in efficient and timely ways. Case studies 9.1 and 9.2 explain how these new developments are being put into practice to realise these benefits.

Discussion

New ways of working that integrate and capitalise on automation are necessary to tackle the growing burden of identifying and synthesising research. New technologies – which range from the mundane (such as identifying duplicates in bibliographic records) to full artificial intelligence (AI) systems – are under constant development and are already assisting various aspects of the evidence curation (see Tip below) and discovery process. It is possible to break these new tools down into two broad categories:

1 Tools which can make existing manual processes more efficient.
2 Tools which aim to change the way systematic reviews are carried out in more fundamental ways by linking tools together and changing the sequencing of activities.

> **TIP:**
> **What is 'curation'?**
> A key concept in this chapter is 'evidence curation'. 'Curation' as an idea has been around a long time and concerns the activities necessary to manage, sort and arrange information. We see current methods for finding and processing evidence as inadequate, since they result in so much repetitive and avoidable work in systematic reviews. We will therefore use the word 'curation' throughout to denote the work necessary to organise research information in a way that facilitates its easy discovery and reuse. In this sense, 'curation' also involves an acknowledgement that research data has value and that this value needs to be protected through fit-for-purpose management.

The following section examines the potential for automation to assist in existing processes. The section after that considers the potential for linking these tools into integrated surveillance systems for LSRs and other types of living evidence, such as guidelines.

How automation can make existing processes more efficient

The systematic review process follows what is now a well-trodden path that, once the research questions have been agreed and the review team established, usually includes the following steps:

- developing the search strategy
- searching databases and other sources and downloading the results
- de-duplication of records
- screening records for eligibility
- full-text document retrieval and screening
- checking bibliographies and citation indexes
- data extraction and quality assessment
- synthesis and write-up of final reports.

This list emphasises the retrieval and curation tasks that occur early in the review process. The development of enabling tools has tended to focus on these tasks since many are repetitive and time-consuming (for example, reference screening) and also more amenable to machine assistance. We will now consider each of the stages in terms of the available tools and their readiness for use in reviews.

Developing the search strategy

As Chapter 7 shows, there has been a proliferation of tools to help with developing search strategies. Previous work has shown that the way that search strategies are developed can impact on the recall of the search (for example, Hausner et al., 2016). In a case study, Stansfield and colleagues (Stansfield, O'Mara-Eves and Thomas, 2017) describe how text analytic software is able to assist in five ways:

1 Improving the precision of the search and so reducing manual effort in screening results.
2 Identifying search terms which can improve the sensitivity and reliability of the search.

3 Assisting with translating strategies between databases (for example, the Polyglot Search Translator, http://crebp-sra.com/#/polyglot).
4 Searching and screening within an integrated system (Mergel, Silveira and da Silva, 2015).
5 Developing search strategies objectively (see also Hausner et al., 2015).

There is interest in using relationships between citations for identifying other relevant studies (for example, Octaviano et al., 2015). Comprehensive citation databases such as Google Scholar (https://scholar.google.co.uk), Microsoft Academic (https://academic.microsoft.com), Scopus (www.scopus.com) and Web of Science (www.wokinfo.com) all offer tools to support this. An important issue to bear in mind – which can be highlighted using new technology – is the care required when following citation trails. Research is often carried out by communities of researchers and if they fail to cite the work of other groups working in the same field, then this kind of pearl growing will not find all relevant pockets of research. A heat map of a citation network of systematic reviews in psychology (Figure 9.1) shows graphically how related research does not always connect, the darker

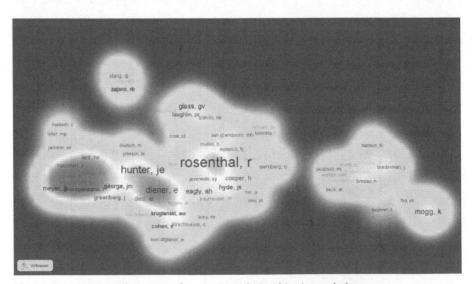

Figure 9.1 *VOSviewer heat map of co-citation relationships in psychology*
Copyright © 2009 - 2018 Nees Jan van Eck and Ludo Waltman
(www.vosviewer.com)

areas of the map indicating a higher occurrence of a particular term or theme. Information specialists should consider using tools to help visualise and identify these kinds of connections to ensure that search methods do not rely exclusively on specific sources and approaches.

Searching databases and other sources and downloading the results

New ways of searching databases are emerging all the time, as Chapter 7 has highlighted with respect to tools for searching PubMed and MEDLINE (for example, PubReMiner). Tool development for the PubMed dataset is particularly common because of its size and the fact that it is freely accessible. Automation tools rely on application programming interfaces (APIs) which enable systematic review tools to access databases 'behind the scenes'. For example, users can search PubMed from within EPPI-Reviewer without needing to visit PubMed directly and Cochrane's Central Register of Studies (which sits behind the public CENTRAL database) also searches sources such as Embase and ClinicalTrials.gov at the programming, rather than user, interface level. Although API access to commercial databases is more com-plicated because of the issues involved in retaining and reusing references, it is becoming more commonplace.

Being able to search databases from within systematic review tools can save the user having to download multiple text files and then reload them for screening. The process of ensuring compatible formats (for example, RIS) can also be more reliable using this route. However, it is when we consider the need for automated searches to facilitate surveillance that API access to databases becomes particularly important. Here, we need regular searches to be run and relevant references retrieved, automatically with minimal user interaction. While some sources, such as PubMed, are relatively unproblematic, others do not offer API access at all, limiting the scope for full implementation of an automated surveillance process at this time.

De-duplication of records

Searching multiple sources inevitably results in the retrieval of duplicate references. Although bibliographic software tools like

EndNote can minimise much of the workload in identifying duplicates, eliminating them altogether is not a simple task. Records entered manually by different providers can contain slightly different information. Some research has been carried out into developing and evaluating de-duplication algorithms (for example, Jiang et al., 2014; Rathbone et al., 2015), but it would be fair to say that further evaluations are required, including increasing the availability of 'gold standard' datasets on which to evaluate new algorithms.

Screening records for eligibility

The ability of text mining and machine learning tools to assist in the screening of records for eligibility has been outlined in Chapter 7. There are two approaches to highlight here in the context of evidence surveillance.

First, the use of 'active learning' – whereby the machine learns the review's inclusion criteria in an iterative fashion alongside human screening (O'Mara-Eves et al., 2015) – is still of relevance when we are updating an existing review. We naturally already have all the screening data generated when the review was originally written and from any subsequent updates. This means that it is possible to build a machine learning classifier to rank the relevance of newly retrieved references at the outset of an update and, because it can utilise more data than are typically available when a new review is conducted, it is likely to perform better too.

Second, the use of study-type machine learning classifiers is now becoming more widespread. These are classifiers which have been trained from large quantities of data (and so are highly accurate) that are able to classify papers according to the type of study they describe. While not all study types are yet covered, there are some high-performing classifiers now which can distinguish between records which do, and do not, describe randomised controlled trials (RCTs) with a high degree of confidence (Cohen et al., 2015; Marshall et al., 2018). Since many systematic reviews in the health sector only include RCTs, being able to eliminate the records which are very unlikely to be describing RCTs can be an efficient way of reducing manual effort.

Full-text document retrieval and screening

Many tools, including generic bibliographic software such as EndNote, now offer the facility to identify and download full-text reports based on citation records. The Digital Object Identifier (DOI) system has transformed this task and the main barrier to full automation is the fact that many documents lie behind journal subscription paywalls. Services such as Crossref are making the identification of these documents more efficient, even if the last phase of document recovery needs to be undertaken manually.

Checking bibliographies and citation indexes

Current tools that allow reviewers to undertake citation searching (and examine both the references cited in a given paper and those that cite it) have two main weaknesses. First, since no tool is truly comprehensive it may be necessary to use multiple services such as Web of Science, Scopus and Google Scholar. Second, extracting the bibliography from a paper and the automated linking of references to one another is challenging; tools often fail to list, for example, all the papers in a given bibliography. That said, the OpenCitations (www.opencitations.net) and Crossref (www.crossref.org) initiatives are gaining ground and these systems are becoming increasingly comprehensive. It is hoped that major publishers, such as Elsevier, could sign up to the consortium (www.opencitations.wordpress.com/2017/11/24/elsevier-references-dominate-those-that-are-not-open-at-crossref). The case for using citation networks would then become even more compelling (Choong et al., 2014), the warning above about relying too heavily on citation trails notwithstanding.

Data extraction and quality assessment

As we move through the review process, the number and maturity of tools for deployment decreases. There is still significant potential to reduce manual workload but it is much more difficult to build an automated data extraction system than it is to build one for screening search results. Every report of a study is unique and identifying even apparently simple information, such as the number of study participants, is quite a challenge. The ExaCT tool aims to extract information from clinical trial reports (Kiritchenko et al., 2010), and the RobotReviewer tool can automate the risk of bias assessment for RCTs (Marshall, Kuiper and Wallace, 2016).

Synthesis and write-up of final reports

While writing the report is currently beyond the capacity of even the most advanced systematic review AI system, some tools do aim to write text around the results of a statistical meta-analysis. Slightly more prosaically, it is recognised that many sections of a systematic review describe standard processes and standardised wording might be entirely appropriate. Currently, support for the needs of LSRs, where information about new studies automatically appears in the right part of the report, is scant, with few alternatives available beyond those for standard systematic reviews.

Creating surveillance systems with automation tools

Until now, this chapter has considered how individual automation tools and technologies can improve the efficiency of existing tasks and support a living evidence workflow. However, the real potential of these technologies to change fundamentally the way evidence is identified, lies in joining them together and considering the up-front strategic identification of relevant research at scale.

Consider the workflow depicted in Figure 9.2 on the next page. This shows the key steps involved in the information retrieval and curation aspects of the review in a continuous process from 'federated search' through to 'synthesis'. Outlined here is a 'living' process that enables surveillance of evidence as it becomes available whether as, for example, published papers or registrations in trials registries. One critical difference between the 'micro' systems described above and the workflow in Figure 9.2 is that a full surveillance system typically operates across wide areas of research, rather than individual reviews; it is concerned with the up-front identification of evidence at scale, rather than the one-off processes which accompany the traditional systematic review process. Instead of reviewers having to periodically interrogate multiple sources to identify whether any relevant evidence has been published, there is now the promise of a system that can prospectively signal when new evidence is available.

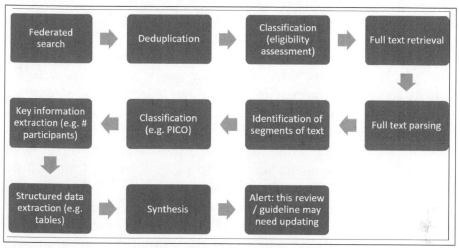

Figure 9.2 *Living Systematic Review and evidence surveillance workflow*

Conceptualising evidence discovery as an up-front process across a domain brings economies of scale. For example, the need for sensitive searches leads to the same studies being examined multiple times by people doing different but related systematic reviews across the globe; for reviews of randomised trials, the same assessments are being made numerous times. Currently, there is no system for ensuring that these assessments do not need to be repeated the next time a given study is retrieved and so systematic reviewers frequently duplicate one another's work. If, however, knowledge generated about a study (whether automated or manual) contributed to a domain-wide map of the evidence base, we would know that if a study is relevant for a particular review then it is also *not* relevant for many other reviews. Thus, a full surveillance system uses information about a study's relevance to one question to ascertain its relevance to others.

One vision for an integrated system involves automated:

- searches of major databases.
- de-duplication.
- full-text retrieval.
- assignment of new research to appropriate reviews.
- data extraction.
- synthesis.

While automated synthesis is unlikely to be as reliable as a human-controlled process, it may be sufficient to indicate whether the 'new' study is likely to impact the review's findings in important ways. For example, if an automated system is able to determine the size of a study – and the direction of its effect – it might be able to alert authors as to the likely impact of the new study in a given review. As the description of tools above has indicated though, the current state of tool development, the limited availability of APIs and the difficulty of obtaining full-text content held behind paywalls, means that a fully automated system is currently unachievable.

Full automation may not be a necessary, or even desirable, goal for an effective evidence surveillance system if moving towards an integrated process (that minimises the duplication of effort and identifies relevant studies up-front) brings significant efficiencies on its own. Critical to the success of such a system are effective tools to ensure knowledge is shared between reviews and not lost and a good interaction between human and machine effort to maximise human input and minimise the expenditure of human effort on tasks which can be automated. Case studies 9.1 and 9.2 on the following pages describe how two evidence surveillance systems are being created to put these innovative ideas into practice.

Case study 9.1: Cochrane Evidence Pipeline

Introduction
Cochrane is an international collaboration of clinicians, researchers, patients, policymakers and others who are concerned with evidence-based decision-making to improve people's health. Central to the work of Cochrane is the production of rigorous systematic reviews which are published in an online library (www.cochranelibrary.com). There are over 7,500 systematic reviews, a significant effort on the part of Cochrane's many thousands of volunteer contributors. Ensuring these reviews are up to date so they continue to be useful for decision makers is an even more formidable challenge.

Duplication of effort is a problem across Cochrane, with individual reviewers and review teams using different systems for their reviews. Cumulatively, they have probably screened more than 40 million references over the past 20 years to find RCTs (mostly) for inclusion in Cochrane reviews; yet there have probably been no more than 2 million RCTs conducted so far in human history. It would be much more efficient to find and collate all RCTs and for reviewers to look in this limited pool than to continually assess the same records, making the same decisions about a reference's eligibility.

This is the problem that the Cochrane Evidence Pipeline has been designed to solve. As Figure 9.3 on page 201 shows, research enters the pipeline at the top and ends in the Cochrane Register of Studies (CRS) ready for inclusion in systematic reviews. In between are a number of stages which enrich the study record with additional information. Critically though, this is a mixture of human and machine effort: no part of the process is expected to be fully automated.

The process starts with research reports (typically references to articles indexed in bibliographic databases) entering the Pipeline. Cochrane's centralised search service supplies the Pipeline with a constraint stream of new research. Not all databases have an API though, so research enters the Pipeline through a mixture of automated and manual searches. Importantly though, the aim is for sensitive searches to be carried out up-front, outside the process of any individual review.

What type of study is this?
The first piece of data enrichment to be applied is the type of study that the report describes. Systematic reviews commonly rely on particular study types to answer specific questions, so identifying the right types of study is more important for a database like the Cochrane Register of Studies than for a more generic database, such as MEDLINE. The Pipeline is currently focused on identifying RCTs and has a machine learning classifier that is able to distinguish accurately between RCTs and non-RCTs (Marshall et al., 2018; Wallace et al., 2017). This classifier was built with data from Cochrane Crowd (http://crowd.cochrane.org/index.html), a citizen-science platform where volunteers help with specific data curation activities (called 'micro-tasks'), including classifying abstracts according to whether they describe RCTs or not. An agreement algorithm ensures a high degree of collective accuracy with sensitivity and precision both exceeding 99%.

Research is first classified by the machine; those records that the machine classifier rates as *possibly* describing RCTs are then examined by Cochrane Crowd and a final determination made as to their eligibility. There is a pleasing symbiosis to this machine-Crowd interaction: the initial machine algorithm that was derived from the efforts of the Crowd is now deployed to reduce the number of abstracts that the Crowd needs to assess. As the dataset examined by the Crowd grows, so the accuracy of the machine algorithm improves in a virtuous circle that is freeing up Crowd resource for other tasks. Other machine classifiers include ones to identify systematic reviews and economic evaluations.

This work in identifying RCTs is already saving reviewers' time and reducing duplication of effort. An increasingly large dataset of previously assessed records is being accumulated against which new search results can be checked. A Cochrane Information Specialist can upload their search results to the database and have them automatically matched against existing records.

A record already assessed as not describing an RCT can be discarded without further manual checks. Remaining records can then be assessed by the machine-Crowd service, leaving very few for review authors to examine (Thomas et al., 2017).

What is this study about?

While identifying the study type is already saving significant reviewer effort, the living evidence process depends on identifying studies relevant to *specific* reviews. The next item in the Pipeline – the enrichment of data by identifying PICO (Population, Intervention, Comparison, Outcome) characteristics – aims to achieve this. PICO precisely describes the scope of a review and is often used as the organising framework for search strategies. If it were possible to classify research studies according to their PICO, it would be possible to pre-allocate them to reviews, thus not only facilitating the updating of existing reviews, but identifying where there might be gaps in the synthesised evidence.

As described in Chapter 8, the Cochrane 'linked data' project has developed a model which encapsulates the PICO structure of clinical trials and a standardised vocabulary to describe their elements in detail (Mavergames, Oliver and Becker, 2013). Developing the standardised vocabulary is a significant effort and an ongoing task: it is linked to terms used in other major thesauri (for example, SNOMED CT, MedRA and RxNorm) and contains many hundreds of thousands of terms.

It is already possible to automate the identification of the broad area of a study (for example, the article is about treatments for heart disease or injuries), but being able to detect the detailed PICO terms (for example, the article is about men aged over 65 at high risk of heart attack) is a challenging task for automation alone and so human and machine are again working together on this problem. At the time of writing, many thousands of Cochrane reviews and their included studies have had their PICO manually classified by Cochrane Information Specialists, thus providing valuable training material for machine learning. In addition, Cochrane Crowd has recently launched a new task which involves identifying specific concepts in abstracts and associating them with PICO elements. Alongside this, machine learning work is analysing the training data and attempting to automate the PICO predictions. Overall accuracy is approaching 50%, which may not yet be sufficient for global roll-out, but does represent good progress, considering how challenging this classification task is (bearing in mind there are hundreds of thousands of terms for the machine to learn from very little training data) (Singh et al., 2017).

What are the data?

The final piece of metadata enrichment in the Evidence Pipeline concerns data extraction. Here, the focus is on one of the most time-consuming and error-prone aspects of the process, namely extracting numeric data. There are two tools under development: one for extracting structured data from tables in PDF documents and the other for extracting numeric data from graphs. Neither tool aims to be completely automated, but both aim to reduce manual effort by providing some automation, for example by having users check results of the machine automation and undertake aspects of the process which would be unreliable if left fully automated.

After the various machine and human processes have enhanced the study record, it is saved in the CRS database and is ready for use in reviews. The ultimate aim is for authors to receive automated alerts when new content is available in their area.

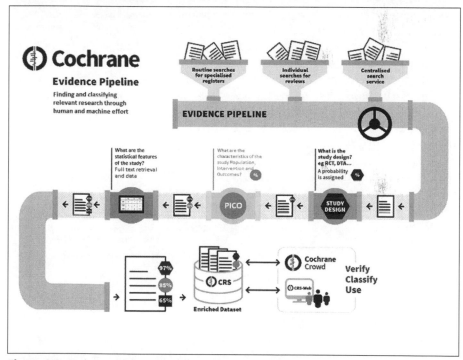

Figure 9.3 *Cochrane Evidence Pipeline* © Cochrane, used with permission

Case study 9.2: The Human Behaviour-Change Project

The Human Behaviour-Change Project (www.humanbehaviourchange.org) shares some characteristics with the Cochrane Evidence Pipeline but aims to take the automation one stage further into the synthesis itself. It is funded by a grant from the Wellcome Trust and is being carried out by a consortium of behaviour change experts from University College London (principal investigator: Professor Susan Michie) and computer scientists from IBM Research, Dublin, and UCL (Michie et al., 2017).

The project is concerned with the discipline of behaviour change, since changing people's behaviour is key across a range of social, health and environmental challenges. It is asking the overarching question: which interventions are effective (for whom, in which circumstances) for achieving behaviour change? In order to help researchers and decision-makers to answer this question it is developing a system that will produce recommendations for potentially useful interventions based on the extant behaviour change literature.

The system thus requires some of the same components as the Cochrane Evidence Pipeline: it needs a system for locating and keeping up to date with research evidence, processes to organise the research and a system for synthesising the evidence and making recommendations to users. The first component for locating research is similar to that employed in the Cochrane Evidence Pipeline: a continuous feed of research. Again, in common with the previous example, an ontology is needed to organise the literature and, in this case, an *ontology of behaviour change interventions* is being developed and widely consulted upon. Research papers are being annotated according to this ontology in order to provide training data for machine learning systems.

This annotation work is designed with future automation in mind and involves selecting specific pieces of text in research reports and associating these snippets of text with a given classification in the ontology (for example, a section in the description of the intervention which communicates to the reader which type of behaviour change intervention is being used). As an example, one behaviour change technique involves the 'self-monitoring of behaviour'. This classification has been applied to the following text from three studies:

- 'Messages are interactive and prompt users to track smoking, report on cravings, and provide smoking status'.
- 'Examples of behavioural treatment strategies used include providing personalised feedback about use of alcohol including comparison of personal level of use to peer norms'.
- 'Participants learned about their smoking habit by writing down time of day, situation, and perceived need for every cigarette smoked before smoking cessation'.

Based on these snippets of text (among many others), machine learning systems can then learn to recognise similar pieces of text and make the association with, in this case, the type of behaviour change intervention being described. The project also aims to automate the process of recognising and extracting results from tables in documents. This is necessary to automate the extraction of accurate statistics describing study findings.

The final component of the project is the system for generating inferences and recommendations for users that are generated by the system reading across the entire field of literature. To automate the synthesis of research in this way, the system will need to have achieved a very high level of reliability in terms of the detailed classification and extraction of results from studies. It will then synthesise the results across studies to generate recommendations using methods which are similar to those employed in existing methods for network meta-analysis (for example, Caldwell, 2014).

Future directions

Case studies 9.1 and 9.2 are both part of a vision for a future of evidence curation and synthesis workflow that changes the current process of evidence discovery in quite fundamental ways.

First, the task of locating evidence is no longer a process specific to individual reviews. Instead, research is identified as soon as it is published (or registered in registries of trials) and the record enhanced with sufficient information for it to be assigned to relevant systematic reviews.

Second, the classification systems being developed and applied go beyond the usual indexing that takes place in some databases (for example, MeSH and Emtree tagging) because they are more structured and *use orientated*, i.e. the domain models for PICO and behaviour change allow the research to be described in ways which precisely describe the characteristics required for synthesis. In the Cochrane Evidence Pipeline, the aim is for the search for relevant studies to start and end with the specification of a PICO question. When the PICO for a given review has been searched for, the system should locate a small number of studies with high precision *and* recall, greatly truncating the current lengthy search and screen process.

The case studies also point to changes in working practices necessary to make them a reality. Both systems rely on the up-front identification of research and seek to eliminate (or at least reduce) the current duplication of effort across review teams. Implementing systems that will achieve these gains in productivity requires both technical interoperability and organizational willingness to invest in systems which facilitate data sharing. At an organizational (and inter-organizational) level there needs to be investment in the up-front organization of research. If the systems are to be sustainable and not require more human effort than can reasonably be made available, tasks which are amenable to automation will need to be automated. If automation efficiencies are to be realised, then specific training datasets will also need to be created, requiring both a commitment to this model of research curation and investment in human annotation. The term 'evidence ecosystem' is quickly gaining currency as it aims to encapsulate this new dynamic of a global system of linked data which has been organised to facilitate its reuse.

The most obvious gains in efficiency appear to come from improving the global discovery and curation of research for use in systematic reviews and decision-making. However, Case study 9.2 also points to a world where the synthesis of research itself may change in the future. AI systems, which digest vast quantities of information and make recommendations for practice, are becoming commonplace and systems which digest data and suggest treatments, diagnoses and prognoses (for example, IBM Watson Oncology (www.ibm.com/ watson/health/oncology-and-genomics/oncology)) are being deployed in practice settings. Despite their possible pivotal and game-changing role, these systems are rarely evaluated in traditional RCTs. One important issue for future research is to develop methodologies and regulatory expectations for this new generation of decision aids.

Conclusion

This chapter has examined moves towards the automation of systematic reviews and the developments underway to support living systematic reviews and guidelines. These processes can be seen as strategic shifts towards evidence surveillance systems that change traditional systematic review methods, moving some elements of study identification outside the processes of any individual review. Few automation systems operate entirely autonomously and most require human intervention to achieve acceptable levels of performance. Realising a new dynamic 'ecosystem' of research evidence will require organizational investment, a willingness to share data and a more strategic and use-orientated way of understanding evidence curation.

Suggestions for further reading

Akl, E. A., Meerpohl, J. J., Elliott, J., Kahale, L. A., Schünemman, H. J. and

Living Systematic Review Network (2017) Living Systematic Reviews: 4. Living guideline recommendations, *Journal of Clinical Epidemiology*, **91**, 47-53.

Elliott, J. H., Synnot, A., Turner, T., Simmonds, M., Akl, E. A., McDonald, S., Salanti, G., Meerpohl, J., MacLehose, H., Hilton, J., Tovey, D., Shemilt, I., Thomas, J. and Living Systematic Review Network (2017) Living Systematic Review: 1. Introduction – the why, what, when, and how, *Journal of Clinical Epidemiology*, **91**, 23-30.

Jonnalagadda, S. R., Goyal, P. and Huffman, M. D. (2015) Automating Data Extraction in Systematic Reviews: a systematic review, *Systematic Reviews*, **4** (1), 78.

Michie, S., Thomas, J., Johnston, M., Mac Aonghusa, P., Shawe-Taylor, J., Kelly, M. P., Deleris, L. A., Finnerty, A. N., Marques, M. M., Norris, E., O'Mara-Eves, A. and West, R. (2017) The Human Behaviour-Change Project: harnessing the power of artificial intelligence and machine learning for evidence synthesis and interpretation, *Implementation Science*, **12** (1), 121.

O'Mara-Eves, A., Thomas, J., McNaught, J., Miwa, M. and Ananiadou, S. (2015) Using Text Mining for Study Identification in Systematic Reviews: a systematic review of current approaches, *Systematic Reviews*, **4** (1), 5.

Simmonds, M., Salanti, G., McKenzie, J., Elliott, J. and Living Systematic Review Network (2017) Living Systematic Reviews: 3. Statistical methods for updating meta-analyses, *Journal of Clinical Epidemiology*, **91**, 38-46.

Thomas, J., Noel-Storr, A., Marshall, I., Wallace, B., McDonald, S., Mavergames, C., Glasziou, P., Shemilt, I., Synnot, A., Turner, T., Elliott, J. and Living Systematic Review Network (2017) Living Systematic Reviews: 2. Combining human and machine effort, *Journal of Clinical Epidemiology*, **91**, 31-37.

Tsafnat, G., Dunn, A., Glasziou, P. and Coiera, E. (2013) The Automation of Systematic Reviews, *BMJ*, **346**, f139.

Tsafnat, G., Glasziou, P., Choong, M. K., Dunn, A., Galgani, F. and Coiera, E. (2014) Systematic Review Automation Technologies, *Systematic Reviews*, **3** (1), 74.

Wallace, B. C., Trikalinos, T. A., Lau, J., Brodley, C. and Schmid, C. H. (2010) Semi-automated Screening of Biomedical Citations for Systematic Reviews, *BMC Bioinformatics*, **11** (1), 55.

References

Bastian, H., Glasziou, P. and Chalmers, I. (2010) Seventy-Five Trials and Eleven Systematic Reviews a Day: How Will We Ever Keep Up?, *PLOS Medicine*, **7** (9), e1000326.

Caldwell, D. M. (2014) An Overview of Conducting Systematic Reviews with Network Meta-analysis, *Systematic Reviews*, **3**, 109.

Choong, M. K., Galgani, F., Dunn, A. G. and Tsafnat, G. (2014) Automatic Evidence Retrieval for Systematic Reviews, *Journal of Medical Internet Research*, **16** (10), e223.

Cohen, A. M, Smalheiser, N. R., McDonagh, M. S., Yu, C., Adams, C. E., Davis, J. M. and Yu, P. S. (2015) Automated Confidence Ranked Classification of Randomized Controlled Trial Articles: an aid to evidence-based medicine, *Journal of the American Medical Informatics Association*, **22** (3), 707-717.

Elliott, J. H., Synnot, A., Turner, T., Simmonds, M., Akl, E. A., McDonald, S., Salanti, G., Meerpohl, J., MacLehose, H., Hilton, J., Tovey, D., Shemilt, I., Thomas, J. and Living Systematic Review Network (2017) Living Systematic Review: 1. Introduction – the why, what, when, and how, *Journal of Clinical Epidemiology*, **91**, 23-30.

Elliott, J. H., Turner, T., Clavisi, O., Thomas, J., Higgins, J. P., Mavergames, C. and Gruen, R. L. (2014) Living Systematic Reviews: an emerging opportunity to narrow the evidence-practice gap, *PLOS Medicine,* **11** (2), e1001603.

Hausner, E., Guddat, C., Hermanns, T., Lampert, U. and Waffenschmidt, S. (2015) Development of Search Strategies for Systematic Reviews: validation showed the noninferiority of the objective approach, *Journal of Clinical Epidemiology,* **68** (2), 191-199.

Hausner, E., Guddat, C., Hermanns, T., Lampert, U. and Waffenschmidt, S. (2016) Prospective Comparison of Search Strategies for Systematic Reviews: an objective approach yielded higher sensitivity than a conceptual one, *Journal of Clinical Epidemiology*, **77**, 118-124.

Jiang, Y., Lin, C., Meng, W., Yu, C., Cohen, A. M. and Smalheiser, N. R. (2014) Rule-based Deduplication of Article Records from Bibliographic Databases, *Database*, 2014, bat086.

Kiritchenko, S., de Bruijn, B., Carini, S., Martin, J. and Sim, I. (2010) ExaCT: automatic extraction of clinical trial characteristics from journal publications, *BMC Medical Informatics and Decision Making*, **10**, 56.

Macleod, M. R., Michie, S., Roberts, I., Dirnagl, U., Chalmers, I., Ioannidis,

J. P. A., Al-Shahi Salman, R., Chan, A-W. and Glasziou, P. (2014)
Biomedical Research: increasing value, reducing waste, *The Lancet*,
383 (9912), 101-104.

Marshall, I., Kuiper, J. and Wallace, B. C. (2016) RobotReviewer: evaluation
of a system for automatically assessing bias in clinical trials, *Journal of the
American Medical Informatics Association*, **23** (1), 193-201.

Marshall, I., Noel-Storr, A., Kuiper, J., Thomas, J. and Wallace B. C. (2018)
Machine Learning for Identifying Randomized Controlled Trials: an
evaluation and practitioner's guide, *Research Synthesis Methods*, **9** (4),
602-614.

Mavergames, C., Oliver, S. and Becker, L. (2013) Systematic Reviews as an
Interface to the Web of (Trial) Data: using PICO as an ontology for
knowledge synthesis in evidence-based healthcare research, *CEUR
Workshop Proceedings*, **994**, 22-26.

Mergel, G. D., Silveira, M. S. and da Silva, S. (2015) A Method to Support
Search String Building in Systematic Literature Reviews Through Visual
Text Mining. In Wainwright, R. L. (ed), *Proceedings of the 30th Annual
ACM Symposium on Applied Computing*, Association for Computing
Machinery, 1594-1601.

Michie, S., Thomas, J., Johnston, M., Mac Aonghusa, P., Shawe-Taylor, J.,
Kelly, M. P., Deleris, L. A., Finnerty, A. N., Marques, M. M., Norris, E.,
O'Mara-Eves, A. and West, R. (2017) The Human Behaviour-Change
Project: harnessing the power of artificial intelligence and machine
learning for evidence synthesis and interpretation, *Implementation
Science*, **12**, 121.

Octaviano, F. R., Felizardo, K. R., Maldonado, J. C. and Fabbri, S. C. P. F.
(2015) Semi-automatic Selection of Primary Studies in Systematic
Literature Reviews: is it reasonable?, *Empirical Software Engineering*,
20 (6), 1898-1917.

O'Mara-Eves, A., Thomas, J., McNaught, J., Miwa, M. and Ananiadou, S.
(2015) Using Text Mining for Study Identification in Systematic Reviews:
a systematic review of current approaches, *Systematic Reviews*, **4**, 5.

Rathbone, J., Carter, M., Hoffmann, T. and Glasziou, P. (2015) Better
Duplicate Detection for Systematic Reviewers: evaluation of Systematic
Review Assistant-Deduplication Module, *Systematic Reviews*, **4**, 6.

Shojania, K. G., Sampson, M., Ansari, M. T., Ji, J., Doucette S. and Moher, D.
(2007) How Quickly Do Systematic Reviews Go Out of Date? A Survival
Analysis, *Annals of Internal Medicine*, **147** (4), 224-233.

Singh, G., Marshall, I. J., Thomas, J., Shawe-Taylor, J. and Wallace, B. C. (2017) A Neural Candidate-Selector Architecture for Automatic Structured Clinical Text Annotation, *Proceedings of the ACM International Conference on Information and Knowledge Management*, 1519-1528.

Stansfield, C., O'Mara-Eves, A. and Thomas, J. (2017) Text Mining for Search Term Development in Systematic Reviewing: a discussion of some methods and challenges, *Research Synthesis Methods*, **8** (3), 355-365.

Thomas, J., Noel-Storr, A., Marshall, I., Wallace, B., McDonald, S., Mavergames, C., Glasziou, P., Shemilt, I., Synnot, A., Turner, T., Elliott, J. and Living Systematic Review Network (2017) Living Systematic Reviews: 2. Combining human and machine effort, *Journal of Clinical Epidemiology*, **91**, 31–37.

Wallace, B. C., Noel-Storr, A., Marshall, I. J., Cohen, A. M., Smalheiser, N. R. and Thomas, J. (2017) Identifying Reports of Randomized Controlled Trials (RCTs) Via a Hybrid Machine Learning and Crowdsourcing Approach, *Journal of the American Medical Informatics Association*, **24** (6), 1165-1168.

10

Training the next generation of information specialists

Michelle Maden and Gil Young

Introduction

The expert searcher, able to deliver high-quality searches in challenging or pressured environments, is central to accessing and utilising information (Lasserre, 2012). One key example is that health care professionals require reliable, evidence-based information to inform 'high quality decision-making, learning, research and innovation to achieve excellent health care and health improvement' (Health Education England, 2014, 9).

Library and information science (LIS) professionals who become expert searchers come from a variety of backgrounds with different types and levels of experiences and training (Booth and Beecroft, 2010; McGowan and Sampson, 2005; Tran, 2017). Training fulfils various roles and it may be required to support:

- New professionals
- Information professionals looking to move into roles who need to improve their search skills
- Information specialists experienced in literature searching but without the relevant discipline knowledge.

(Booth and Beecroft, 2010; Tran, 2017)

Different types of expert searcher roles have different degrees of involvement in searching, ranging from roles in which the main focus is on searching (for example, information specialists supporting the production of systematic reviews), to roles where searching is embedded within a wider role description (for example, clinical librarians). Consequently, they will have individual learning and development needs.

This chapter will focus on the knowledge, skills and attributes required of an expert searcher. It will look at how LIS professionals acquire and develop them through training and continuing professional development. It will highlight the extent to which higher education LIS programmes prepare graduates for expert searcher roles; how LIS professionals prepare themselves for the different roles; the subject and contextual knowledge and skills required; and how different approaches to training and development can help LIS professionals acquire the types of knowledge and skills required.

Knowledge and skills required of the expert searcher

To begin to understand the training needs of an expert searcher, we must first recognise what knowledge and skills the role requires. In the absence of a formal expert searcher qualification, frameworks such as the Systematic Review Competency Framework (Townsend et al., 2017), Competencies for Librarians Consulting on Systematic Reviews (Jewell, Foster and Dreker, 2017) and the Peer Review of Electronic Search Strategies (PRESS) guideline document (McGowan et al., 2016; Sampson et al., 2009) identify expert searcher competencies (see Table 10.1 opposite). Such frameworks and guidance are useful for identifying gaps in expert searcher knowledge and skills and for prioritising training needs (Townsend et al., 2017). They highlight the need for knowledge (for example, how databases are indexed), advanced information skills (for example, using methodological search filters) and analytical skills (for example, refining research questions, evaluating the impact of proximity operators).

The focus of these frameworks and guidance is on the knowledge and skills required in formulating, conducting, managing and documenting the search within the context of systematic reviews. The Medical Library Association (MLA) in the USA has a policy statement (MLA, 2005) outlining a set of professional competencies which apply to wider expert searcher roles (for example, clinical librarians). In

Table 10.1 *Summary of competencies for expert searchers involved in systematic reviews**

Competencies (Jewell, Foster and Dreker, 2017; McGowan et al., 2016; Sampson et al., 2009; Townsend et al., 2017)	Knowledge and Skills
Understanding systematic review foundations and processes	Systematic review processes, methodologies and guidance (e.g. PRISMA)
Formulating the review question	Frameworks for question formulation (e.g. PICO, SPICE) Communicating with clients or end users to refine research questions
Formulating and conducting searches	Carrying out scoping searches Identifying search terms (keywords and thesaurus terms) Identifying and selecting databases and other sources Search strategies for different systematic review topics (e.g. public health, service delivery, clinical review topics) and methodologies (e.g. qualitative reviews, realist reviews, mixed-methods reviews) Supplementary search techniques (e.g. citation searching) Search strategy techniques (e.g. Boolean logic, proximity operators, truncation, limits) Methodological search filters (i.e. hedges) Evaluating and validating the search strategy (spelling or search combination errors, sensitivity analysis) Communicating search details and progress
Managing the search and results	Saving searches, auto-alerts, updating searches Reference management software Screening software Retrieving articles
Reporting the search	Documenting the search and retrieval process Writing for publication

* The focus here is only on the competencies in the frameworks that specifically relate to the role of the expert searcher rather than the wider role librarians can contribute in systematic reviews (for example, involvement with critical appraisal or data extraction).

addition to the information and analytical skills outlined in the competency frameworks, the MLA policy statement and others (Booth and Beecroft, 2010; Lyon et al., 2015; McGowan and Sampson, 2005; Tan and Maggio, 2013) highlight attributes such as time management and confidence in making relevancy judgements when assessing the appropriateness of the search strategy, when to stop searching and in filtering search results. As well as improved confidence in search skills, Booth (2007) highlights a lack of confidence amongst LIS professionals about moving into unfamiliar roles as a major barrier and calls for the inclusion of confidence as a development need. These points are examined in more depth below.

The importance of context in training expert searchers

Expert searchers work in a variety of roles, for example, supporting systematic review and guideline production, delivering specialist question and answer services, providing professionals with literature searches to support evidence-based practice and research. Training of the expert searcher needs to go beyond the acquisition and application of information and analytical skills to consider the context within which searching takes place (Booth and Beecroft, 2010; Lyon et al., 2015; Tan and Maggio, 2013; Tran, 2017). This involves consideration of the discipline and the wider structural environment.

Expert searchers supporting systematic reviews need an under-standing of how different types of systematic review (for example, systematic reviews of broad-based interventions, realist reviews or qualitative reviews) require the application of different information retrieval techniques to effectively locate the evidence. Searching for systematic reviews of complex interventions or realist reviews often extends beyond the usual scoping and searching for studies, to involve searching for theories to inform systematic reviews (for example, searching for theory in Booth and Carroll, 2015), as we saw in Chapter 2.

Systematic reviews on public health topics are a good example of where an expert searcher would need to be aware of context, different types of reviews and other types of search techniques. The searcher requires an understanding of public health terminology, the lack of standardisation in indexing public health topics (Cooper et al., 2014), familiarity with the multidisciplinary nature of public health ques-tions, types of evidence likely to be available and public health issues, policies and procedures (Alpi, 2005; Tran, 2017). The generic competencies might be similar to expert searchers in other areas but learning about all of these contextual factors is essential to applying them effectively in a systematic search.

Expert searchers in clinical question and answer roles require an understanding of the context in which questions are asked and how clinicians work (Booth and Beecroft, 2010). Clinical librarians often undertake very complex systematic searches to support patient care and research. A study investigating the lived experiences of clinical librarians undertaking literature searches at the point of care (Lyon et al., 2015) found that training was requested in medical terminology, general medical knowledge, laboratory test values, drug names, clinical culture and institutional politics. Studies also highlight the need for clinical librarians to manage emotional stress resulting from their involvement in direct patient care (Lyon et al., 2015; Tan and Maggio, 2013). Providing search results to busy health care professionals may also require additional skills in critical appraisal and synthesis. Case study 10.1 highlights the generic and contextual training needs of clinical librarian expert searchers.

Training of the expert searcher therefore should incorporate both the fundamental knowledge and skills required to undertake searches but also the contextual knowledge and attributes required to prepare them for different working environments (Booth, 2007). The next section will explore the extent to which different education and training models offer generic and more tailored options in supporting professional development.

Case study 10.1: The clinical librarian as an expert searcher, by Pip Divall, Clinical Librarian Service Manager

The Clinical Librarian Service at University Hospitals of Leicester NHS Trust has been in existence since 1999. Clinical librarians join care teams on their ward rounds, in multidisciplinary case conferences, at educational meetings and journal clubs to understand the information needs of the teams and provide the best available evidence to underpin clinical decision-making and assist in research. Some of the expert searching will take place 'on the job' while working outside of the library.

All our Clinical Librarian Service team are expected to have a formal qualification in Library and Information Studies, or equivalent, and we have found that while a grounding in medical information and terminology can be incredibly useful as a starting point, this can be learned. In particular, a clinical librarian needs detailed understanding of the clinical area in which they are working. For example, in areas such as gastroenterology or surgery it is useful to be able to identify basic anatomy so as to be able to select phrases and synonyms that will get the results that clinicians need. In the early stages of my career, an open medical dictionary and a basic textbook on the body system I was searching were essentials. A quick orientation on the topic is always helpful and so much the better if you are able to glean this directly from the team or individual asking the question. I have found it especially useful for clinicians to sketch out visual representations when it comes to questions on anaesthetic nerve blocks and orthopaedic procedures.

The confidence to ask questions when you are unsure about the topic or to sort out mistakes cannot be understated. Completely misunderstanding the topic and needing to start again from scratch can be frustrating for both the requester and the searcher. The ability to think around an issue and consider synonyms is essential. This comes with a knowledge of the topic and broad medical vocabulary, experience of searching biomedical databases and familiarity with thesaurus terms, all of which can be developed over time.

Traditional reference interviews, as learned during a degree programme, can become less common as you learn more about a clinical area and become embedded with a team. However, communication skills are always important, as is quickly establishing rapport with teams. As medical staff rotate around a hospital or geographical area, it means you can often be re-building and renewing relationships. This type of work can be difficult to train for and different cultures within different teams may mean an individual clinical librarian needs to treat each team they work with differently.

Having colleagues who are experienced searchers helps to bounce ideas around and discuss what terms and phrases can be helpful to find the information needed. I liken searches to thinking around solutions to crossword puzzles; it is about finding as many words as possible that could fit and make sense of the question. Sometimes talking out loud about an issue can lead to the 'Eureka!' moment.

All our search strategies are stored in an online database and it is possible to check against others' work on similar topics and learn more about their choices of combinations and controlled language. When time allows, the team will tackle the same question for continuing professional development and comparison purposes. This usually shows that while we may approach each question in different ways, we often find the results have a significant overlap.

The ability to swiftly include and exclude articles from a database search means utilising critical appraisal skills on abstracts, which is less intensive than reading the full text of articles, though sometimes this is necessary to select whether the article answers the clinicians' questions. Skills in summarising and synthesising information are incredibly important and where possible the team have made use of attending externally provided training from a variety of providers, both electronic learning and face-to-face.

The role of each clinical librarian evolves over time and we have found that more and more we are being asked to form part of the authorship teams for systematic reviews. This has meant even more on-the-job learning as we check our own work against standards of searching and learn from peers outside of my organization.

New members joining the team are given as much opportunity as possible for training through shadowing colleagues and looking for suitable external training. However, cost-effectiveness of external training is always a consideration in a busy hospital and must always be balanced against the needs of the whole team.

Education and training of the expert searcher

Traditionally, information professionals first encounter search skills instruction when undertaking higher education LIS programmes. Few studies have investigated the extent to which such programmes teach the knowledge and skills required of expert searchers (Smith and Roseberry, 2013). A content analysis and review of the subject matter taught in courses on expert searching in domain-independent American Library Association (ALA) accredited programmes found that while expert searching continues to be a relevant part of the curriculum, the extent to which it is taught may vary across programmes (Smith and Roseberry, 2013).

While LIS programmes help to lay the foundations for expert searcher roles through an understanding of search theory and transferable information and analytical skills, a gap exists between the fundamentals taught within an artificial environment and their application in 'real-life' (Nicholson, 2005). Vieira and Dunn (2005) observe that, 'it takes more than continuing education to make an expert searcher. Expertise is the synthesis of ability and knowledge and not knowledge alone'. This view is further supported by the results of a survey of 167 librarians working in roles supporting information needs at the clinical point of care (Lyon et al., 2015), which found that nearly 70% of respondents were self-taught and 31.2% were mentored by another librarian.

This apparent disparity between the fundamentals taught in LIS programmes and their application in a 'real-life' environment is explained by Carol Tenopir (DiMattia, 2007). In an interview of faculty members who teach online searching, Tenopir makes the following distinction between searcher 'education' and 'training':

There is a difference in philosophy between education and training…
Education focuses on the underlying fundamentals with specific systems

as examples. Training focuses on the specific systems and their features. We try to emphasize education, with some training or pointing to training materials and lab exercises to reinforce the training aspect.

(DiMattia, 2007, 35)

The SPECTRAL (SPECialist TRaining in clinical question Answering for Informaticists/Librarians) project (Booth and Beecroft, 2010) identified four major deficiencies in the training provision of LIS professionals delivering clinical question and answer services:

1 A lack of co-ordination in the delivery of a single course.
2 The need to tailor generic courses to meet specialist roles (e.g. clinical librarian).
3 The need for quality assurance standards.
4 The need for competencies.

While work has begun on developing searching standards (McGowan et al., 2016; Sampson et al., 2009) and competencies (Jewell, Foster and Dreker, 2017; Townsend et al., 2017), these relate specifically to searching within a systematic review context.

Tailored formal training to support librarians in, or moving into, expert searcher roles is available (Lyon et al., 2015). Typically, this type of training may be delivered by LIS professional organizations, universities or specialist organizations (for example, the Centre for Reviews and Dissemination in the UK). However, it continues to be implemented on an ad-hoc, unco-ordinated basis or is embedded within wider systematic review programmes or workshops or is only available to internal employees (for example, Tran, 2017). There is currently a lack of formal education or training leading to professional qualifications or accreditation for the expert searcher (Lasserre, 2012). In a review of educational processes on expert searching, Lasserre (2012) calls for expert searcher education to be reviewed by health library organizations at an international level.

However, several authors (Booth, 2007; Jankowski, 2016; Tran, 2017) argue that while information skills can be taught, they question whether contextual knowledge and attributes such as confidence, the ability to make relevancy judgements on filtering results or when to stop searching can be formally taught. Such 'real-world' attributes are more likely to develop through experience, mentoring or observing practice within the context in which the expert searcher works (Booth, 2007; Tran, 2017; Vieira and Dunn, 2005). In which case, accreditation rather than a qualification may be the preferred route of continued professional development for the expert searcher.

Context-led training

Context-led training offers participants the opportunity to learn through experiencing a real-life searching environment. This is often delivered using a peer-led or peer-to-peer training model whereby participants learn from and with each other. Learning may take place through observation (Vieira and Dunn, 2005); formal teaching (Sbaffi, Hallsworth and Weist, 2018); or informal mentoring programmes (Lyon et al., 2015; Tran, 2017). Multiple approaches may be adopted and training may be delivered in-house, via external networks or online, as we explore in the next sections.

Observation

Learning through observation may involve observing the searching practice of others or having experts observe your own practice (Vieira and Dunn, 2005, and see Case study 10.1). More experienced searchers help those with less experience to develop their search skills by providing feedback on, for example, search errors, use of proximity operators and database syntax. More importantly, experienced searchers can help those new to the subject area develop contextual knowledge and skills. For example, those with more experience will be familiar with nuances in subject terminology, the suitability of database search features such as age tags and subheadings in high recall search strategies (McGowan and Sampson, 2005; Vieira and Dunn, 2005). Feedback from 'subject experts' or mentors can help develop relevancy judgement skills and presentation skills.

Vieira and Dunn (2005, 71) also observe that 'user comments and feedback are critical because they come from clients. They are the arbiters of the search results.' User feedback is essential in determining the relevance and usefulness of the search. This is particularly important when demonstrating the impact of searches.

Peer-led/peer-to-peer teaching

Peer-led/peer-to-peer training can be delivered using formal taught methods. Studies have evaluated this approach in improving search skills in health care (Young, McLaren and Maden, 2017; Tran, 2017). Tran (2017) described using a peer-based approach (NICE Evidence Search Student Champions Scheme: www.nice.org.uk/get-involved/student-champions) to deliver information literacy training among health care undergraduates in the UK. After first being trained by staff from the National Institute for Health and Care Excellence (NICE) in using Evidence Search (www.evidence.nhs.uk), which is a web portal providing evidence-based resources, student champions then cascaded face-to-face training to their peers. Using their knowledge of the curriculum, assignments and clinical placements, the student champions enhanced the learning experience by choosing examples with practical relevance to the participants. After the training, student champions and participants reported increased searching confidence (Sbaffi, Hallsworth and Weist, 2018; Tran, 2017).

Increased confidence with searching and teaching of search skills were reported by librarians involved in the evaluation of an innovative, online peer-led/peer-to-peer training course to provide health care librarians with the knowledge, skills and practical examples to help them provide an effective literature search service (Maden, Young and McLaren, 2016; Young, McLaren and Maden, 2017). Case study 10.2 outlines the development and evaluation of a Massive Open Online Course (MOOC) in developing the knowledge and skills of expert searchers.

Case study 10.2: The Library and Information Health Network Northwest (LIHNN) Introduction to Literature Searching Massive Open Online Course (MOOC)

A MOOC is a 'free at the point of delivery' innovative online educational resource. MOOCs aim to develop peer learning networks using a variety of social media, supported by video lectures, discussion boards and open educational resources. The LIHNN Literature Searching MOOC aimed to provide librarians with the knowledge, skills and examples to provide an effective literature search service (see Figure 10.1 on page 220). The MOOC was funded by Health Education England and was a pilot project that ran for six weeks. 679 librarians from different sectors (for example, health, academic, public) and students took part.

An experienced searcher led the content development in consultation with other searchers of varying levels of experience. The content was delivered using a variety of formats including audio-led PowerPoint, interactive exercises and quizzes, videos and peer-to-peer discussion. Participants valued the use of real-life searching examples throughout that ensured the training was directly relevant and immediately applicable to current practice (see Figure 10.2), with one stating, 'the MOOC was really practical, it felt like everything I was learning would be used in day to day situations' (Maden, Young and McLaren, 2016, 16).

Participants were encouraged to share their own experiences, templates, resources and tips via the discussion board and a wiki (http://lihnnmooclitsearch.pbworks.com). The large number of experienced searchers who participated enhanced the experience further by sharing their searching wisdom and practical examples. Sharing of good practice and tips in this way goes beyond what can often be taught in more formal workshops.

Although new content was released weekly, participants could dip in and out as needed and the content remains open access (Maden, Young and McLaren, 2015). This flexible approach recognises that individuals learn at different paces and acknowledges that librarians may undertake training during their normal busy working day, as one participant commented: 'going at my own pace, dipping in and out of sessions, the step by step approach enabled me to consolidate my learning before moving on to the next topic' (Maden, Young and McLaren, 2016, 15).

At the end of the MOOC, participants reported feeling better equipped and more confident about undertaking expert searches:

> I have personally seen an increase over the last year in offers for me to participate in systematic reviews. I put this down to my increased knowledge in the subject which presumably comes over as confidence when training or talking to colleagues about their searching requirements.
> (Maden, Young and McLaren, 2017, 8)

The MOOC offered an opportunity for health care librarians to refresh their searching knowledge and skills. Above all, the MOOC was useful for librarians without health sector experience looking to move into a new searching role. Evidence from an impact evaluation found the MOOC met these aims:

> This MOOC filled in the gaps in my knowledge and I was able to use this knowledge to get a promotion from working on the library front desk to now teaching literature searching to students and researchers.
> (Young, McLaren and Maden, 2017, 316)

The MOOC was a cost-effective way of providing in-depth context-led search skills training to an international audience. Based on the 294 people who responded to the evaluation at the end of the MOOC, the cost was £68.72 per person. Taking into account the 679 people who registered for the MOOC in January 2016 the cost per person dropped to £29.45. As of March 2018, 893 people were registered, dropping the cost per person to just £22.40.

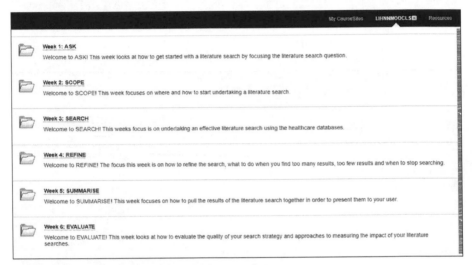

Figure 10.1 *Weekly content of the MOOC screen-shot*

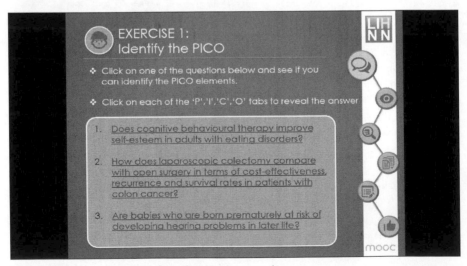

Figure 10.2 *Example exercise from the MOOC screen-shot*

Mentoring

Mentoring is a common approach used in LIS to develop continuing professional skills. By placing the mentee's needs at the centre of the learning process, mentoring offers an informal learning experience sensitive to changes to the working context of the expert searcher (Booth, 2007; Rowley et al., 2015). In offering a tailored learning experience by focusing on specific needs and challenges encountered within practice, mentoring can help to address different levels of expert searcher experiences and training (Booth and Beecroft, 2010; Tran, 2017).

Mentoring is particularly useful for developing confidence in professionals new to the expert searcher role or for those moving into a new area. Tran (2017) and Lyon et al. (2015) suggest that a non-pressured environment is ideal for building confidence in search skills and in coping with different searching environments. As well as using mentors with searching expertise, Lyon et al. (2015), for example, advocate the use of clinical mentors in preparing clinical librarians for the emotional stresses in working on ward rounds.

Online training

In an era when library finances are being squeezed, online training offers a viable alternative to face-to-face training, which often incurs both direct costs (for example, workshop fees, travel and subsistence) and indirect costs (for example, time away from the desk) (Gore and Jones, 2015; Jankowski, 2008; Young, McLaren and Maden, 2017; see also Case study 10.1). Online training options may offer both generic and context-led (peer-led/peer-to-peer) training. These include webinars (for example, Cochrane (n.d.) *Learning Live: a webinar programme*), e-learning modules, MOOCs (as explored in Case study 10.2) and the use of Skype for mentoring (Tran, 2017).

Online training can provide a more flexible, non-pressured approach to developing search skills, offering training at the point of need with the opportunity to 'view again' to help consolidate learning and promote the sharing of searchers' experiences and resources.

Benefits of context-led training

Since learning takes place within a 'real-life' environment, context-led training is directly relevant and applicable to practice and is highly valued by participants (Lyon et al., 2015; Maden, Young and McLaren, 2016; Maden, Young and McLaren, 2017; Sbaffi, Hallsworth and Weist, 2018; Tran, 2017; Vieira and Dunn, 2005). Aside from developing skills that are difficult to teach in an artificial environment, one of the main benefits is that it allows for the sharing of knowledge and expertise that only those involved in searching in a particular context would understand (Lyon et al., 2015; Maden, Young and McLaren, 2016; Maden, Young and McLaren, 2017). This not only includes searching tips and tricks, but more practical tips for expert searchers working in more specialised roles. For instance, Lyon et al. (2015) mention that clinical librarians should wear clothing with pockets and comfortable shoes when taking part on ward rounds.

Tran (2017) highlights the continuous two-way learning process of peer-led or peer-to-peer training. According to Tran (2017), an individual's approach to searching reflects their previous training, experiences and backgrounds. It is likely that different searchers will approach the same task differently. Mentors as well as mentees therefore have an opportunity to learn new approaches and skills (Tran, 2017).

Finally, from an organizational point of view, context-led training can be accommodated within the working day, in the workplace and, aside from staff time, it can be provided at minimal or no cost (Vieira and Dunn, 2005).

Keeping up to date with advances in expert search methods

Evolving expert searcher roles and advances in searching methodologies (for example, text mining, searching for complex topics) make it essential that knowledge and skills are kept up to date. As well as attending training workshops, expert searcher knowledge can be acquired and improved through reading (Jankowski, 2008; Jankowski, 2016; McGowan and Sampson, 2005; Vieira and Dunn, 2005). Keeping up to date with new approaches in expert search methods published in journal articles or conference proceedings, for example, is important since systematic review guidance on searching may not necessarily incorporate new and emerging searching methodologies.

Traditionally, keeping up to date involved the setting up of search alerts to track new literature added to databases. More recently with the advent of social media, following the Twitter accounts or blogs of individuals and organizations with an interest in advancing search methodologies or sharing searcher expertise is another useful way of identifying new and innovative searching techniques and issues.

Pre-conference workshops, conferences or network events may offer training for the expert searcher (Jankowski, 2008; Jankowski, 2016). For example, the Evidence Synthesis Research Network (www.bmh. manchester.ac.uk/research/institutes-centres/evidence-synthesis), run in association with NICE and the University of Manchester in the UK, brings together researchers, guideline developers and information specialists with an interest in systematic reviews to share knowledge and expertise. Past events have covered improving the precision of search strategies for guideline surveillance, when to stop searching and text mining.

Future directions

This chapter has highlighted several recommendations for further research and practice.

Research

- Identifying the different training needs associated with different expert searcher roles is essential. This will require a mapping exercise of expert searcher roles and responsibilities (e.g. supporting systematic reviews, guideline development, question and answer services, clinical librarians).
- Training needs should be informed not only by trainees' perceptions of what is expected but by those with experience of expert searcher roles and by the users requesting searches.
- Involving expert searchers in designing training content can ensure it is practical and relevant to their needs.
- There is a lack of accredited professional training for the expert searcher. This chapter echoes earlier calls made to explore a more

co-ordinated approach to the delivery of training for the expert searcher at higher education and professional organization level (Booth and Beecroft, 2010).

Practice

- It is essential that librarians looking to move into expert search roles are equipped with both an understanding of the fundamentals of searching as well as appropriate contextual knowledge and skills.
- While an understanding of the fundamentals of searching is often taught in LIS degree programmes, training in the contextual knowledge and skills specific to the roles within which expert searchers may work and developing searching confidence can be undertaken using observational techniques, peer-led/peer-peer teaching, mentoring and through real-life experience.
- Training needs between individuals may differ depending on their background, experience and the type of work they undertake, therefore a tailored approach to training using multiple methods (e.g. observation and mentoring) should be considered.
- Delivery of expert searcher training should consider the wider environmental context and barriers (e.g. time, cost) to attending training. Delivery methods offering flexible approaches to learning (e.g. MOOCs, online peer networks) can help overcome barriers.

Conclusion

Given the different levels of search experience, training and the various types of expert searcher roles, training the next generation of expert searchers is a challenging prospect. While the fundamentals of searching knowledge and skills are often cultivated during LIS degree programmes, a gap exists between what can be taught in an artificial environment and the contextual knowledge, skills (for example, relevance judgements) and attributes (for example, confidence) required to perform expert searches in practice. Contextual knowledge and skills are more likely to develop through 'on-the-job' training and experience. Furthermore, different expert searcher roles may place greater emphasis on acquiring different skills, therefore training needs to be tailored to meet individual needs. How these needs are best met (for example, via observation, mentoring, online training) will also require consideration of the wider organizational context.

Suggestions for further reading

Booth, A. and Beecroft, C. (2010) The SPECTRAL Project: a training needs analysis for providers of clinical question answering services, *Health Information and Libraries Journal*, **27** (3), 198-207.

Foster, M. J. and Jewell, S. T. (eds) (2017) *Assembling the Pieces of a Systematic Review: a guide for librarians*, Rowman and Littlefield.

Maden, M., Young, G. and McLaren, L. (2015) *The LIHNN Literature Searching MOOC*. www.coursesites.com/s/_LIHNNMOOCLS

Sampson, M., McGowan, J., Cogo, E., Grimshaw, J., Moher, D. and Lefebvre, C. (2009) An Evidence-based Practice Guideline for the Peer Review of Electronic Search Strategies, *Journal of Clinical Epidemiology*, **62** (9), 944-952.

Townsend, W. A., Anderson, P. F., Ginier, E. C., Maceachern, M. P., Saylor, K. M., Shipman, B. L. and Smith, J. E. (2017) A Competency Framework for Librarians Involved in Systematic Reviews, *Journal of the Medical Library Association*, **105** (3), 268-275.

References

Alpi, K. M. (2005) Expert Searching in Public Health, *Journal of the Medical Library Association*, **93** (1), 97-103.

Booth, A. (2007) New Breed or Different Species: is the 21st century health information professional generic or specific?
www.researchgate.net/publication/242083690_New_Breed_Or_
Different_Species_Is_The_21st_Century_Health_Information_
Professional_Generic_Or_Specific

Booth, A. and Beecroft, C. (2010) The SPECTRAL Project: a training needs analysis for providers of clinical question answering services, *Health Information and Libraries Journal*, **27** (3), 198-207.

Booth, A. and Carroll, C. (2015) Systematic Searching for Theory to Inform Systematic Reviews: is it feasible? Is it desirable?, *Health Information and*

Libraries Journal, **32** (3), 220-235.

Cochrane (n.d.) *Learning Live: a webinar programme.*
www.training.cochrane.org/cochrane-learning-live-webinar-programme

Cooper, C., Levay, P., Lorenc, T. and Craig, G. M. (2014) A Population
Search Filter for Hard-to-reach Populations Increased Search Efficiency
for a Systematic Review, *Journal of Clinical Epidemiology*, **67** (5), 554-559.

DiMattia, S. (2007) How We Teach (or Should Teach) Online Searching,
Online, **31** (2), 34-38.

Gore, G. C. and Jones, J. (2015) Systematic Reviews and Librarians: a primer
for managers, *The Canadian Journal of Library and Information Practice and
Research*, **10** (1).

Health Education England (2014) Knowledge for Healthcare: a
development framework for NHS library and knowledge services in
England 2015-2020.
https://hee.nhs.uk/sites/default/files/documents/Knowledge_for_
healthcare_a_development_framework_2014.pdf

Jankowski, T. A. (2008) *The MLA Essential Guide to Becoming an Expert
Searcher: proven techniques, strategies, and tips for finding health information*,
ALA Neal-Schuman.

Jankowski, T. A. (2016) *Expert Searching in the Google Age*, Rowman and
Littlefield.

Jewell, S. T., Foster, M. J. and Dreker, M. (2017) The Art of Puzzle Solving.
In Foster, M. J. and Jewell, S. T. (eds), *Assembling the Pieces of a Systematic
Review: a guide for librarians*, Rowman and Littlefield.

Lasserre, K. (2012) Expert Searching in Health Librarianship: a literature
review to identify international issues and Australian concerns, *Health
Information and Libraries Journal*, **29** (1), 3-15.

Lyon, J. A., Kuntz, G. M., Edwards, M. E., Butson, L. C. and Auten, B. (2015)
The Lived Experience and Training Needs of Librarians Serving at the
Clinical Point-of-Care, *Medical Reference Services Quarterly*, **34** (3), 311-333.

Maden, M., Young, G. and McLaren, L. (2015) *The LIHNN Literature
Searching MOOC*. www.coursesites.com/s/_LIHNNMOOCLS

Maden, M., Young, G. and McLaren, L. (2016) *LIHNN Introduction to
Literature Searching MOOC.*
https://www.lihnnclinicallibs.files.wordpress.com/2017/04/lihnn_mooc_
evaluation_report_revj16.pdf

Maden, M., Young, G. and McLaren, L. (2017) *LIHNN Literature Searching
MOOC – Follow-up Survey.*

https://lihnnclinicallibs.wordpress.com/2017/04/04/lihnn-introduction-to-literature-searching-mooc-follow-up-survey

McGowan, J. and Sampson, M. (2005) Systematic Reviews Need Systematic Searchers, *Journal of the Medical Library Association*, **93** (1), 74-80.

McGowan, J., Sampson, M., Salzwedel, D. M., Cogo, E., Foerster, V. and Lefebvre, C. (2016) PRESS Peer Review of Electronic Search Strategies: 2015 guideline statement, *Journal of Clinical Epidemiology*, **75**, 40-46.

Medical Library Association (2005) Role of Expert Searching in Health Sciences Libraries, *Journal of the Medical Library Association*, **93** (1), 42-44.

Nicholson, S. (2005) Understanding the Foundation: the state of generalist search education in library schools as related to the needs of expert searchers in medical libraries, *Journal of the Medical Library Association*, **93** (1), 61-68.

Rowley, J., Johnson, F., Sbaffi, L. and Weist, A. (2015) Peer-based Information Literacy Training: insights from the NICE Evidence search student champion scheme, *Library and Information Science Research*, **37** (4), 338-345.

Sampson, M., McGowan, J., Cogo, E., Grimshaw, J., Moher, D. and Lefebvre, C. (2009) An Evidence-based Practice Guideline for the Peer Review of Electronic Search Strategies, *Journal of Clinical Epidemiology*, **62** (9), 944-952.

Sbaffi, L., Hallsworth, E. and Weist, A. (2018) Peer Teaching and Information Retrieval: the role of the NICE Evidence search student champion scheme in enhancing students' confidence, *Health Information and Libraries Journal*, **35** (1), 50-63.

Smith, C. and Roseberry, M. (2013) Professional Education in Expert Search: a content model, *Journal of Education for Library and Information Science*, **54** (4), 255-269.

Tan, M. C. and Maggio, L. A. (2013) Expert Searcher, Teacher, Content Manager, and Patient Advocate: an exploratory study of clinical librarian roles, *Journal of the Medical Library Association*, **101** (1), 63-72.

Townsend, W. A., Anderson, P. F., Ginier, E. C., MacEachern, M. P., Saylor, K. M., Shipman, B. L. and Smith, J. E. (2017) A Competency Framework for Librarians Involved in Systematic Reviews, *Journal of the Medical Library Association*, **105** (3), 268-275.

Tran, A. (2017) In-house Peer Supported Literature Search Training: a public health perspective, *Health Information and Libraries Journal*, **34** (3), 258-262.

Vieira, D. L. and Dunn, K. (2005) Peer Training in Expert Searching: the observation effect, *Journal of the Medical Library Association,* **93** (1), 69-73.

Young, G., McLaren, L. and Maden, M. (2017) Delivering a MOOC for Literature Searching in Health Libraries: evaluation of a pilot project, *Health Information and Libraries Journal,* **34** (4), 312-318.

11

Collaborative working to improve searching

Siw Waffenschmidt and Elke Hausner

Introduction

Systematic reviews need the right people at the right time because they 'benefit from team working, and co-production is an essential part of high-quality research synthesis' (Uttley and Montgomery, 2017). The review team should therefore be multidisciplinary and include methodological experts, content experts and information specialists (Institute of Medicine, 2011). Close collaboration is not only required between project team members but also between information specialists.

The first part of this chapter summarises the different phases of collaboration between information specialists and the review authors, discusses some of the challenges, highlights the main issues, and describes the different work settings. The next part of the chapter explains why collaboration between information specialists is required, in which areas and to what extent. The section on information specialists starts with collaboration on a day-to-day level and then looks at the value of local, national and international collaboration for developing information retrieval methods. We are grateful to Justin Clark for contributing Case study 11.2.

Collaboration between information specialists and review authors

Collaboration in the different phases of a systematic review

This section shows how information specialists are involved in the production of a systematic review and the different points of collaboration with review authors. Successful collaboration requires detailed project co-ordination, as set out in Table 11.1.

Table 11.1 *Collaboration between information specialists and review authors*

Production phases of a systematic review	Collaboration between information specialists and review authors
Project planning	• Conducting exploratory searches • Agreeing on methods • Estimating costs and other resources.
Information retrieval	• Conducting information retrieval • Documenting information retrieval.
Study selection	• Selecting tools for study selection, including data management • Ordering the literature.
Reporting and publication	• Reporting information retrieval in the systematic review • Distributing the systematic review.

Project planning phase

The first stage of a new project will usually be tricky and information specialists should remember that 'the initial planning stages of the review can be difficult but with guidance can lead to starting a valuable research project' (Foster and Jewell, 2017). Systematic reviews usually start with the writing of a protocol setting out how it will be conducted. The protocol is an opportunity to discuss who will perform each role, as well as being a technical document detailing the specific methods to be used. A good protocol will include, among other things, information on the roles and responsibilities of the review team members, the research question, the information retrieval and data analysis methods to be applied and the project timetable (O'Connor et al., 2014).

Conducting exploratory searches

An exploratory search, which can be conducted once or several times during the course of review production, is a targeted search for suitable information on a topic and supports the acquisition of knowledge and the exploratory examination of the corresponding evidence (see Grant and Booth, 2009). The goal of the search is to determine whether and to what extent studies on the topic of interest are available and what evidence level they have; for this purpose, for example, a search for existing systematic reviews might be conducted. The search ends as soon as the information required is retrieved, meaning it differs fundamentally from the comprehensive retrieval expected for a full systematic review. Even if information specialists do not always conduct exploratory searches themselves, they should be informed about the databases and information systems used and be able to explain these tools to the review authors.

Agreeing on methods

In the planning phase, the review team should also determine which type of review will be produced; Grant and Booth (2009) describe 14 different types, from a rapid review to a full systematic review. Depending on the type of review, information retrieval may need to take different approaches and the information specialist should advise the project team on the most appropriate search methods for the type of review, as discussed in Chapter 2.

All systematic reviews should be registered, for example in PROSPERO (www.crd.york.ac.uk/prospero), and the project team should determine who is responsible for this task. Furthermore, adherence to standards for the design, conduct and reporting of systematic reviews, for example the PRISMA statement (Liberati et al., 2009), needs to be ensured and, if applicable, review-specific changes discussed.

Estimating costs and other resources

After gaining an overview of the review topic and the available evidence, the project team should be able to estimate the costs and other resources required for the project and draft a timetable for the review. For this purpose, the information specialist should provide the following information or advice:

1 **Selecting databases and other information sources.** The project team needs to determine which information sources should be used and which team member is responsible for which task. As

searches in bibliographic databases and trial registries require comprehensive data management and documentation, they are usually conducted by an information specialist. However, in some settings the information specialist's role is restricted to providing basic guidance on developing a search strategy (Gore and Jones, 2015). If searching or screening sources requires in-depth content knowledge, then it is more meaningful for this task to be performed by the review authors with appropriate support from information specialists. These sources include making requests to study authors or pharmaceutical companies, searching regulatory websites, handsearching journals or screening reference lists of relevant publications.

2 **Estimating the number of hits to be screened and studies to be included.** Searches in bibliographic databases and trial registries produce the most hits and, as the number retrieved varies greatly depending on the topic, it is important to estimate the number of hits to be expected for screening. This number markedly affects not only the amount of resources required but also the resulting number of studies for inclusion in the review. The information specialist should provide both estimates, the latter in collaboration with the review authors.

3 **Costs of full-text articles and database licences.** On the basis of previous projects, the information specialist should estimate the budget required for obtaining full-text articles from scientific journals and access to databases. From our experience at the Institute for Quality and Efficiency in Health Care (IQWiG) in Germany, it is estimated for systematic reviews in health technology assessments (HTAs) that about 10% of references screened at the title and abstract stage are subsequently ordered for screening at the full-text stage. In addition, the information specialist should list the relevant databases that are free of charge and indicate the costs for those that are not (see Chapter 4). The review protocol should be drafted taking the above information into account.

Information retrieval phase

After finalising the protocol, the production of the actual review begins and the information retrieval is conducted. A precondition for a high-quality review is that the complete search process is documented in enough detail in real time, so that information retrieval can be reported accurately and is reproducible (Rader et al., 2014). This is especially important if more than one person is involved in information retrieval. For this purpose, all relevant information pertaining to the searches (for example, databases searched, search terms and filters used, reference management tools used) should be included in a data management plan (Foster and Jewell, 2017).

The review authors' contribution to developing the search strategy depends on the information retrieval method. If an objective approach is applied, such as one using text-analytic procedures to identify free-text terms and subject headings through frequency analysis (EUnetHTA, 2017), their contribution is often restricted to evaluating the relevance of individual references. The information specialist should ask the authors to contribute additional search terms or synonyms when the search approach is more subjective.

Study selection phase

Information specialists should also be familiar with screening tools as they usually deposit the references in one of these tools, for example Covidence (www.covidence.org) and EPPI-Reviewer (http://eppi.ioe. ac.uk/cms/Default.aspx?alias=eppi.ioe.ac.uk/cms/er4). The review team should determine whether the information specialist is respon-sible for the import and export of references, as well as how to present the results of the screening process. If the information specialist is responsible for ordering the full-text articles, they can often be uploaded directly into the tool used.

Reporting and publication phase

The project team should also specify which team members draft which sections of the protocol and the review. The information specialist provides current guidelines on reporting information retrieval (for example, Liberati et al., 2009; Mullins et al., 2013; Sampson et al., 2008). Either the information specialist drafts the sections on information retrieval in the methods and results section of the review or provides the relevant data and details. In the latter case, the sections should be quality assured by an information specialist. Before the start of the project, it should be clarified whether the information specialist is listed as an author, which is usually the case (Gore and Jones, 2015; Ludeman et al., 2015; McGowan and Sampson, 2005).

The information specialist may also be responsible for distributing the systematic review, such as publishing it on the organization's website or submitting it to external databases and library catalogues.

Challenges of collaborating with review authors

Information specialists often report methodological and interpersonal challenges when collaborating on systematic reviews (Nicholson, McCrillis and Williams, 2017). These can be largely avoided if the following issues are taken into account and clear agreements are concluded before the start of a project.

Organizational challenges

Collaboration is more difficult if the information specialist is not considered to be an equal member of the review team, which is especially the case if organizational structures for efficient collaboration are lacking. This may result in the information specialist being only sporadically informed about relevant project developments (for example, changes in content or timetable), which can make it difficult to perform the searches well.

In addition, an information specialist usually works on several projects simultaneously, meaning that in-depth involvement in an individual project can be difficult. Furthermore, most of the information retrieval is completed at the beginning of the project and the close collaboration with the review team usually ends with data extraction. It may be several months between an information specialist being involved in searching for a project and the review actually being published.

Methodological challenges

Initially, the review authors are often unable to clearly define the research question according to a standard framework for addressing questions (see Table 2.1 in Chapter 2), such as the PICO of 'Population, Intervention, Comparison, Outcomes' that is commonly used in health care topics. For instance, the question 'What are the best treatment forms for diabetes?' might be interesting but cannot be addressed meaningfully in a systematic review. Likewise, authors initially often hesitate to restrict the search to certain study types if they are unsure which types of evidence might be useful or how much of it there might be. This usually results in additional work for the information specialist as no appropriate study filters can be selected and subsequently the search strategy may change.

Difficulties also arise if the review authors want to change the methods previously specified in the protocol. If methods are changed during the review process, these changes must be documented and the information specialist informed so that potential effects on information retrieval can be taken into account. Methodological issues especially arise if the review is not a systematic review (see Grant and Booth (2009) for other review types) with standardised procedures for the retrieval and synthesis of information. Some types of review require extensive discussions regarding their implementation (see Chapter 2).

Interpersonal challenges

Challenges also arise if the project team does not have enough members or experts. This may cause problems with quality assurance (for example, in the study selection and data extraction process) or lead to methodological flaws (for example, conducting inappropriate statistical tests when a statistician is missing (Ioannidis et al., 2014)).

Major challenges arise if inexperienced researchers are used as project managers, especially if they are not adequately supervised. In the academic environment, this can result in premature project termination; Ludeman et al. (2015) found that of 37 systematic review requests received by librarians at a large university, only 22 searches had been completed and only three reviews had been published or submitted for publication.

Information specialists are often the first point of contact for review authors, and collaboration often involves areas beyond actual information retrieval, such as informing authors about the general standards for conducting a review, including the requirement to register prospectively the review and to follow reporting guidelines such as PRISMA. In summary, information specialists often spend 'a significant amount of time educating researchers on methodology' (Nicholson, McCrillis and Williams, 2017, 389).

Key points for successful collaboration

Successful collaboration between the information specialist and the review authors requires that the points in the 'to-do' list set out in Table 11.2 are clarified and the necessary documents provided.

Table 11.2 *Points to clarify for successful collaboration*

Requirements	Actions
Specify the review team members, the timetable and the review process	• Clarify the responsibilities of each team member • Ensure clear and frequent communication within the project team • Establish a data management plan (including the reference management software and screening tools to be used)
Finalise the protocol	• Define a clear research question • Confirm the inclusion and exclusion criteria (type of research (e.g. RCT, cohort study) with sound methods) • Clarify the type of review (Foster and Jewell, 2017)
Adhere to international standards and internal agreements	• Register the review • Adhere to PRISMA or other appropriate standards • Clarify authorship of the information specialist

Working in different settings

The way in which information specialists work with review authors largely depends on the type of setting they work in.

General trained librarians

One type of information specialist is the general trained librarian in a traditional library setting who provides support to systematic reviews (McGowan and Sampson, 2005). A survey has shown that of 157 Association of Academic Health Sciences Libraries (AAHSL) in the

USA, 79 offer a search or support service for systematic reviews on their website (Anderson, Ginier and Mani, 2016). They are faced with major challenges in information retrieval for systematic reviews, as they are often confronted with students or junior researchers who are not familiar with standard processes (Nicholson, McCrillis and Williams, 2017) and communication is frequently poor. In addition, information retrieval often comprises only a small part of their work and so it is more difficult to keep up to date with all the latest developments.

Research-embedded settings

The second type refers to information specialists who are either trained librarians or have a different professional background and work in a research-embedded setting (Greyson et al., 2013). Large HTA organizations or research institutes generally employ their own information specialists who are members of review teams. They may be organised in a separate Information Management Unit (for example, as in the Canadian Agency for Drugs and Technologies in Health (CADTH) or IQWiG) or they can be directly allocated to a department. They spend most of their time with information retrieval and have little or no involvement in traditional library work.

Collaboration between information specialists

The first part of this chapter showed how close collaboration between information specialists and review authors is important and we will now look at why collaboration between information specialists is required and the value it brings to systematic reviews.

Day-to-day collaboration

The following section outlines the different levels and topics of collaboration, depending on whether the information specialists work alone or in a team of peers. Collaboration between information specialists is required to provide support and quality control as well as to distribute the workload more evenly within a team. In addition, the exchange of knowledge between information specialists is crucial in the continually developing field of information retrieval.

It is easier to allocate specific tasks if an information specialist team is available, depending on the knowledge, experience and preferences of the individual team members. For example, one team member is responsible for keeping up to date with searches in study registries, certain bibliographic databases or with search filters; while another manages checklists and ensures that internal documentation and reporting requirements are met. A further information specialist could co-ordinate the development of overall standards such as Standard Operating Procedures (SOPs) and checklists to ensure consistent and high-quality work. Table 11.3 provides examples of practical collaboration on day-to-day activities, showing how a team of information specialists might tackle the issues, along with suggestions for people who are the only expert searcher in their organization.

Table 11.3 *Practical collaboration of information specialists on day-to-day activities*

Tasks	Typical example	How to implement this as an information specialist team	Alternative approach for a single information specialist
Select the appropriate method for information retrieval	Select appropriate search sources, search filters, etc.	Develop standard procedures for different kinds of reviews based on established manuals or the current literature (any deviations must be discussed by the team)	Make decisions on the basis of established manuals (any deviations must be discussed by the review team)
Conduct searches	Peer review search strategies using the PRESS checklist (McGowan et al., 2016; Sampson et al., 2009)	The task is performed by an information specialist who has not been involved in the project	Collaborate with external information specialists, e.g. through PRESSforum (www.pressforum.pbworks.com); the task can also be performed by another project team member if appropriate
Write internal Standard Operating Procedures or guidance for specific tasks	Provide a template with items that should be reported in a systematic review (e.g. flowchart, search strategies)	A specified team member is responsible for reporting issues on information retrieval, including: • Defining the main reporting items on the basis of guidelines, e.g. PRISMA (Liberati et al., 2009)	Define reporting items and discuss them with the review team Develop and maintain a template based on established manuals

(Continued)

Table 11.3 *Continued*

Tasks	Typical example	How to implement this as an information specialist team	Alternative approach for a single information specialist
		• Developing and maintaining a reporting template according to feedback • Keeping up to date with ongoing developments through the review team, other colleagues or reading current literature	
Keep up to date with technical issues in databases, registries and other information sources	Provide import and export filters for the reference management systems Keep up to date with search features and interfaces	A certain team member is responsible for saving all filters, writing guidance for usage and maintenance Another team member maintains ongoing relationships with database/interface providers when needed	Document and modify filters for the day-to-day work Contact database/interface providers when needed
Keep up to date with the literature on information retrieval	Use auto-alerts to identify the current literature on information retrieval	A team member is responsible for the surveillance of important information sources (e.g. through PubMed alerts or important conference proceedings) A team member then needs to assess the potential consequences of the new research for information retrieval Another task is to distribute the information obtained to all team members (e.g. via annual reports or journal clubs) and to the review team	Work with established manuals or online sources providing current information such as SuRe Info (http://vortal.htai.org/?q=sure-info) See also Table 13.5 in Chapter 13 for a table of useful journals to monitor
Collect routine data for research on information retrieval	Evaluate search filters for specific conditions or populations (e.g. children)	Develop an archive with completed search strategies and references included in projects completed: • Save, evaluate and reuse search strategies for recurring topics	All searches should be saved for reuse and analysis.

(Continued)

Table 11.3 *Continued*

Tasks	Typical example	How to implement this as an information specialist team	Alternative approach for a single information specialist
		• Collect the references included in previous systematic reviews as a test set that can be used to check or evaluate search filters • Provide guidance for other team members on the use of information • Consistently document the results of evaluations.	

The case studies show that the ideas in Table 11.3 have been put into practice in quite different ways. Case study 11.1 describes the collaboration across a team of information specialists and Case study 11.2 shows what can be achieved when an information specialist works alone.

Case study 11.1: Information Management Unit at IQWiG

The team consists of four librarians, five information specialists and one unit head. They are service providers for the whole of IQWiG (with around 140 researchers), which is an HTA agency for Germany.

The librarians are mainly responsible for managing subscription journals and accessing bibliographic databases, ordering journal articles (approximately 8,000 per year), checking the style of reference lists of all IQWiG products and distributing IQWiG reports (for example, to PubMed, HTA database and Trip database).

The information specialists are responsible for all systematic searches conducted at IQWiG and are involved in project teams for each review. Their professional background varies: some are trained librarians, while others have various health care or health science degrees. They conduct preliminary searches, select information sources, develop, conduct and peer review systematic searches, organise reference management (mainly via EndNote), support the reporting of information retrieval in IQWiG reports and are involved in the multi-stage internal quality assurance process. One information specialist is responsible for all information retrieval tasks in a project. This person is supervised by a second information specialist who is also responsible for quality control and is a substitute during absence.

Besides project work, the information specialists are also involved in methodological work, for example drafting and updating the sections on information retrieval methods in the IQWiG methods paper (Institute for

Quality and Efficiency in Health Care, 2009; 2017) as well as the EUnetHTA guideline on the process of information retrieval for systematic reviews on clinical effectiveness (EUnetHTA, 2017). They are also involved in various other information retrieval projects (for example, Hausner et al., 2012; Hausner et al., 2015; Hausner et al., 2016; Knelangen et al., 2018; Waffenschmidt et al., 2013).

The team regularly assesses new publications on information retrieval and visits the main national and international meetings (for example, HTAi or the Cochrane Colloquium).

The team also routinely collects data and will collate the relevant references and save the accession numbers, study registry entries and identification numbers from each completed project. These data can be used to answer specific methodological questions to improve future topics. Examples of their use have been published in various articles and conference proceedings (for example, Hausner, 2015; Hausner et al., 2017; Waffenschmidt et al., 2013; Waffenschmidt and Groen, 2014).

The following list provides an overview of the unit's internal and IQWiG meetings:

- Weekly meetings of information specialists involved in review teams to discuss all current projects and methodological issues.
- Bi-weekly meetings with the whole unit about developments at IQWiG and to discuss methodological, technical or organizational issues.
- Weekly meetings of the IQWiG review team; the information specialist assigned attends these meetings until the searches are completed and the review team have started to extract data from the retrieved articles – after this point, further information retrieval topics will not usually be discussed.
- The unit head or their substitute represents the unit in IQWiG's methods and management meetings.

Case study 11.2: The Research Information Specialist at the Centre for Research in Evidence-Based Practice (CREBP), Bond University, Australia, by Justin Clark

The Centre for Research in Evidence-Based Practice (CREBP) at Bond University in Australia (www.crebp.net.au) has six full time research staff, six part-time researchers and between five to ten PhD students, as well as a research information specialist. CREBP produces approximately ten systematic reviews per year, along with other types of research articles, many of which require a search to be conducted. The information specialist also works with the Cochrane Acute Respiratory Infections Group supporting authors by designing or peer reviewing search strategies, updating searches and providing de-duplicated search results for approximately 30 reviews per year. When the information specialist is a co-author on a systematic review or a research paper they track down the full text of studies and, when time permits or necessity requires, they will screen the search results for relevant studies, critically appraise studies and extract data, as well as provide critical feedback on the manuscript.

The information specialist also provides workshops (both for Bond University and Cochrane) on how to conduct a search for a systematic review and searching for high-quality evidence.

Justin Clark, the current information specialist, has a professional background as a health librarian, with over ten years' experience working in hospitals and universities. He stays current by conducting methodological research around information retrieval and presents at international and national meetings, such as the Cochrane Colloquium and the Health Libraries Australia Professional Development Day.

It can be difficult to obtain feedback and peer review of search strategies. This is overcome by forming a strong working relationship with the University Library and the health librarians who work there, as well as by uploading search strategies to the PRESS (Peer Reviewed Electronic Search Strategies) Forum.

Local collaboration

As outlined in Table 11.3, when only one information specialist works on a project, there is an increased need for general collaboration and networking with people from other organizations to ensure high-quality products. However, information specialist teams should also engage in collaboration opportunities within the team and with teams in other organizations.

There are different ways of organising collaboration, depending on the country, the setting (for example, HTA agency, university, hospital) or the focus of the work (for example, guideline development, HTAs or rapid evidence assessments). As examples, we present collaboration opportunities on a local, national or international level through meetings or working groups. Case study 11.3 illustrates a successful example of a local collaborative initiative.

Case study 11.3: Ottawa Valley Health Libraries Association (OVHLA)
OVHLA (http://ovhla.chla-absc.ca) is an active local chapter of the Canadian Health Libraries Association (Farrah et al., 2016). They meet at least once a year. Professional development through the informal sharing of knowledge and continuing education has always been a key activity of OVHLA. Other activities include sharing resources, a journal club and a mini-conference. Networking and socialising provide another focus as a way of sharing ideas and discussing common problems.

National collaboration

The health librarian associations are well organised and demonstrate the kinds of activities that can be planned on a national basis. They have regular meetings and working groups where specific topics can be discussed. Three of the main associations are:

- Medical Library Association (www.mlanet.org) - Systematic Reviews Special Interest Group (in the USA)
- Canadian Health Libraries Association (www.chla-absc.ca)
- European Association for Health Information and Libraries (http://eahil.eu).

The various meetings of these associations differ in focus. In the more general library meetings, information retrieval is one topic among many. They can be attended to obtain a more general understanding of information retrieval and the basic skills required. The specialised meetings also address highly specific topics and offer workshops to acquire particular information retrieval skills.

International collaboration

Depending on the topic, there are different ways to collaborate. The main organizations for systematic review methods are Cochrane, the Campbell Collaboration and Health Technology Assessment international (HTAi). Cochrane and HTAi both have a strong focus on information retrieval. Usually their meetings provide special sessions and workshops for information retrieval, which are extremely useful for learning about general methodological aspects and developments as well as for acquiring specific information retrieval skills. These two organizations also have information specialist groups:

- Cochrane Information Specialist group (www.community.cochrane.org/organizational-info/resources/ resources-groups/information-specialists-portal) Although this is a closed group, non-Cochrane information specialists may join the email list and participate in the group's meetings at the annual Cochrane Colloquium. Case study 9.1 in Chapter 9 looks in more depth at how information specialists are collaborating with review teams to develop exciting solutions to information retrieval challenges.

- HTAi Interest Group on Information Retrieval (IRG) (www.htai.org/interest-groups/information-retrieval)
  The IRG is a well-established group within HTAi. The group has more than 150 members and organises beginner and advanced workshops on information retrieval at its annual meetings. It also has a mailing list and bi-annual newsletters. In addition, a subgroup produces the web resource 'Summarized Research in Information Retrieval for HTA' (SuRe Info, http://vortal.htai.org/? q=sure-info), which provides research-based information relating to the information retrieval aspects of producing systematic reviews and health technology assessments. Membership of HTAi is required to join the meetings, but the pre-meeting IRG workshops can be booked by non-HTAi members. The mailing list is open for non-members and the web resource SuRe Info is free of charge. SuRe Info might focus on HTAs but a lot of the publications it lists are of general interest to anyone interested in systematic searching.

Future directions

Information specialists need to be flexible and team-orientated and tackle new challenges with new ideas. They perform highly specialised tasks and thus require regular further training and exchanges with other information specialists. It will be important for them to maintain these various roles in the future.

It might have been assumed that information retrieval would become easier over time due to the increasing digitisation of knowledge and the availability of so much information on the internet. The opposite seems to be the case with the work becoming more complex and technical. We have seen in Case study 9.1 in Chapter 9 that information specialists can play a vital role in helping review teams avoid 'data deluge' and harness the potential benefits of technology. Expert searching requires highly specialised knowledge and there is a clear need for someone on a review team with the appropriate skills. Collaboration is an important component of maintaining this professional standing, since information specialists are expected to work in an evidence-based way, discuss their work with the scientific community, publish it and read and act on those findings.

Conclusion

To provide the optimum input into the project team of a systematic review, information specialists should be aware of the needs of the review authors. Before being involved in a project, information specialists should ensure that the standards to be applied have been specified and then work with the team to develop an appropriate protocol. There can be some organizational, methodological and interpersonal challenges to collaborating well with the review team and the information specialist will need to be a good communicator to overcome these.

Working in a team of other information specialists offers many obvious advantages. Information specialists who are the only expert searcher in their organization have opportunities to collaborate with the review teams and to network with other information specialists. There are networks at local, national and international levels that can foster good relations and help to promote best practice in information retrieval methods.

Suggestions for further reading

Booth, A. and Brice, A. (eds) (2004) *Evidence-based Practice for Information Professionals: a handbook*, Facet Publishing.

Brettle, A. and Urquhart, C. (2012) *Changing Roles and Contexts for Health Library and Information Professionals*, Facet Publishing.

Foster, M. J. and Jewell, S. T. (2017) *Assembling the Pieces of a Systematic Review: guide for librarians*, Rowman & Littlefield (Medical Library Association Books).

References

Anderson, P. F., Ginier, E. C. and Mani, N. S. (2016) Systematic Review Services on Health Sciences Library Websites. In Medical Library Association (ed.) (2016) *Mosaic '16: poster abstracts*, 13-18 May 2016,

Toronto, Canada, 298. www.mlanet.org/d/do/6882

European Network for Health Technology Assessment (EUnetHTA) (2017) Process of Information Retrieval for Systematic Reviews and Health Technology Assessments on Clinical Effectiveness. www.eunethta.eu/process-of-information-retrieval-for-systematic-reviews-and-health-technology-assessments-on-clinical-effectiveness

Farrah, K., Ford, C., Cunningham, J. and Skuce, J. (2016) Reflections on Turning Forty: a historical review of the Ottawa Valley Health Libraries Association, *Journal of the Canadian Health Libraries Association*, **37** (1), 12-16.

Foster, M. J. and Jewell, S. T. (eds) (2017) *Assembling the Pieces of a Systematic Review: guide for librarians*, Rowman & Littlefield (Medical Library Association Books).

Gore, G. C. and Jones, J. (2015) Systematic Reviews and Librarians: a primer for managers, *The Canadian Journal of Library and Information Practice and Research*, **10** (1), 1-16.

Grant, M. J. and Booth, A. (2009) A Typology of Reviews: an analysis of 14 review types and associated methodologies, *Health Information and Libraries Journal*, **26** (2), 91-108.

Greyson, D., Surette, S., Dennett, L. and Chatterley, T. (2013) 'You're Just One of the Group When You're Embedded': report from a mixed-method investigation of the research-embedded health librarian experience, *Journal of the Medical Library Association*, **101** (4), 287-297.

Hausner, E. (2015) How Fast is Indexing in the MEDLINE Segment of PubMed Compared to Embase? [Poster], *HTAi 2015: global efforts in knowledge transfer; HTA to health policy and practice*, 15-17 June 2015, Oslo, Norway.

Hausner, E., Guddat, C., Hermanns, T., Lampert, U. and Waffenschmidt, S. (2015) Development of Search Strategies for Systematic Reviews: validation showed the noninferiority of the objective approach, *Journal of Clinical Epidemiology*, **68** (2), 191-199.

Hausner, E., Guddat, C., Hermanns, T., Lampert, U. and Waffenschmidt, S. (2016) Prospective Comparison of Search Strategies for Systematic Reviews: an objective approach yielded higher sensitivity than a conceptual one, *Journal of Clinical Epidemiology*, **77**, 118-124.

Hausner, E., Knelangen, M., Sanders, L. and Waffenschmidt, S. (2017) Methodological Quality of HTA reports [Poster], *HTAi 2017: XIV Annual Meeting*, 17-21 June 2017, Rome, Italy.

Hausner, E., Waffenschmidt, S., Kaiser, T. and Simon, M. (2012) Routine Development of Objectively Derived Search Strategies, *Systematic Reviews*, **1**, 19.

Institute for Quality and Efficiency in Health Care (IQWiG) (2009) *General Methods for the Assessment of the Relation of Benefits to Costs – Version 1.0 – 19 November 2009*. www.iqwig.de/download/General_Methods_ for_the_Assessment_of_the_Relation_of_Benefits_to_Costs.pdf

Institute for Quality and Efficiency in Health Care (IQWiG) (2017) *General Methods – Version 5.0*. www.iqwig.de/en/methods/methods-paper.3020.html

Institute of Medicine (USA) Committee on Standards for Systematic Reviews of Comparative Effectiveness Research; Eden, J., Levit, L., Berg, A. and Morton, S. (eds), (2011) *Finding What Works in Health Care: standards for systematic reviews*, The National Academies Press. www.nap.edu/catalog/13059/finding-what-works-in-health-care-standards-for-systematic-reviews

Ioannidis, J. P., Greenland, S., Hlatky, M. A., Khoury, M. J., Macleod, M. R., Moher, D., Schulz, K. F. and Tibshirani, R. (2014) Increasing value and reducing waste in research design, conduct, and analysis, *The Lancet*, **383** (9912), 166-175.

Knelangen, M., Hausner, E., Metzendorf, M. I., Sturtz, S. and Waffenschmidt, S. (2018) Trial Registry Searches for RCTs of New Drugs Required Registry-specific Adaptation to Achieve Adequate Sensitivity, *Journal of Clinical Epidemiology*, **94**, 69-75.

Liberati, A., Altman, D. G., Tetzlaff, J., Mulrow, C., Gøtzsche, P. C., Ioannidis, J. P., Clarke, M., Devereaux, P. J., Kleijnen, J., Moher, D. and the PRISMA Group (2009) The PRISMA Statement for Reporting Systematic Reviews and Meta-analyses of Studies that Evaluate Healthcare Interventions: explanation and elaboration, *BMJ*, **339**, b2700.

Ludeman, E., Downton, K., Shipper, A. G. and Fu, Y. (2015) Developing a Library Systematic Review Service: a case study, *Medical Reference Services Quarterly*, **34** (2), 173-180.

McGowan, J. and Sampson, M. (2005) Systematic Reviews Need Systematic Searchers, *Journal of the Medical Library Association*, **93** (1), 74-80.

McGowan, J., Sampson, M., Salzwedel, D. M., Cogo, E., Foerster, V. and Lefebvre, C. (2016) PRESS Peer Review of Electronic Search Strategies: 2015 guideline statement, *Journal of Clinical Epidemiology*, **75**, 40-46.

Mullins, M. M., DeLuca, J. B., Crepaz, N. and Lyles, C. M. (2013) Reporting

Quality of Search Methods in Systematic Reviews of HIV Behavioral Interventions (2000-2010): are the searches clearly explained, systematic and reproducible?, *Research Synthesis Methods*, **5** (2), 116-130.

Nicholson, J., McCrillis, A. and Williams, J. D. (2017) Collaboration Challenges in Systematic Reviews: a survey of health sciences librarians, *Journal of the Medical Library Association*, **105** (4), 385-393.

O'Connor, A. M., Anderson, K. M., Goodell, C. K. and Sargeant, J. M. (2014) Conducting Systematic Reviews of Intervention Questions I: writing the review protocol, formulating the question and searching the literature, *Zoonoses and Public Health*, **61** (Suppl 1), 28-38.

Rader, T., Mann, M., Stansfield, C., Cooper, C. and Sampson, M. (2014) Methods for Documenting Systematic Review Searches: a discussion of common issues, *Research Synthesis Methods*, **5** (2), 98-115.

Sampson, M., McGowan, J., Cogo, E., Grimshaw, J., Moher, D. and Lefebvre, C. (2009) An Evidence-based Practice Guideline for the Peer Review of Electronic Search Strategies, *Journal of Clinical Epidemiology*, **62** (9), 944-952.

Sampson, M., McGowan, J., Tetzlaff, J., Cogo, E. and Moher, D. (2008) No Consensus Exists on Search Reporting Methods for Systematic Reviews, *Journal of Clinical Epidemiology*, **61** (8), 748-754.

Uttley, L. and Montgomery, P. (2017) The Influence of the Team in Conducting a Systematic Review, *Systematic Reviews*, **6** (1), 149.

Waffenschmidt, S. and Groen, L. (2014) Validation of the 'NOTing OUT' Corrao Filter Strategy in MEDLINE with Primary Publications Included in Systematic Reviews [Poster], *11th Annual Meeting of Health Technology Assessment international (HTAi): optimizing patient-centered care in an era of economic uncertainty*, 13-18 June 2014, Washington D. C., USA.

Waffenschmidt, S., Janzen, T., Hausner, E. and Kaiser, T. (2013) Simple Search Techniques in PubMed are Potentially Suitable for Evaluating the Completeness of Systematic Reviews, *Journal of Clinical Epidemiology*, **66** (6), 660-665.

12

Communication for information specialists

Margaret Sampson

Introduction

This chapter will examine elements of communication in our role as expert searchers. First, interprofessional communication and communicating as part of a team will be examined from the framework of core professional competencies. The practical use of peer communication to assure or improve search quality will be examined with the PRESS checklist. Next will be a discussion of presenting search results to gain maximum impact.

The chapter will go on to examine ways to increase discoverability, reproducibility and reusability of our work through mechanisms such as protocol registration, open access publication and data deposit. These are key to clear, complete, transparent scientific communication. The role of social media, broadly defined, in professional communication in support of search will also be discussed.

Our advances through formal research studies in methods of searching need to be communicated to professional audiences, both in library science and, more broadly, through academic communication or knowledge translation. Finally, future directions for research and practice will be suggested and conclusions and key points for reflection will be presented.

Interprofessional communication

'Interdisciplinary communication' is defined in the Medical Subject Heading (MeSH) term as:

> Communication, in the sense of cross-fertilization of ideas, involving two or more academic disciplines (such as the disciplines that comprise the cross-disciplinary field of bioethics, including the health and biological sciences, the humanities, and the social sciences and law). Also includes differences in patterns of language usage in different academic or medical disciplines. (National Library of Medicine, 2018)

Chapter 11 has shown just how important this collaboration with other members of the review team can be to maintaining the professional standing of the expert searcher.

Understanding training and expectations for communication can be very helpful. CanMEDS is a Canadian framework that identifies and describes the abilities physicians require to meet effectively the health care needs of the people they serve (Royal College of Physicians and Surgeons of Canada, 2011). The overarching competency is that of medical expert, but the first specific role is that of communicator (see Case study 12.1). These role expectations can be paraphrased to describe the role of the searcher in the reference interview (see Case study 12.2). While this example relates to the medical context and is based on a

---

Case study 12.1: CanMEDS Framework – Communicator

'Physicians enable patient-centred therapeutic communication by exploring the patient's symptoms, which may be suggestive of disease, and by actively listening to the patient's experience of his or her illness. Physicians explore the patient's perspective, including his or her fears, ideas about the illness, feelings about the impact of the illness, and expectations of health care and health care professionals. The physician integrates this knowledge with an understanding of the patient's context, including socio-economic status, medical history, family history, stage of life, living situation, work or school setting, and other relevant psychological and social issues. Central to a patient-centred approach is shared decision-making: finding common ground with the patient in developing a plan to address his or her medical problems and health goals in a manner that reflects the patient's needs, values, and preferences. This plan should be informed by evidence and guidelines.'

Available at www.royalcollege.ca/rcsite/canmeds/framework/canmeds-role-communicator-e.

formal framework, it can be helpful to consider the communication practices and expectations of other fields, whether in health science, social science, computer science, public policy or law, for example.

Case study 12.2: Application of the CanMEDS Framework to the reference interview

Information specialists enable investigator-centred communication by exploring the investigator's stated research need, which may be suggestive of a research question answerable by one or more evidence synthesis approaches, and by actively listening to the investigator's experience of his or her project. Searchers explore the investigator's perspective, including his or her concerns about successfully completing the project, and expectations of the literature search and the information specialist. The searcher integrates this knowledge with an understanding of the research context, including resources available to support the review, the investigator's prior research experience, the research experience of the investigator's mentors or supervisors, timeframe, the organizational setting (such as clinical or academic) and other relevant contextual issues. Central to an investigator-centric approach is shared decision-making: finding common ground with the investigator in developing a search plan to address their research problems and goals in a manner that reflects the investigator's needs, resources and preferences. This plan should be informed by evidence and guidelines.

Communication competencies

We saw in Table 10.1 in Chapter 10 that communication features prominently in the competencies in which expert searchers involved in systematic reviews require training. Communication runs through the systematic review process, from communicating with the team to refine the research question in the early stages, keeping colleagues up to date on the progress of the search and responding to queries about the search details, to writing for publication and communicating the final results.

In the competencies framework for systematic review searchers (Townsend et al., 2017) communication competencies are framed in two ways. These are team communication and communicating to professional audiences. Team communication skills are needed to understand the task at hand and to provide support tailored to the needs of the research group, thereby optimising their likelihood of successfully completing their project. Skilled communication of research methods and results to professional audiences are necessary to ensure that these users of evidence products can understand and critically appraise the evidence.

Team communication

Team communication and effective project management requires negotiation on the scope of the information specialist's role within the systematic review, which might be limited to conducting the searches or may extend to providing methodological consulting and assuming the responsibilities of co-authorship. It may involve advising on technological support for collaborative aspects of reviewing and communication of nuances (including timelines) of exhaustive literature searches. Some searchers will work almost exclusively with expert teams, but others will support researchers with a range of experience.

Early communications should establish where the researchers are in their planning and what help they may need to get to the point where you can develop the search. These consultations provide an opportunity to assess the researcher's level of expertise and, in the case of new researchers, the degree of support they have from engaged supervisors. It may be possible to refer the research to other professionals such as epidemiologists, methodologists or statisticians, who can provide additional support in developing a protocol. Such referrals can greatly increase the chance that the project will be a success.

Early communications also provide the opportunity to build rapport with the review team which will be helpful during the search development process. Communicating that you are interested in their topic, that you intend to work closely with them and that their success is important to you will be very helpful in setting the stage for designing the search. Case study 12.3 shows how these principles have been put into practice in the early stages of a new project.

> **Case study 12.3: First meeting with the review team**
> Some teams will have little or no experience working with an information specialist to develop a complex search and may not know what to expect or hold assumptions that are unhelpful. Therefore, I try to be clear about my work flow and what participation I need from them. For example, I insist on meeting with the principal investigator for the project as I find I get a better understanding of the topic, project objectives, resources and timelines than if I meet with an intermediary. If the principal investigator wants me to work

with a research associate or graduate student later in the process, I ask that they participate in our first meeting.

I generally begin a first meeting by asking the investigators to tell me a little about the topic. As I am a hospital librarian, the topic is usually medical and I can signal my level of understanding by asking for clarification on points I don't understand but that I think are important. Practising physicians are experienced at communicating medical topics both to their peers and to patients and their families. Most are quick to gauge my level of comprehension and adjust their communication accordingly.

Next, I will generally explore their impression of how much literature is available on their topic and I will have asked them to provide references for any known relevant studies in advance of the meeting. I determine if they have searched for existing systematic reviews and I may do a quick search for such prior work during our meeting. Many will have prepared a list of keywords I should search and a list of databases they want to use, thinking that this is expected. I briefly explain the process I use to discover search terms, in part working from the indexing of the known relevant studies they provide. Often the databases proposed are simply copied from a colleague's grant application and the investigators have no direct experience with them. I will therefore share with them suggestions of those databases that I think can contribute meaningfully to the project and discuss whether they are willing to adjust their selection – most are.

I ask when they would like the search completed, but I am also clear what my availability is like and that I want to time the actual running of the search to when they are fully prepared to start screening the results. I may need to communicate both the importance of such 'just in time' searching and, for a less experienced team, provide guidance on the practical steps needed to get screening underway, such as selecting a screening platform, devising screening criteria and recruiting and training screeners.

As that first meeting concludes, I communicate my next steps: that I will develop the search and be in contact with them if I would like any clarification or encounter situations that need decisions, that I will have the search peer reviewed, then finalise it, prepare the database of results and provide records for screening as well as a search log and methods write up. Generally, at this stage, when the investigators have a better picture of what my role will be and what is involved in the searching, we discuss whether my contribution to the review will result in authorship or acknowledgement.

Communicating to professional audiences

Townsend's second competency featuring communication is that of reporting; communicating literature search methods and results according to established standards so that they are suitable for publication and are replicable (Townsend et al., 2017). The professional audience that is the target of this communication is the user of the evidence product and that may be practitioners in the field, guideline developers or policymakers. You will be communicating to other search professionals who may need to critically appraise, replicate or update your search in the future, but that typically is not the primary audience. In health sciences, such professional communication is governed by reporting guidelines that specify what information about a study should be presented and where in the document it should be found.

A rigorous methodology for developing such communication standards includes reviewing the relevant evidence and consulting experts through the Delphi method (a forecasting method based on the results of questionnaires sent to a panel of experts) (Moher et al., 2010). Health science journals widely endorse Preferred Reporting Items for Systematic Reviews and Meta-Analyses (PRISMA), a reporting guideline for systematic reviews (Moher et al., 2009). Research shows that reviews published in journals endorsing PRISMA are more completely communicated (Panic et al., 2013).

PRISMA sets out the core elements that enable the reader to critically appraise the work and to allow someone skilled to replicate the research. PRISMA includes the minimum details of the search: the database used, platform, dates of the search and database coverage, a transcript of the principal database search strategy and details of non-database methods used, such as contacting experts or checking reference lists (Liberati et al., 2009). While PRISMA is not the only source of guidance for search reporting (Sampson et al., 2008), it is the only rigorously developed one. PRISMA was developed for health care but its use is wider than that and it provides useful guidance on the minimum information about the search that should be communicated, regardless of the context, if the goals of supporting critical appraisal and replication are to be achieved.

PRISMA is not specific to search reporting and does not cover all possible search elements that could be reported. To remedy these limitations, PRISMA Search was registered in February 2016 (www.equator-network.org/library/reporting-guidelines-under-development/#57). It may be that there are additional elements of the search process that must be recorded and communicated to ensure methods are transparent and reproducible, for example the search procedures for systematic web searching (Stansfield, Dickson and Bangpan, 2016).

Peer review as professional communication

Peer review ensures quality at the earliest and final stages of research, funding applications or protocols and journal publication. PRISMA states that one reason for presenting the full search strategy for the main bibliographic database is to enable peer review (Liberati et al., 2009). Given the expertise required to craft complex searches (McGowan and Sampson, 2005), peer review becomes an important aspect of professional communication. Having important searches reviewed by peers (other expert searchers) has been shown to:

- yield additional relevant retrievals in 20 of 47 searches (43%) and was judged to have improved the number of relevant articles found (Spry, Mierzwinski-Urban and Rabb, 2013).
- identify lack of use of, or missing, subject headings or thesauri terms, the omission of free-text terms including synonyms in over a quarter of searches examined (Wong, Paisley and Carroll, 2013).
- detect typographical errors, incorrectly combined line numbers, inappropriate subject heading explosions and errors in the use of study design filters (Allen et al., 2011).

In a study by Revelo and Paynter, over 80% of respondents viewed the use of a structured review of searches by peers as helpful, while none found it limiting (Revelo and Paynter, 2012). The person undertaking peer review can benefit from having contextual information from the searcher, such as how various search-related decisions were reached, to evaluate more effectively the subjective elements of the search (Craven and Levay, 2011).

Peer review of searches belongs outside the established peer review points for journal articles for two reasons. First, the peer review needs to be done by a search expert because of its technical nature. Second, the search needs to be peer reviewed at an early stage because a poor search would undermine the rest of the study and it would be too late if this was not picked up until the traditional point of the article being peer reviewed after submission to a journal. Rectifying any problems detected during journal peer review would cause significant delay and additional work for the review team.

The PRESS checklist (McGowan et al., 2016a; 2016b) provides a framework for such peer review of searches. In teaching PRESS to information specialists, we focus on professionalism in review and that the goal is not to 'mark' the search or use your expertise to redevelop it, but to examine it methodically to ensure it addresses the research question, has all essential terminology, reasonable and properly applied limits, and is free from clerical errors that would negatively affect the retrieval.

Now that we have established how peer review can benefit expert searchers, we can consider how to find a peer who will engage with you to do the review. For those who have close colleagues with the necessary knowledge base, the choice is easy and some organizations will mandate internal review as part of the quality assurance process. Otherwise PRESSforum (www.pressforum.pbworks.com) or listservs may be useful for finding reviewers. Issues such as how many reviews should be obtained (one is the norm), whether only the search of the main database will be reviewed, and if re-review of revised search strategies is required, are agreed between the search author and the peer reviewer, rather than being determined by PRESS.

The peer review of search shares a few things with peer review of protocols, grants and finished manuscripts. The review should be professional, respectful and focused on improving the product. Traditional peer reviews are often the basis for go/no go decisions, such as whether a project receives funding or whether a paper is accepted for publication. For this reason, peer reviews are often blinded (although the evidence for that is not compelling) and competing interests are formally addressed to help ensure objective review. While peer reviewers of searches may recommend that a search must be revised before use, they typically do not have the power to block its use. The review relationship is therefore more collegial. PRESS, for example, is designed for direct communication between searcher and reviewer, with no intermediary. This requires trust and the trust dividend is efficiency (Covey and Merrill, 2006). The review is handled as a professional communication, and can be fast and inexpensive.

Academic communication

As creators of evidence, we need to continually build the research base for our work, asking important questions and answering them rigorously and then communicating those results. As a professional community, we need to think about, discuss and ideally fund research that explores important questions and then communicate those results to our profession or to a broader audience. We can also answer smaller questions that can be addressed with few resources and Case study 12.4 shows how a relatively simple research idea could be effectively communicated to a wider audience.

Case study 12.4: Removing duplicates on the Ovid platform

I have been using server-side duplicate removal on the Ovid platform for about 18 months. The Ovid (www.ovid.com) user can open several databases at once and develop a search customised for each database, for example using the subject headings and limits for that source. When that search is run with several databases open, the searcher can isolate the records from that database. After repeating this process for each database, the database-specific sets can be combined and the 'Remove duplicates' command is issued. Users can set preferences as to which database record is retained when the duplicates are removed (Kwon et al., 2015). For each project, we have documented the number of records from each database before and after the online duplicate removal step. Several additional passes of downloaded records were made after they were imported into Reference Manager, a reference manager no longer commercially available but with robust duplicate detection features. Now, with the help of a library technician student, we are compiling those numbers across all projects.

The results may suggest that online duplicate removal is sufficient, that the small number of duplicates picked up through the second, offline de-duplication is not worth the bother. With a little extra work, I can write up the methods, findings and limitations and disseminate that either through formal publication or more casual social media outlets. By building data collection into the workflow, I am able to test objectively whether I have found efficiency. If I have, then taking the time to communicate that will leverage my efforts and allow others to consider whether this adjustment might be helpful in their work. Ideally, someone will try to replicate my findings.

We need to consider publishing in journals targeted to the broader audience to ensure that our advances have maximum uptake and impact. The topic of Case study 12.4, duplicate removal, has a limited audience and could be effectively communicated through an expedient manner and targeting those who do searches. Other findings, such as those that would support a significant shift in how or when we search, may benefit from a larger audience and should be published in epidemiology or methods journals, as the following example shows.

My reference manager software contains those articles that I pay attention to. I have 510 references where the record contains the terms 'librarian' or 'information specialist'. Informal analysis of these shows that for journals where I have retained five or more papers (accounting for 212 papers in all), 42% come from library journals (*Bulletin of the Medical Library Association, Evidence Based Library and Information Practice, Health Information and Libraries Journal, Journal of the Medical Library Association* and *Medical Reference Services Quarterly*), while 58% come from epidemiology or research methods journals (*BMC Medical Research Methodology, Journal of Clinical Epidemiology, Research Synthesis Methods* and *Systematic Reviews*), including one general medical journal (*BMJ*).

Scientific communication

The goal of communicating searches and search results for maximum impact means we should think of their potential future use as well as the project on which we are currently working. We will consider the importance of scientific communication by discussing discoverability, reproducibility, reusability, registration, open-access publication and data deposit.

Registering a review protocol is an important first step. The communication of a protocol and search plan contributes to the credibility and impact of the evidence synthesis project. Duplication of effort is common in the systematic review world (Siontis, Hernandez-Boussard and Ioannidis, 2013). Registering a protocol will mean that others can discover the project before it is completed and published, thereby avoiding wasteful duplication. Advance communication of the analysis plan, through protocol registration, makes it easier to detect when the data analysis has been manipulated. Such selective reporting can involve omission of some outcomes, selecting the most favourable result from multiple measures or from multiple data transformations of a measure or reporting only certain subpopulations (Page, McKenzie and Forbes, 2013).

Cochrane has long published protocols of systematic reviews. More recently, the Prospective Register of Systematic Reviews (PROSPERO) initiative (www.crd.york.ac.uk/prospero) allows any systematic review with health-related outcomes to be prospectively registered. Cochrane and PROSPERO are searchable and serve as a useful starting point for any information specialist asked to conduct the search for a review. If another review is already in progress, reviewers can be encouraged to select another topic or join forces with the project already underway. As the searcher on the review, you will benefit from having a clearly thought out and complete protocol with pre-specified questions and eligibility criteria and you will expect to participate in developing the search plan.

Search reuse

Searches, or components of them, such as the search terms used to represent a particular concept (for example, the Population element in a PICO question), may be reused by others. The value of search sharing has been recognised (de Jonge and Lein, 2015; Saleh, Ratajeski and LaDue, 2014; Walkerdine and Rodden, 2001), but possibly only the InterTASC ISSG Search Filter Resource (https://sites.google.com/a/ york.ac.uk/issg-search-filters-resource/home) is widely used (Lefebvre et al., 2013). PRESSforum has been suggested as a platform for reusable search components (de Jonge and Lein, 2015) and indeed has peer reviewed searches on file. The blog *PubMed Search Strategies*, with contributors Christina L. Wissinger, Cindy Schmidt, Concepción Campos-Asensio, Lorie Kloda, Patricia Heckmann and Patricia J. Erwin (www.pubmedsearches.blogspot.com), shares numerous PubMed strategies.

Whatever the platform used for such professional communications, reporting the search and background information on how it was developed and validated will support reuse of well-developed search components. Simply citing the source of components or filters you have used will go a long way, but any peer review or validation efforts (Sampson and McGowan, 2011) will also be useful to someone wishing to reuse a component and will add to the impact of your work.

Open science

Open science is a term describing a number of trends in the creation and communication of science, including:

- innovations in communication technology that serve as infrastructure to make science more transparent

- demands by the public to improve access to knowledge for everyone
- changes in how we measure research impact, such as Altmetrics, which give a fuller picture of the conversation around a publication rather than just the number of citations it receives (Piwowar, 2013)
- new opportunities for collaborative research (Fecher and Friesike, 2014).

Science open to greater scrutiny provides a rich research base and expands the potential for collaboration while helping to ensure the same study is not unknowingly conducted twice (House of Commons Science and Technology Committee, 2013). Infrastructure such as the Systematic Review Data Repository (SRDR) (Ip et al., 2012; Li et al., 2015) or functionality within systematic review platforms, such as that offered by DistillerSR (Evidence Partners Inc., Ottawa, Canada), can make some data available, typically screening records and extracted data. These systems do not necessarily share metadata about the project, such as the protocol, search strategies or other decisions made during the research process. This limits the utility of these resources for the searcher and thus we must look for more complete solutions to meet our communication needs.

There are several options for more complete data deposit. Many universities have institutional repositories, which can archive dissertations, publications and datasets, often curated by the institutional librarians. Public repositories exist, often focused in particular disciplines (for example, www.science.gc.ca). Journals will make supplemental information available online. When depositing data with a journal, the author should consider whether assigning copyright for the article would also apply to the accompanying material. A Creative Commons (CC) licence places the dataset entirely in the public domain and has been recommended for biomedical datasets associated with journal articles (Hrynaszkiewicz and Cockerill, 2012).

The benefits of depositing data with the journal are that there will be a direct link from the article to the associated data and the data will become available when the article is published. However, repositories such as Dryad (www.datadryad.org) will provide a digital object identifier (DOI) that can be published in the article, effectively providing such a link (American Psychological Association, 2012), and place an embargo on the dataset until the publication of the associated article. Journal editors agree that such deposit does not constitute prior publication (Krleza-Jerić and Lemmens, 2009). Data files should be in a generic format such as a comma separated CSV text file format rather than the proprietary format. As well, documentation of the variables and their coding should be made available (Hrynaszkiewicz and Cockerill, 2012). RIS format makes sense for references and provides for some annotation (such as source database and eligibility status) in discretionary fields.

As well as supporting more completely communicated scholarly research, open science involves new kinds of partnership and collaboration, new tools and new approaches to intellectual property. These developments lead to initiatives such as Altmetrics, BioMed Central, Creative Commons, Mendeley, Zotero, Research ID and highly visible initiatives such as the Human Genome Project (Friesike et al., 2015). Case study 12.5 is an example of a small research project that has adopted the principles of open science.

Case study 12.5: Using Open Science Framework to communicate a small research study

Open Science Framework (OSF) is an initiative that covers the entire research cycle, providing integrated prospective registration and open data deposit. It is a complete platform with features to support the management of research projects, housing documents and datasets and integrating with other cloud-based services such as Dropbox and Google Docs. Each element of a project can be open to all, only to team members or embargoed.

I registered the small study described in Case study 12.4, calling it 'The Utility of Ovid Online Duplicate Removal for Building Databases for Systematic Reviews'. To register, I completed a template which had important protocol elements: hypothesis, study design, sample size, data collection methods, variables and the analysis plan. I was asked to declare what access I had to the data before registering as this helps to determine if I could have pre-selected outcomes that looked most promising. I then submitted this registration for review and very quickly got some feedback on areas that needed clarification, such as this comment, 'Your hypotheses indicate that you will be measuring % more work for screeners. Please describe how this measure will be created. Thank you!' and 'Please either fully pre-specify your follow-up analyses or move them to the Exploratory analysis section. Each analysis in the Statistical models and Follow-up analyses sections must be fully pre-specified, conducted according to the pre-registration, and reported in the final manuscript. Thank you!' Not much wiggle room here! I tightened things up and resubmitted.

On submission, I was asked if I should make the registration public immediately or after an embargo. I opted for immediate release. Embargoing protects your research idea while still providing a time-stamped statement of your research intentions that can be compared with the final publication. After registration, I was free to start exploring the data the student had assembled and I could post that data to OSF, granting read-only or read-write access to co-investigators or anyone else. I have left all elements of the project open to all (www.osf.io/3hnes). At the time of writing, several iterations of the protocol and the original and cleaned datasets have been posted. The dataset is still in proprietary format.

As an example of using OSF for a finished project, see the data deposited for a study I have been involved in looking at the epidemiology of systematic reviews (Page et al., 2016). All screened and included references are supplied (although not in an optimal format); the extracted data and the code used to run the data analysis are available for review or re-analysis. A link to these files (www.osf.io/rw3q5) is provided in the front matter of the article.

Using social media and technology effectively

We can think beyond Facebook, Twitter and YouTube and broadly define social media to include user communities such as listservs (for example, Expertsearcher, MedLib and CanMedLib). Social media, as we saw in Chapter 6, can be excellent for professional communications. For example, at 2:05pm today as I was writing this, a request went out on a Canadian listserv for a peer reviewer for a search on seasonal flu vaccine uptake among the elderly. At 2:40pm we were notified that a reviewer had come forward.

The wiki-based online community PRESSforum (www.pressforum. pbworks.com) provides an option for searchers wanting to connect with peer reviewers. Searchers can join the community and post search strategies that they want to have peer reviewed. A submission form provides a standardised means of communicating background information that would help a peer to evaluate the search against the six elements of PRESS. Other members can select a search they would like to review, download the submission, assess it and communicate their feedback by re-uploading the completed review. PRESSforum is premised on reciprocity, as are many social media sites (Lewis, 2015), and may give the new professional an opportunity to contribute while building their network and getting useful feedback on their searches.

ORCID (Open Researcher and Contributor ID) is a useful tool for facilitating scholarly communication (www.orcid.org). ORCID provides the researcher with a unique number that will permanently and uniquely identify them. This number is a persistent digital identifier that serves as authority control. As an example, my ORCID ID is 0000-0003-2550-9893. Searching this ID yields a list of my works and distinguishes me from all the other people who publish under the name 'Margaret Sampson'. It is free to sign up for an ID and I can now use it when I publish articles to show it is definitely by me. It is particularly useful if you have a common name to distinguish you from other people, if you have published under slightly different versions of your own name (such as Mike or Michael) or indeed if you have changed your name. Clearly, we can use the IDs ourselves, but we can also encourage the researchers we support to register with ORCID and update their profile with grants received, journal publications, conference presentations and other scholarly publications.

Future directions

What does the future hold? As the pace of research production continues to increase and updating becomes more and more challenging, the idea of the living systematic review holds great appeal (see Chapter 9). Now, as the conduct of reviews moves online and can benefit from techniques such as automation and crowd sourcing, the idea is coming to fruition (Thomas et al., 2017). While the impact of machine learning is now being felt in the relevance assessment of systematic reviews, this will likely expand into search updating and only later into the initial searching to establish the evidence base. What is certain is that we will be increasingly called upon to make our work both transparent and reusable. This will require ever higher levels of documentation and communication of our search methods, their development and validation.

Conclusion

Information specialists who are involved with systematic reviews and other evidence synthesis methods participate in complex teams and we need to employ a range of consulting and interpersonal communication skills in our work. We also collaborate with other professionals in the field to ensure we maximise the quality of our work, through such processes as peer review. We document and communicate our methods to provide transparency and maximise the impact of our work. We must be consumers of evidence as well as finders and producers of evidence, staying up to date with methods and research in this continually evolving field. Many recent changes relate to the opening of science, a trend that naturally aligns with systematic review searching, as an enabler of complete identification of relevant studies. We can further this trend by participating in it, opening our own methods and sharing our data.

Suggestions for further reading

Derr, J. (2000) *Statistical consulting: a guide to effective communication*, Duxbury Press.
United Nations Educational, Scientific and Cultural Organization (2017) *Open access for librarians* [e-learning course], UNESCO Knowledge Societies Division Open Access Programme. www.unesco.org/new/en/communication-and-information/access-to-knowledge/open-access-to-scientific-information.

References

Allen, A., Misso, K., Riemsma, R. and Kleijnen, J. (2011) Appraisal of Search Strategies in Industry Submissions for Technology Appraisal (ASSIST): reviewing search methods of industry submissions to NICE using a structured checklist, *19th Cochrane Colloquium*, 19-22 October 2011, Madrid, Spain. https://abstracts.cochrane.org/2011-madrid/appraisal-search-strategies-industry-submissions-technology-appraisal-assist-reviewing
American Psychological Association (2012) Electronic Sources and Locator Information. In *Publication Manual of the American Psychological Association*, 6th edn, American Psychological Association, 187-188.
Covey, S. M. R. and Merrill, R. R. (2006) *The Speed of Trust : the one thing that changes everything*, Free Press.
Craven, J. and Levay, P. (2011) Recording Database Searches for Systematic

Reviews – What is the Value of Adding a Narrative to Peer-Review Checklists? A Case Study of NICE Interventional Procedures Guidance, *Evidence Based Library and Information Practice*, **6** (4), 72-87.

de Jonge, G. and Lein, R. K. (2015) Sharing Literature Search Blocks: status and ideas for a cooperative solution, *Journal of EAHIL*, **11** (3), 11-14.

Fecher, B. and Friesike, S. (2014) Open Science: one term, five schools of thought. In Bartling, S. and Friesike, S. (eds), *Opening Science*, Springer International Publishing.

Friesike, S., Widenmayer, B., Gassmann, O. and Schildhauer, T. (2015) Opening Science: towards an agenda of open science in academia and industry, *The Journal of Technology Transfer*, **40** (4), 581-601.

House of Commons Science and Technology Committee (2013) *Clinical Trials*, The Stationery Office Limited. https://publications.parliament.uk/pa/cm201314/cmselect/cmsctech/104/104.pdf

Hrynaszkiewicz, I. and Cockerill, M. J. (2012) Open by Default: a proposed copyright license and waiver agreement for open access research and data in peer-reviewed journals, *BMC Research Notes*, **5** (1), 494.

Ip, S., Hadar, N., Keefe, S., Parkin, C., Iovin, R., Balk, E. M. and Lau, J. (2012) A Web-based Archive of Systematic Review Data, *Systematic Reviews*, **1**, 15.

Krleza-Jerić, K. and Lemmens, T. (2009) 7th Revision of the Declaration of Helsinki: good news for the transparency of clinical trials, *Croatian Medical Journal*, **50** (2), 105-110.

Kwon, Y., Lemieux, M., McTavish, J. and Wathen, N. (2015) Identifying and Removing Duplicate Records from Systematic Review Searches, *Journal of the Medical Library Association*, **103** (4), 184-188.

Lefebvre, C., Glanville, J., Wieland, L. S., Coles, B. and Weightman, A. (2013) Methodological Developments in Searching for Studies for Systematic Reviews: past, present and future?, *Systematic Reviews*, **2**, 78.

Lewis, S. C. (2015) Reciprocity as a Key Concept for Social Media and Society, *Social Media + Society*, **1** (1), 1-2.

Li, T., Vedula, S. S., Hadar, N., Parkin, C., Lau, J. and Dickersin, K. (2015) Innovations in Data Collection, Management, and Archiving for Systematic Reviews, *Annals of Internal Medicine*, **162** (4), 287-294.

Liberati, A., Altman, D. G., Tetzlaff, J., Mulrow, C., Gøtzsche, P. C., Ioannidis, J. P., Clarke, M., Devereaux, P. J., Kleijnen, J., Moher, D. and the PRISMA Group (2009) The PRISMA Statement for Reporting

Systematic Reviews and Meta-analyses of Studies that Evaluate Health Care Interventions: explanation and elaboration, *PLOS Medicine*, **6**, (7) e1000100.

McGowan, J. and Sampson, M. (2005) Systematic Reviews Need Systematic Searchers, *Journal of the Medical Library Association*, **93** (1), 74-80.

McGowan, J., Sampson, M., Salzwedel, D. M., Cogo, E., Foerster, V. and Lefebvre, C. (2016a) *PRESS Peer Review of Electronic Search Strategies Guideline: explanation and elaboration*, Canadian Agency for Drugs and Technologies in Health. www.cadth.ca/resources/finding-evidence/press

McGowan, J., Sampson, M., Salzwedel, D. M., Cogo, E., Foerster, V. and Lefebvre, C. (2016b) PRESS Peer Review of Electronic Search Strategies: 2015 guideline statement, *Journal of Clinical Epidemiology*, **75**, 40-46.

Moher, D., Liberati, A., Tetzlaff, J., Altman, D. G. and the PRISMA Group (2009) Preferred Reporting Items for Systematic Reviews and Meta-analyses: the PRISMA statement, *Annals of Internal Medicine*, **151** (4), 264-269.

Moher, D., Schulz, K. F., Simera, I. and Altman, D. G. (2010) Guidance for Developers of Health Research Reporting Guidelines, *PLOS Medicine*, **7** (2), e1000217.

National Library of Medicine (2018) Interdisciplinary Communication. Retrieved 26 January 2018 from: www.ncbi.nlm.nih.gov/mesh/?term=interprofessional+communication

Page, M. J., McKenzie, J. E. and Forbes, A. (2013) Many Scenarios Exist for Selective Inclusion and Reporting of Results in Randomized Trials and Systematic Reviews, *Journal of Clinical Epidemiology*, **66** (5), 524-537.

Page, M. J., Shamseer, L., Altman, D. G., Tetzlaff, J., Sampson, M., Tricco, A., Catalá-López, F., Li, L., Reid, E. K., Sarkis-Onofre, R. and Moher, D. (2016) Epidemiology and Reporting Characteristics of Systematic Reviews of Biomedical Research: a cross-sectional study, *PLOS Medicine*, **13** (5), e1002028.

Panic, N., Leoncini, E., de Belvis, G., Ricciardi, W. and Boccia, S. (2013) Evaluation of the Endorsement of the Preferred Reporting Items for Systematic Reviews and Meta-Analysis (PRISMA) Statement on the Quality of Published Systematic Review and Meta-Analyses, *PLOS ONE*, **8** (12), e83138.

Piwowar, H. (2013) Altmetrics: value all research products, *Nature*, **493**, (7431), 159.

Revelo, R. and Paynter, R. (2012) *Peer Review of Search Strategies – Methods Research Reports,* Agency for Healthcare Research and Quality (USA). www.ncbi.nlm.nih.gov/books/NBK98353

Royal College of Physicians and Surgeons of Canada (2011) CanMEDS Framework – CanMEDS: better standards, better physicians, better care. www.royalcollege.ca/rcsite/canmeds/canmeds-framework-e

Saleh, A. A., Ratajeski, M. A. and LaDue, J. (2014) Development of a Web-Based Repository for Sharing Biomedical Terminology from Systematic Review Searches: a case study, *Medical Reference Services Quarterly,* **33** (2), 167-178.

Sampson, M. and McGowan, J. (2011) Inquisitio Validus Index Medicus: a simple method of validating MEDLINE systematic review searches, *Research Synthesis Methods,* **2** (2), 103-109.

Sampson, M., McGowan, J., Tetzlaff, J., Cogo, E. and Moher, D. (2008) No Consensus Exists on Search Reporting Methods for Systematic Reviews, *Journal of Clinical Epidemiology,* **61** (8), 748-754.

Science.gc.ca (2011) *Open Access: Research Data. Research Funding Collaboration - Policies and Guidelines.* www.sshrc-crsh.gc.ca/about-au_sujet/policies-politiques/open_access-libre_acces/index-eng.aspx

Siontis, K. C., Hernandez-Boussard, T. and Ioannidis, J. P. A. (2013) Overlapping Meta-analyses on the Same Topic: survey of published studies, *BMJ,* **347**, f4501.

Spry, C., Mierzwinski-Urban, M. and Rabb, D. (2013) Peer Review of Literature Search Strategies: does it make a difference?, *Canadian Health Libraries Association (CHLA) Conference,* 22-25 May 2013, Saskatoon, Saskatchewan, Canada.

Stansfield, C., Dickson, K. and Bangpan, M. (2016) Exploring Issues in the Conduct of Website Searching and Other Online Sources for Systematic Reviews: how can we be systematic?, *Systematic Reviews,* **5** (1), 191.

Thomas, J., Noel-Storr, A., Marshall, I., Wallace, B., McDonald, S., Mavergames, C., Glasziou, P., Shemilt, I., Synnot, A., Turner, T., Elliott, J. and Living Systematic Review Network (2017) Living Systematic Reviews: 2. Combining human and machine effort, *Journal of Clinical Epidemiology,* **91**, 31-37.

Townsend, W. A., Anderson, P. F., Ginier, E. C., MacEachern, M. P., Saylor, K. M., Shipman, B. L. and Smith, J. E. (2017) A Competency Framework for Librarians Involved in Systematic Reviews, *Journal of the Medical Library Association,* **105** (3), 268-275.

Walkerdine, J. and Rodden, T. (2001) Sharing Searches: developing open support for collaborative searching. In Hirose, M. (ed.), *Human Computer Interaction – INTERACT '01*, IOS Press, 140-147.

Wong, R., Paisley, S. and Carroll, C. (2013) Assessing Searches in NICE Single Technology Appraisals: practice and checklist, *International Journal of Technology Assessment in Health Care*, **29** (3), 315-322.

13

The information specialist as an expert searcher

Alison Brettle

Introduction

Information specialists play a key role in undertaking the searching for systematic reviews. This chapter traces the context, background and history of how the role has evolved over the last 20 years, before considering the challenges and debates facing today's expert searchers. Examples from the literature and practice will be used to highlight the debates before a summary of future directions for research and practice for expert searchers concludes the chapter.

The evolving role of the information specialist

Opportunities provided by evidence-based practice and systematic reviews

Evidence-based practice (EBP), with its emphasis on finding evidence, offered information specialists a wide range of opportunities for using and promoting their skills. For over 20 years, information specialists have been encouraged to undertake new roles and demonstrate their expertise within the EBP context (Falzon and Booth, 2001; Harris, 2005; McGowan and Sampson, 2005; Medical Library Association, 2005; Palmer, 1996). These roles have mainly focused on using traditional information skills in teaching others to find evidence and searching for evidence on behalf of others (both for individual patient care and within a systematic review context). There is some evidence of role development using critical appraisal, research and management skills and outreach roles (Brettle, 2009; Brettle and Urquhart, 2011).

The main focus of this chapter is on the role of the information specialist as an expert searcher within the context of systematic reviews. This role has been documented over time (Beverley, Booth and Bath, 2003; Spencer and Eldredge, 2018), although it has not been fully explored or evaluated.

Evidence-based practice itself has evolved from its origins in medicine, across health care to a means of decision-making in a wide range of other professions from librarianship (Koufogiannakis and Brettle, 2016) to policing (Sherman, 1998). The systematic review, although around since the 1970s, gained significant momentum in the late 1990s with interest from policymakers (Moher, Stewart and Shekelle, 2015) and organizations such as Cochrane (www.cochrane.org) and the Centre for Reviews and Dissemination (www.york.ac.uk/crd) and more recently the EPPI-Centre (http://eppi.ioe.ac.uk/cms), the Campbell Collaboration (www.campbellcollaboration.org) and the Joanna Briggs Institute (www.joannabriggs.org). The key feature of a systematic review is the use of formal and explicit methods which describe, at the outset, the question to be answered, the search for evidence and the assessment and synthesis of the evidence (Moher, Stewart and Shekelle, 2015). The aim is to reduce bias and in terms of searching this is achieved by undertaking a comprehensive literature search, hence the potential role for an expert searcher.

Over time, new models of systematic review have evolved (see Chapter 2). These have not replaced the original systematic review model (based on evaluating the effectiveness of an intervention), rather they have emerged in response to policymakers' and other stake-holders' needs for information, for which the existing systematic review model does not quite fit (Moher, Stewart and Shekelle, 2015). These include:

> ... the rapid review, when time is of the essence; the scoping review, when an overview of a broad field is needed; and the realist review, where the question of interest includes how and why complex social interventions work in certain situations, rather than assume they either do or do not work at all. (Moher, Stewart and Shekelle, 2015)

These newer types of review and the subsequent developments in review methods have implications for expert searchers. These will be described, together with searchers' responses to dealing with them, within this chapter.

Documenting the role of the expert searcher

The role of the expert searcher within evidence-based practice, and particularly within systematic reviews, has been documented since 2003 when the Medical Library Association in the USA released a policy statement (MLA, 2005) that defined expert searching. It articulated the role of health sciences librarians in the provision of expert searching and put forward a number of high impact areas where health librarians should be providing expert searching. These include:

- complex or unusual cases
- research support
- basic science research
- institutional support for patient safety or litigation
- key business and academic decisions
- scholarship and grant applications
- best practice identification and development
- evidence-based interfaces to the medical record
- patient education support and information therapy (MLA, 2005, 43).

The expert searcher role within systematic reviews was not explicitly made within the MLA policy statement, although guidance for conducting systematic reviews stresses the importance of comprehensive literature searches and recommends that they are conducted by experienced information specialists (for example, Centre for Reviews and Dissemination, 2009).

Beverley, Booth and Bath (2003) identified ten roles that librarians could play within the systematic review process, including literature searcher (covering resource selection, search term selection and developing highly sensitive search strategies to reduce potential bias). The roles of reference manager and document supplier, which arguably form part of expert searching, were also highlighted (Beverley,

Booth and Bath, 2003). McGowan and Sampson (2005) also argued that librarians who conduct searches for systematic reviews must be experts. They described the methods, knowledge and skills required for searching within systematic reviews, suggesting they need to understand the specifics about data structure and functions of bibliographic and specialised databases, as well as the technical and methodological issues of searching (McGowan and Sampson, 2005). More recently, Spencer and Eldredge (2018) documented reference management, de-duplication of search results, evaluating search strategies, search planning, question formulation, search reporting, resource selection, search filter development and protocol development amongst the 18 distinct roles that information professionals play within systematic reviews.

However, in practice, documenting roles does not really highlight the complexity of the tasks involved in expert searching, nor does it provide the expert searcher with guidance on how to approach the task. This does not mean there is no help or evidence, but, as shown below, it is widely scattered within the literature. Case study 13.1 highlights some of the issues encountered in practice when advising a review team as an expert searcher.

Case study 13.1: Counselling young children aged 4-10 years

I was recently commissioned to undertake a comprehensive search of the evidence for counselling young children aged 4-10 years. The search provided the basis of a systematic scoping review that would provide an evidence base to underpin a competency framework being developed by the British Association of Counselling and Psychotherapy. In undertaking the search, I needed to:

- Select appropriate resources to search (which databases and other sources would be the most useful and could be searched within the time and money available).
- Select appropriate keywords and thesaurus terms for each of the resources, which involved selecting from over 60 potentially relevant thesaurus terms related to counselling and psychotherapy (not an easy task if you are not a counsellor or do not understand the intricacies and politics around the different areas of the profession).
- Decide on an appropriate means of retrieving articles relating to younger children rather than teenagers or adolescents, without missing relevant articles.

- Decide on an appropriate means of reducing the set of results from over 5,000 to a manageable number, either through appropriate limiters (such as by study design) or by the most efficient means of combining keywords (for example, establishing if removing 'cognitive therapy' would exclude relevant evidence).

All these choices required testing through scoping searches, reviewing the results and uploading onto reference management software. Communicating my findings through discussions with the review team were also necessary, as each choice had the potential to impact on the volume of evidence retrieved. Missing evidence could potentially impact on the eventual competencies included in the framework. Including too many therapies within the search had the potential to make the framework irrelevant to particular groups of counsellors.

All these tasks and decisions fit with the expert searcher role outlined in the literature, but simple guides outlining procedures or what happens in the 'search part' of a systematic review are lacking when compared to guidance for the critical appraisal and other subsequent parts of systematic reviews.

Evidence for the role of expert searcher

Although the role of expert searcher within systematic reviews has been documented, recent studies suggest that their involvement is not high, with studies quoting ranges from 7% (Vassar et al., 2017) or 11% (Meert, Torabi and Costella, 2016) to 51% (Koffel, 2015). Evidence of the effectiveness or value of librarians as expert searchers is lacking (Brettle, 2009). Zhang, Sampson and McGowan (2006) established that when the person responsible for searching within a systematic review was listed as an author, searches were less prone to errors, but as the qualifications of the authors were poorly reported, it was impossible to determine whether it was information specialists or other professionals who were responsible for this improved contribution. More recent research (Koffel, 2015) suggests that involving librarians is linked to better quality searches, but this only correlated librarian involvement with adherence to guidance rather than the effectiveness of the searches. Librarian involvement has also been linked to better reporting of search strategies (Meert, Torabi and Costella, 2016).

According to McGowan and Sampson (2005, 74), 'search methodology must be based on research about retrieval practices, and it is vital that expert searchers keep informed about, advocate for, and, moreover, conduct research in information retrieval'. Information specialists are increasingly researching a range of issues in relation to searching and systematic reviews. This contributes to the evidence base around searching for systematic reviews and improves the quality of searches undertaken. As described in the next sections, research undertaken by expert searchers includes:

- developing and improving search filters
- improving the quality of searching within systematic reviews
- refining the reporting of search strategies.

Developing and improving search filters

The history of search filter development is relatively long with the first studies appearing in the mid-1990s, often conducted by those involved in expert searching themselves. An overview that highlighted and critiqued filters, their designs and testing was published (Jenkins, 2004), but this is likely to be dated now. Expert searchers are well placed to develop search filters as they are potential heavy users of them in practice. Filters seek to improve search accuracy and performance and have been developed to retrieve particular study designs (for example, Boynton et al., 1998; Haynes et al., 1994; White et al., 2001) and more recently to locate population groups (for example, Campbell, Dorgan and Tjosvold, 2014; Cooper et al., 2014) and geographical locations (Ayiku et al., 2017). Search filters are commonly used by expert searchers as part of guideline development (Damarell et al., 2011) and these expert searchers are also developing tools to critically appraise the quality of their filters (Bak et al., 2009; Glanville et al., 2008). The quality of the filter is crucial and retrospectively checking whether using a filter affected the results of the review (for example, Cooper et al., 2014) is a means of determining whether the filter (or indeed the expert searcher) is making an impact on the review.

Improving the quality of searching within systematic reviews

Systematic review guidance lists which resources to search when conducting searches for systematic reviews, but this guidance is not evidence-based (Brettle, 2009) and does not cover the specifics of how to search. Expert searchers have begun to develop this evidence base and the increasing number of topics and case studies suggests that there is not one searching model to be employed across systematic reviews. Most of this research is case study-based but it begins to build a picture of the evidence, provides some guide to searching and confirms that systematic searching can be complex. This section just provides an overview of some of the research available and many other papers are available.

Table 13.1 shows the types of issues information specialists have examined in effectiveness reviews.

Table 13.1 *Examples of research for effectiveness reviews*

Topic	References
Trials and trial registries	Crumley et al., 2005
Searching non-English publications	Moher et al., 2005 Pham et al., 2005
Rapid versus exhaustive searches	Featherstone et al., 2015 Royle and Waugh, 2003

Table 13.2 shows examples of the research that has been conducted regarding improving the quality of searches.

Table 13.2 *Examples of research on search quality*

Topic	References
Improving precision	Sampson, Tetzlaff and Urquhart, 2011
Comparative recall	Bramer et al., 2013
Adequacy or optimal combinations of databases	Aagaard, Lund and Juhl, 2016 Beyer and Wright, 2013 Brettle and Long, 2001 Greenhalgh and Peacock, 2005 Lawrence, 2008 Sampson et al., 2003 Stevinson and Lawlor, 2004 Suarez-Almazor et al., 2000 Taylor et al., 2007
Searching for theory	Booth and Carroll, 2015
Locating qualitative research	Wright, Golder and Lewis-Light, 2015

Table 13.3 on the next page illustrates examples of topic-focused research.

Table 13.3 *Examples of topic-focused research*

Topic	References
Type and value of resources for social care systematic reviews	Brettle and Long, 2001 Golder, Mason and Spilsbury, 2008 Long et al., 2002 McNally and Alborz, 2004 Ogilvie et al., 2005 Stansfield and Liabo, 2017 Taylor et al., 2007 Wright, Golder and Lewis-Light, 2014
Searching for topics in medical education	Haig and Dozier, 2003
Searching in social science reviews	Papaioannou et al., 2009 Woodman et al., 2010
Searching in public health	Stansfield, Brunton and Rees, 2014
Maternal mortality and morbidity	Betran et al., 2005
Identifying evidence on criminal justice topics	Tompson and Belur, 2016

Information specialists have examined the value of going beyond databases and using supplementary techniques to ensure more comprehensive searches, as we saw in Chapters 3 and 4. Table 13.4 provides examples of what this research has included.

Table 13.4 *Examples of research into other search techniques*

Topic	References
Conducting website searches	Stansfield, Dickson and Bangpan, 2016
Comparing handsearching to electronic searching	Hopewell et al., 2007
The contribution of grey literature	Hartling et al., 2017

The developments highlighted in these tables were crucial for moving systematic reviews away from health care and into a wider range of other domains. Initial search guides, such as from Cochrane, met the needs of effectiveness reviews but a different set of approaches was needed for broad-based topics (see Chapter 3). It was up to information professionals to decide how the wider questions, multiple stakeholder perspectives and qualitative study designs could be incorporated into search methods, through such approaches as selecting an optimum range of databases or using other search techniques. Expert searchers were then in a good position to engage with newer types of review (see Chapter 2) and to tackle the additional challenges these bring, such as considering literature which may be outside the focus of the review (to achieve theoretical saturation), a focus on specificity rather than sensitivity and the need to continue searching throughout the review (Briscoe, 2014).

Refining the reporting of search strategies

Clear reporting of a search enables a reader to determine the comprehensiveness and extent of bias within the search (and potentially the systematic review). Clear reporting of searches also enables other expert searchers to build on previous searches. Information specialists have highlighted discrepancies in reporting search strategies in systematic reviews (Booth, 2006; Faggion et al., 2016; Mullins et al., 2014; Sampson et al., 2008; Toews, 2017; Yoshii et al., 2009) and have been developing standards to improve reporting (Atkinson et al., 2015; Rader et al., 2014). These improvements include, as discussed in Chapter 12, guidelines for peer reviewing search strategies (McGowan et al., 2016, Sampson et al., 2009). Furthermore, information specialists have been associated with improved reporting of searches (Meert, Torabi and Costella, 2016; Rethlefsen et al., 2015).

There is further work to do, however, as search strategies are not always widely reported in practice (indeed the PRISMA guidance (Moher et al., 2009) states that only the strategy from one database needs to be reported), which is not helpful to those designing or updating searches.

Expert searchers as part of a team

> Expert searchers are an important part of the systematic review team, crucial throughout the review process – from the development of the proposal and research question to publication.
>
> (McGowan and Sampson, 2005, 74)

These roles are not always documented within the literature (even within an acknowledgement or authorship on a published paper) so the role and its extent may well be underplayed. It is not clear to what extent expert searchers develop their roles outside the searching element of a systematic review. Case study 13.2 gives an idea of the roles that information specialists may actually play in a systematic review, which could go beyond a narrow range of tasks assigned to an expert searcher.

Case study 13.2: Physical activity in the workplace

A systematic review on physical activity in the workplace was commissioned to provide evidence for a national guideline in England (NICE, 2008). The literature searches were conducted by information specialists, while a different expert searcher collaborated with public health experts and other researchers to actually undertake the systematic review.

This happened from a chance conversation between myself as an information specialist (or expert searcher) and a colleague with research expertise in workplace physical activity. The researcher was interested in bidding for the review to underpin the guidance but had no experience or knowledge of conducting systematic reviews. From this chance conversation, we collaborated to write the funding proposal, then once this was obtained I guided the team in developing a protocol and managing the whole review process. I also trained the project team in all aspects of the review process and shared in the tasks of screening, data extraction and critical appraisal before collaborating on the synthesis and report writing (Dugdill et al., 2008). I took a similar approach in other projects relating to systematic reviews in counselling and psychotherapy (Brettle, Hill and Jenkins, 2008; Hill and Brettle, 2005) and for these I also played a more traditional expert searcher role by conducting the literature searching.

My experience contrasted with the literature available at the time and to some extent in the present day. Indeed, at the time, an article about the librarian's role within systematic reviews suggested that it was unlikely that information specialists would be able to undertake roles such as critical appraisal for reviews of health topics due to lack of expertise (Beverley, Booth and Bath, 2003). This is not the case: information professionals can develop research and critical appraisal skills and are therefore well placed to develop significant roles within the whole of the systematic review process.

In addition to searching roles, Beverley, Booth and Bath (2003) identified information professionals playing roles within systematic reviews that included project leader, project manager, literature searcher, reference manager, document supplier, critical appraiser, data extractor, data synthesiser, report writer and disseminator. The role of teaching others to undertake systematic reviews has also been identified (Harris, 2005; Spencer and Eldredge, 2018).

Librarians are becoming increasingly involved in undertaking and publishing systematic reviews on librarianship and information science topics (Spencer and Eldredge, 2018), which provides opportunities to develop skills outside their searching comfort zone but on topics that are familiar and important to them. This was very much an approach used within the team of clinical librarians who published a review evaluating the clinical librarian services (Brettle et al., 2011) and who then went on to use those skills to undertake a broader research project generating impact data on the wide-scale outcomes to which clinical librarians contribute (Brettle, Maden and Payne, 2016).

Future directions

It is evident from documenting the role of information professionals and expanding the evidence base that expert searching has developed alongside the changing nature and methods of systematic reviews. In practice, there is little guidance on the development or the 'nuts and bolts' of the search strategies themselves, suggesting, as discussed in Chapter 10, that 'expert searching' is experiential and subjective, as well as complex.

One way forward would be to rethink the need to be 'comprehensive' in searching or perhaps, to be more accurate, consider what we mean by 'comprehensiveness' in expert searching. As discussed in Chapter 2, it may be more appropriate to sometimes think in terms of retrieving a representative sample of literature. The current evidence suggests that we need to think about the topic and type of evidence required rather than expecting to follow a fixed set of instructions for each review; for example, it was shown that for effectiveness reviews, the majority of studies could be located using a small number of databases (Royle and Waugh, 2003), whereas another study has shown that 30% of trials are unpublished (Brassey, 2016).

As systematic reviews and systematic searching have developed over the last 20 years, so has technology. This has brought potential challenges and solutions. In terms of challenges, not only is the volume of published studies increasing, but the means of publishing is also changing as evidence is made available online and publicised via social media. One solution that has been proposed is the use of text mining, machine learning and other computational techniques (Stansfield and

Liabo, 2017; Stansfield, O'Mara-Eves and Thomas, 2015). The potential deluge of data from unpublished sources (see Chapter 5) requires a new set of skills to find and incorporate it into evidence syntheses. Chapters 8 and 9 have demonstrated that expert searchers can be responsive to new technology, making sure that they seize the opportunity to mould new processes and start to establish new roles, rather than perceiving these changes as a threat.

These questions could form the basis of a research agenda for expert searching, which will need to go hand in hand with how systematic review methods are developing. In practice, expert searchers need to inform the evidence base regarding the value of different approaches to searching and ensure that search guidance is relevant to newer types of review and broad-based topics. Publishing this work is a means of raising the profile of the expert searcher as well as sharing best practice. Table 13.5 opposite provides a list of selected journals that are useful for both reading new articles and submitting new research about expert searching. It is important that we find ways of determining the effectiveness and impact of searching on the review process. It would be particularly beneficial to establish methods that measure effectiveness by linking the contribution of the expert searcher to the conclusions of the systematic review.

Conclusion

This chapter has shown that evidence-based practice and systematic reviews have provided an opportunity for information professionals to demonstrate their value as expert searchers. This role has developed along with systematic review methods. Systematic reviews are becoming increasingly complex and this provides challenges and opportunities for searchers. Expert searchers need to continue developing their own evidence base to ensure that searches are effective and meet the needs of different types of reviews. At the same time expert searchers can consider developing their skills to take on additional roles within systematic review teams or research. Information skills are widely transferable (Brettle, 2009; Brettle and Urquhart, 2011) and there is no reason why information specialists cannot take on appraisal and research roles within systematic reviews as described above.

Suggestions for further reading

Table 13.5 *Selected journals for keeping up to date with expert searching*

Journal title	Website
BMC Medical Research Methodology	https://bmcmedresmethodol.biomedcentral.com
Environmental Evidence	https://environmentalevidencejournal.biomedcentral.com
Evidence Based Library and Information Practice	https://journals.library.ualberta.ca/eblip/index.php/EBLIP
Evidence and Policy	http://policy.bristoluniversitypress.co.uk/journals/evidence-and-policy
Health Information and Libraries Journal	www.onlinelibrary.wiley.com/journal/14711842
Journal of Clinical Epidemiology	www.journals.elsevier.com/journal-of-clinical-epidemiology
Journal of the European Association for Health Information and Libraries	www.eahil.eu/jeahil
Journal of the Medical Library Association	www.jmla.mlanet.org/ojs/jmla
Qualitative Health Research	http://journals.sagepub.com/home/qhr
Research Synthesis Methods	www.onlinelibrary.wiley.com/journal/17592887
Systematic Reviews	https://systematicreviewsjournal.biomedcentral.com

References

Aagaard, T., Lund, H. and Juhl, C. (2016) Optimizing Literature Search in Systematic Reviews: are MEDLINE, EMBASE and CENTRAL enough for identifying effect studies within the area of musculoskeletal disorders?, *BMC Research Methodology*, **16** (1), 161.

Atkinson, K. M., Koenka, A. C., Sanchez, C. E., Moshontz, H. and Cooper, H. (2015) Reporting Standards for Literature Searches and Report Inclusion Criteria: making research syntheses more transparent and easy to replicate, *Research Synthesis Methods*, **6** (1), 87-95.

Ayiku, L., Levay, P., Hudson, T., Craven, J., Barrett, E., Finnegan, A. and Adams, R. (2017) The MEDLINE UK Filter: development and validation of a geographic search filter to retrieve research about the UK from OVID MEDLINE, *Health Information and Libraries Journal*, **34** (3), 200-216.

Bak, G. Mierzwinski-Urban, M., Fitzsimmons, H., Morrison, A. and Maden-Jenkins, M. (2009) A Pragmatic Critical Appraisal Instrument for Search

Filters: introducing the CADTH CAI, *Health Information and Libraries Journal*, **26** (3), 211-219.

Betran, A. P., Say, L., Gulmezoglu, A. M., Allen, T. and Hampson, L. (2005) Effectiveness of Different Databases in Identifying Studies for Systematic Reviews: experience from the WHO systematic review of maternal morbidity and mortality, *BMC Medical Research Methodology*, **5** (1), 6.

Beverley, C. A., Booth, A. and Bath, P. A. (2003) The Role of the Information Specialist in the Systematic Review Process: a health information case study, *Health Information and Libraries Journal*, **20** (2), 65-74.

Beyer, F. R. and Wright, K. (2013) Can We Prioritise which Databases to Search: a case study using a systematic review of frozen shoulder management, *Health Information and Libraries Journal*, **30** (1), 49-58.

Booth, A. (2006) Brimful of STARLITE: towards standards for reporting literature searching, *Journal of the Medical Library Association*, **94** (4), 421-429.

Booth, A. and Carroll, C. (2015) Systematic Searching for Theory to Inform Systematic Reviews: is it feasible? Is it desirable?, *Health Information and Libraries Journal*, **32** (3), 220-235.

Boynton, J., Glanville, J., McDaid, D. and Lefebvre, C. (1998) Identifying Systematic Reviews in MEDLINE: developing an objective approach to search strategy design, *Journal of Information Science*, **24** (3), 137.

Bramer, W. M., Giustini, D., Kramer, B. M. R. and Anderson, P. F. (2013) The Comparative Recall of Google Scholar Versus PubMed in Identical Searches for Biomedical Systematic Reviews: a review of searches used in systematic reviews, *Systematic Reviews*, **2**, 115.

Brassey, J. (2016) *Threats to traditional systematic reviews*. http://blogs.bmj.com/bmj/2016/06/15/jon-brassey-threats-to-traditional-systematic-reviews

Brettle, A. (2009) *Exploring the Roles, Effectiveness and Impact of Health Information Professionals within Evidence Based Practice*, PhD Thesis, University of Salford. http://usir.salford.ac.uk/12960

Brettle, A., Hill, A. and Jenkins, P. (2008) Counselling in Primary Care: a systematic review of the evidence, *Counselling and Psychotherapy Research*, **8** (4), 207-214.

Brettle, A. J. and Long, A. F. (2001) Comparison of Bibliographic Databases for Information on the Rehabilitation of People with Severe Mental Illness, *Bulletin of the Medical Library Association*, **89** (4), 353-362.

Brettle, A., Maden-Jenkins, M., Anderson, L., McNally, R., Pratchett, T.,

Tancock, J., Thornton, D. and Webb, A. (2011) Evaluating Clinical Librarian Services: a systematic review, *Health Information and Libraries Journal*, **28** (1), 3-22.

Brettle, A. J., Maden, M. and Payne, C. (2016) The Impact of Clinical Librarian Services on Patients and Health Care Organizations, *Health Information and Libraries Journal*, **33** (2), 100-120.

Brettle, A. and Urquhart, C. (eds) (2011) *Changing Roles and Contexts for Health Library and Information Professionals*, Facet Publishing.

Briscoe, S. (2014) *Literature Searching for Realist Reviews*. https://blogs.exeter.ac.uk/realisthive/2014/06/09/literature-searching-for-realist-reviews

Campbell, S., Dorgan, M. and Tjosvold, L. (2014) Creating Provincial and Territorial Search Filters to Retrieve Studies Related to Canadian Indigenous Peoples from OVID MEDLINE, *Journal of the Canadian Health Library Association*, **35** (1), 5-10.

Centre for Reviews and Dissemination (2009) *Systematic Reviews: CRD's guidance for undertaking reviews in healthcare*, Centre for Reviews and Dissemination University of York. www.york.ac.uk/crd/guidance

Cooper, C., Levay, P., Lorenc, T. and Craig, G. M. (2014) A Population Search Filter for Hard-to-reach Populations Increased Search Efficiency for a Systematic Review, *Journal of Clinical Epidemiology*, **67** (5), 554-559.

Crumley, E. T., Wiebe, N., Cramer, K., Klassen, T. P. and Hartling, L. (2005) Which Resources Should be Used to Identify RCT/CCTs for Systematic Reviews: a systematic review, *BMC Medical Research Methodology*, **5**, 24.

Damarell, R. A., Tieman, J., Sladek, R. M. and Davidson, P. M. (2011) Development of a Heart Failure Filter for Medline: an objective approach using evidence-based clinical practice guidelines as an alternative to hand searching, *BMC Medical Research Methodology*, **11** (1), 1.

Dugdill, L., Brettle, A., Hulme, C., McCluskey, S. and Long, A. F. (2008) Workplace Physical Activity Interventions: a systematic review, *International Journal of Workplace Health Management*, **1** (1), 20-40.

Faggion, C. M., Wu, Y. C., Tu, Y. K. and Wasiak, J. (2016) Quality of Search Strategies Reported in Systematic Reviews Published in Stereotactic Radiosurgery, *The British Journal of Radiology*, **89** (1062), 20150878.

Falzon, L. and Booth, A. (2001) REALISE-ing their Potential? Implementing Local Library Projects to Support Evidence-based Health Care, *Health Information and Libraries Journal*, **18**, 65-74.

Featherstone, R. M., Dryden, D. M., Foisy, M., Guise, J. M., Mitchell, M. D.,

Paynter, R. A., Robinson, K. A., Umscheid, C. and Hartling, L. (2015) Advancing Knowledge of Rapid Reviews: an analysis of results, conclusions and recommendations from published review articles examining rapid reviews, *Systematic Reviews*, **4**, 50.

Glanville, J., Bayliss, S., Booth, A., Dundar, Y., Fernandes, H., Fleeman, N. D., Foster, L., Fry-Smith, A., Golder, S., Lefebvre, C., Miller, C., Paisley, S., Payne, L., Price, A. and Welch, K. (2008) So Many Filters, So Little Time: the development of a search filter appraisal checklist, *Journal of the Medical Library Association*, **96** (4), 356-361.

Golder, S., Mason, A. and Spilsbury, K. (2008) Systematic Searches for the Effectiveness of Respite Care, *Journal of the Medical Library Association*, **96** (2), 147-152.

Greenhalgh, T. and Peacock, R. (2005) Effectiveness and Efficiency of Search Methods in Systematic Reviews of Complex Evidence: audit of primary sources, *BMJ*, **331** (7524), 1064-1065.

Haig, A. and Dozier, M. (2003) BEME Guide No. 3: Systematic searching for evidence in medical education – Part 1: Sources of information, *Medical Teacher*, **25** (4), 352-363.

Harris, M. (2005) The Librarian's Roles in the Systematic Review Process: a case study, *Journal of the Medical Library Association*, **93** (1), 81-87.

Hartling, L., Featherstone, R., Nuspl, M., Shave, K., Dryden, D. M. and Vandermeer, B. (2017) The Contribution of Databases to the Results of Systematic Reviews: a cross sectional study, *BMC Medical Research Methodology*, **16** (1), 127.

Haynes, R. B., Wilczynski, N., McKibbon, K. A., Walker, C. J. and Sinclair, J. C. (1994) Developing Optimal Search Strategies for Detecting Clinically Sound Studies in MEDLINE, *Journal of the American Medical Informatics Association*, **1** (6), 447-458.

Hill, A. and Brettle, A. (2005) The Effectiveness of Counselling with Older People: results of a systematic review, *Counselling and Psychotherapy Research*, **5** (4), 265-272.

Hopewell, S., Clarke, M., Lefebvre, C. and Scherer, R. (2007) Handsearching Versus Electronic Searching to Identify Reports of Randomized Trials, *Cochrane Database of Systematic Reviews*, **2**, MR000001.

Jenkins, M. (2004) Evaluation of methodological search filters—a review, *Health Information and Libraries Journal*, **21** (3), 148-163.

Koffel, J. B. (2015) Use of Recommended Search Strategies in Systematic

Reviews and the Impact of Librarian Involvement: a cross sectional survey of recent authors, *PLOS ONE*, **10** (5), e0125931.

Koufogiannakis, D. and Brettle, A. (eds) (2016) *Being Evidence Based in Library and Information Practice*, Facet Publishing.

Lawrence, D. W. (2008) What is Lost When Searching Only One Literature Database for Articles Relevant to Injury Prevention and Safety Promotion?, *Injury Prevention*, **14** (6), 401-404.

Long, A. F., Godfrey, M., Randall, T., Brettle, A. and Grant, M. J. (2002) *Developing Evidence Based Social Care Policy and Practice. Part 3: feasibility of undertaking systematic reviews in social care*, Project Report, University of Leeds, Nuffield Institute for Health, Leeds. http://usir.salford.ac.uk/13071

McGowan, J. and Sampson, M. (2005) Systematic Reviews Need Systematic Searchers, *Journal of the Medical Library Association*, **93** (1), 74-80.

McGowan, J., Sampson, M., Salzwedel, D. M., Cogo, E., Forester, V. and Lefevbre, C. (2016) PRESS Peer Review of Electronic Search Strategies: 2015 guideline statement, *Journal of Clinical Epidemiology*, **75**, 40-46.

McNally, R. and Alborz, A. (2004) Developing Methods for Systematic Reviewing in Health Services Delivery and Organization: an example from a review of access to health care for people with learning disabilities. Part 1. Identifying the literature, *Health Information and Libraries Journal*, **21** (3), 182-192.

Medical Library Association (2005) Role of Expert Searching in Health Sciences Libraries: policy statement by the Medical Library Association adopted September 2003, *Journal of the Medical Library Association*, **93** (1), 42-44.

Meert, D., Torabi, N. and Costella, J. (2016) Impact of Librarians on Reporting of the Literature Searching Component of Pediatric Systematic Reviews, *Journal of the Medical Library Association*, **104** (4), 267-277.

Moher, D., Liberati, A., Tetzlaff, J., Altman, D. G. and the PRISMA Group (2009) Preferred Reporting Items for Systematic Reviews and Meta-Analyses: the PRISMA statement, *PLOS Medicine*, **6** (7), e10000097.

Moher, D., Pham, B., Lawson, M. L. and Klassen, T. P. (2005) The Inclusion of Reports of Randomized Trials Published in Languages Other than English in Systematic Reviews, *Health Technology Assessment (Winchester, England)*, **7** (41), 1-90.

Moher, D., Stewart, L. and Shekelle, P. (2015) All in the Family: systematic reviews, rapid reviews, scoping reviews, realist reviews, and more,

Systematic Reviews, **4**, 183.

Mullins, M. M., DeLuca, J. B., Crepaz, N. and Lyles, C. M. (2014) Reporting Quality of Search Methods in Systematic Reviews of HIV Behavioural Interventions (2000-2010): are the searches clearly explained, systematic and reproducible?, *Research Synthesis Methods,* **5** (2), 116-130.

National Institute for Health and Clinical Excellence (2008) *Intervention guidance on workplace health promotion with reference to physical activity,* NICE. www.nice.org.uk/Guidance/PH13

Ogilvie, D., Hamilton, V., Egan, M. and Petticrew, M. (2005) Systematic Reviews of Health Effects of Social Interventions: 1. Finding the evidence: how far should you go?, *Journal of Epidemiology and Community Health,* **59** (9), 804-808.

Palmer, J. (1996) Effectiveness and Efficiency: new roles and new skills for health librarians, *Aslib Proceedings,* **48** (10), 247-252.

Papaioannou, D., Sutton, A., Carroll, C., Booth, A. and Wong, R. (2009) Literature Searching for Social Science Systematic Reviews: consideration of a range of search techniques, *Health Information and Libraries Journal,* **27** (2), 114-122.

Pham, B., Klassen, T. P., Lawson, M. L. and Moher, D. (2005) Language of publication restrictions in systematic reviews gave different results depending on whether the intervention was conventional or complementary, *Journal of Clinical Epidemiology,* **58**, 769-776.

Rader, T., Mann, M., Stansfield, C., Cooper, C. and Sampson, M. (2014) Methods for Documenting Systematic Review Searches: a discussion of common issues, *Research Synthesis Methods,* **5** (2), 98-115.

Rethlefsen, M. L., Farrell, A. M., Osterhaus Trzasko, L. C. and Brigham, T. J. (2015) Librarian Co-authors Correlated with Higher Quality Reported Search Strategies in General Internal Medicine Systematic Reviews, *Journal of Clinical Epidemiology,* **68** (6), 617-626.

Royle, P. and Waugh, N. (2003) Literature Searching for Clinical and Cost-effectiveness Studies Used in Health Technology Assessment Reports Carried Out for the National Institute for Clinical Excellence Appraisal System, *Health Technology Assessment,* **7** (34).

Sampson, M., Barrowman, N. J., Moher, D., Klassen, T. P., Pham, B., Platt, R., St John, P. D., Viola, R. and Raina, P. (2003) Should Meta-analysts Search Embase in addition to MEDLINE?, *Journal of Clinical Epidemiology,* **56** (10), 943-955.

Sampson, M., McGowan, J., Cogo, E., Grimshaw, J., Moher, D. and

Lefevbre, C. (2009) An Evidence Based Practice Guideline for the Peer Review of Electronic Search Strategies, *Journal of Clinical Epidemiology*, **62** (9), 944-952.

Sampson, M., McGowan, J., Tetzlaff, J., Cogo, E. and Moher, D. (2008) No Consensus Exists on Search Reporting Methods for Systematic Reviews, *Journal of Clinical Epidemiology*, **61** (8), 748-754.

Sampson, M., Tetzlaff, J. and Urquhart, C. (2011) Precision of Healthcare Systematic Review Searches in a Cross-sectional Sample, *Research Synthesis Methods*, **2** (2), 119-125.

Sherman, L. (1998) *Evidence-Based Policing*, Ideas in American Policing Series, Police Foundation.

Spencer, A. J. and Eldredge, J. D. (2018) Roles for Librarians in Systematic Reviews: a scoping review, *Journal of the Medical Library Association*, **106** (1), 46-56.

Stansfield, C., Brunton, G. and Rees, R. (2014) Search Wide, Dig Deep: literature searching for qualitative research: an analysis of the publication formats and information sources used for four systematic reviews in public health, *Research Synthesis Methods*, **5** (2), 142-151.

Stansfield, C., Dickson, K. and Bangpan, M. (2016) Exploring Issues in the Conduct of Website Searching and Other Online Sources for Systematic Reviews. How Can We Be Systematic?, *Systematic Reviews*, **5** (1), 191.

Stansfield, C. and Liabo, K. (2017) Identifying Social Care Literature: case studies from guideline development, *Evidence Based Library and Information Practice*, **12** (3), 114-131.

Stansfield, C., O'Mara-Eves, A. and Thomas, J. (2015) Reducing Systematic Review Workload Using Text Mining: opportunities and pitfalls, *Journal of EAHIL*, **11** (3), 8-10.

Stevinson, C. and Lawlor, D. A. (2004) Searching Multiple Databases for Systematic Reviews: adding value or diminishing returns?, *Complementary Therapies in Medicine*, **12** (4), 228-232.

Suarez-Almazor, M. E., Belseck, E., Homik, J., Dorgan, M. and Ramos-Remus, C. (2000) Identifying Clinical Trials in the Medical Literature with Electronic Databases: MEDLINE alone is not enough, *Controlled Clinical Trials*, **21** (5), 476-487.

Taylor, B., Wylie, E., Dempster, M. and Donnelly, M. (2007) Systematically Retrieving Research: a case study evaluating seven databases, *Research on Social Work Practice*, **17** (6), 697-706.

Toews, L. C. (2017) Compliance of Systematic Reviews in Veterinary

Journals with Preferred Reporting Items for Systematic Reviews and Meta-Analysis (PRISMA) Literature Search Reporting Guidelines, *Journal of the Medical Library Association*, **105** (3), 233-239.

Tompson, L. and Belur, J. (2016) Information Retrieval in Systematic Reviews: a case study of the crime prevention literature, *Journal of Experimental Criminology*, **12** (2), 187-207.

Vassar, M., Yerokhin, V., Sinnet, P. M., Weiher, M., Muckelrath, H., Carr, B., Varney, L. and Cook, G. (2017) Database Selection in Systematic Reviews: an insight through clinical neurology, *Health Information and Libraries Journal*, **34** (2), 156-164.

White, V. J., Glanville, J. M., Lefebvre, C. and Sheldon, T. A. (2001) A Statistical Approach to Designing Search Filters to Find Systematic Reviews: objectivity enhances accuracy, *Journal of Information Science*, **27** (6), 357-370.

Woodman, J. M., Harden, A., Thomas, J., Brunton, J., Kavanagh, J. and Stansfield, C. (2010) Searching for Systematic Reviews of the Effects of Social and Environmental Interventions: a case study of children and obesity, *Journal of the Medical Library Association*, **98** (2), 140-146.

Wright, K., Golder, S. and Lewis-Light, K. (2015) What Value is the CINAHL Database When Searching for Systematic Reviews of Qualitative Studies?, *Systematic Reviews*, **4**, 104.

Yoshii, A., Plaut, D. A., McGraw, K. A., Anderson, M. J. and Wellik, K. E. (2009) Analysis of the Reporting of Search Strategies in Cochrane Systematic Reviews, *Journal of the Medical Library Association*, **97** (1), 21-29.

Zhang, L., Sampson, M. and McGowan, J. (2006) Reporting the Role of the Expert Searcher in Cochrane Reviews, *Evidence Based Library and Information Practice*, **1** (4), 3-16.

14

Conclusion: where do we go from here?

Paul Levay and Jenny Craven

Methods, technology and people

The first part of this book described the developments that are taking place in the methods of systematic searching. The methods have been applied in many subject areas beyond evidence-based medicine. Chapter 2 considered qualitative evidence, realist reviews and mixed methods, while Chapter 5 covered the value of unpublished data and grey literature. Chapter 3 set out some of the techniques that have been applied in broad-based topics, such as in the social sciences, Chapter 4 showed how to choose sources across a range of disciplines and Chapter 6 highlighted the potential to use social media in a range of topics.

Methods have been established in topic areas beyond the scope of this book. One productive area has been environmental management, where techniques and sources are being tested, discussed and applied. There is guidance on doing an ecological synthesis (Bayliss and Beyer, 2015) and systematic searching for environmental evidence (Livoreil et al., 2017) that has assessed the role of grey literature (Haddaway and Bayliss, 2015). There have been similar efforts in the topic area of food and feed safety to understand the types of evidence required (European Food and Safety Authority, 2010) and how it might be systematically identified (Wood et al., 2018). The challenge is to continue developing methods in new directions that are appropriate to the subject and types of evidence that it generates. Information specialists will need to both stay up to date with innovations in evidence synthesis and lead the response in terms of adapting information retrieval practice.

New processes and systems are being built to exploit the full potential of technology. The text mining tools described in Chapter 7 highlighted that it may not be feasible to maintain a clear demarcation between the search and screening process as the information specialist may need to work with results sorted by algorithms, use relevance ranking or help to decide which cut-off points to use. Chapter 8 showed that we may no longer need to think of systematic reviews in terms of whole documents and that it may be fruitful to consider the evidence in more granular terms. Chapter 9 has shown how automation is revolutionising the way evidence is identified across whole subject areas and can be integrated efficiently into reviews using classification systems. We are moving beyond a system where technology is just introduced at established points in the existing systematic review process. Working practices cannot stay the same if these up-front surveillance systems and text mining tools are widely adopted.

Methodological and technological progress means that the knowledge and skills required to be an effective information specialist are evolving. We saw in Chapter 10 that the role of expert searcher requires a combination of technical skills, along with an awareness of contextual factors and confidence. The most effective approach to developing expert searchers is likely to see peer support and mentoring used to complement formal training. Training itself needs to account for different learning styles and barriers to learning so that information specialists have a range of options, such as online networks and MOOCs. It seems that a system of accreditation, rather than qualifications, may help to support continuing professional development in this field.

No matter how systematic reviewing develops, communication and collaboration will remain as important to information specialists as their technical knowledge. We need to be receptive to change to be able to seize the opportunities presented by new technology. Systematic reviews can use multi-disciplinary specialists and this can create some complex team structures that are held together through good communication, as we saw in Chapter 12. Our professional status, as highlighted in Chapter 11, requires us to share knowledge and collaborate with each other locally, nationally and internationally. It is through communication and collaboration that we can ensure that information retrieval practice is, and remains, evidence-based.

There are certainly challenges to collaborating with review teams, but it is through communication skills, learning to negotiate and team working that we can contribute most effectively to systematic reviewing (Nicholson, McCrillis and Williams, 2017). As Chapter 13 suggested, the information specialist does not necessarily need to see their role as one confined to the search alone. The fact that a review question is difficult to turn into a search strategy may alert the team to something that needs revising in their review protocol. The information specialist in this situation should help to refine the research question and advise on the appropriate methods. It takes confidence to provide these insights, engage with the methods and potentially challenge the direction of the review.

The theme of this book has been to show that systematic searching depends on having information professionals in place to make the most of the opportunities arising from new methods and technology. There is a clear need for someone with the appropriate skills to ensure that a systematic review starts with a systematic search. We have guidelines on systematic searching, but no two reviews will ever be the same and information professionals will always need to tailor their searches appropriately. The case studies in this book provide numerous practical examples of information professionals improving results and making a positive difference to systematic reviewing. We hope these examples inspire new ideas and lead to new practice.

Systematic reviews need systematic searches. Systematic searchers need to be flexible, creative and at the forefront of innovation.

References

Bayliss, H. R. and Beyer, F. R. (2015) Information Retrieval for Ecological Syntheses, *Research Synthesis Methods,* **6** (2), 136-148.

European Food and Safety Authority (2010) Application of Systematic Review Methodology to Food and Feed Safety Assessments to Support Decision Making, *EFSA Journal,* **8** (6), 1637.

Haddaway, N. R. and Bayliss, H. R. (2015) Shades of Grey: two forms of grey literature important for reviews in conservation, *Biological Conservation*, **191**, 827-829.

Livoreil, B., Glanville, J., Haddaway, N. R., Bayliss, H., Bethel, A., Flamerie de Lachapelle, F., Robalino, S., Savilaakso, S., Zhou, W., Petrokofsky, G. and Frampton, G. (2017) Systematic searching for environmental evidence using multiple tools and sources. *Environmental Evidence*, **6**, 23.

Nicholson, J., McCrillis, A. and Williams, J. D. (2017) Collaboration Challenges in Systematic Reviews: a survey of health sciences librarians, *Journal of the Medical Library Association*, **105** (4), 385-393.

Wood, H., O'Connor, A., Sargeant, J. and Glanville, J. (2018) Information Retrieval for Systematic Reviews in Food and Feed Topics: a narrative review, *Research Synthesis Methods*, **9** (4), 527-539.

Glossary

Active learning

A semi-automated process used in screening search results which uses inclusion and exclusion decisions made by human selectors to predict the likelihood of the remaining records being relevant (or not). The machine learns the inclusion criteria of the review in an iterative fashion alongside human screening.

Altmetrics

A system that tracks the attention that research outputs such as scholarly articles and datasets receive online. Altmetrics (alternative metrics) are measures of the impact of published research beyond traditional citations (for example, journal impact factors). Altmetrics use a score based on factors such as the number of times and where an article has been mentioned.

Application Programming Interfaces (APIs)

A piece of software that lets one program access or control another program. APIs allow applications to share data without requiring developers to share software code. APIs can enable systematic review tools to access databases 'behind the scenes'.

Artificial intelligence

Intelligence demonstrated by a machine rather than humans or other animals (natural intelligence). The machine performs functions associated with the human mind, such as learning and problem solving.

BeHEMoTh

An overall approach and question framework that offers a structured and systematic way to search for theory to inform a systematic review.

Bias

The systematic, rather than random, deviation of study results from the true results, caused by the way the study is designed, conducted or reported.

CanMEDS

A physician competency framework that defines the necessary competencies for all areas of medical practice and provides a comprehensive foundation for medical education and practice in Canada.

CIMO

An acronym used for management and/or realist review questions to specify the elements of Context, Intervention, Mechanisms and Outcomes.

Citation searching

Citation searching can help to identify additional evidence. Backward citation searching (also called reference harvesting) involves reviewing the bibliography of references cited in studies identified for inclusion in a systematic review. Forward citation searching is searching for additional publications that cite articles known to be relevant (including those identified as relevant to a systematic review).

CLUSTER

A structured approach to searching for directly related papers (sibling reports) or loosely associated (kinship) papers to inform an understanding of context and/or conceptual underpinnings of a particular intervention of interest.

Collocation

Collocation is a sequence of words or terms that occur often together more than would be expected by chance. It is often used in text mining.

Data extraction

Once the search results have been screened the review team will have a list of the publications that are relevant to their research question. The next step is to extract the data from these studies, usually using the full text. A data extraction form is used to ensure that the relevant data is extracted from each study in a consistent way so that they can be compared. This might include extracting detailed data on the population, intervention, comparison and outcomes across a set of studies.

Data management plan

A data management plan helps to control the information generated during a research project. Systematic reviews result in a lot of information and it requires a process that threads through the entire project to manage it. The person conducting the searches needs to keep track of those result numbers and all information pertaining to the searches. Inclusion and exclusion decisions also need to be managed, as does the data extraction process. A data management plan provides information about reference management software, screening tools, statistical software and data extraction tools to handle the data. The goal is to document all aspects of the search to ensure transparent reporting.

Evidence curation

The work necessary to organise research information in a way that facilitates its easy discovery and reuse, which acknowledges that research data has value and this value needs to be protected through fit-for-purpose management.

Exploratory searches

An exploratory search is a targeted search for suitable data. The search ends as soon as the information required is available. This kind of searching thus differs fundamentally from comprehensive information retrieval for a full systematic review.

Granularity

A way to describe identifiable sub-components of the information we are working with and how many sub-components into which the information can be usefully separated.

Grey literature

Literature that is not formally published in sources such as books or journal articles. It is usually protected by intellectual property rights and of sufficient quality to be collected and preserved but it is not controlled by commercial publishers. Grey literature can be in print or electronic information and it includes technical reports, theses, conference proceedings and reports from governments, charities and other organizations.

Health Technology Assessment (HTA)

An independent assessment of the effectiveness, costs and broader impacts of health care treatments and tests, often used by those who plan, commission or provide services.

Knowledge graph

An interconnected network of information presented in a graph.

Linked data

To join up data in a more efficient manner than simply indexing and linking documents. It is a set of best practices for publishing structured data online, rather than a particular technology, standard or technique.

Living systematic review

A systematic review which is continually updated, incorporating relevant new evidence as it becomes available.

Logistics review

A literature review that uses the widest possible range of sources to establish what resources, skills, premises, etc., are required to implement a particular intervention.

Machine learning

Involves teaching a program about relevance by indicating which records are relevant and which are not. The system should eventually be able to identify further relevant records automatically.

Mapping review

A review covering the nature and extent of the literature, mapping the ideas, arguments and concepts from a body of literature. The results are often presented as an evidence map.

Medical Subject Headings (MeSH)

A controlled vocabulary in which a hierarchy of terms is used to define medical subject terms. It is organised by the National Library of Medicine in the USA. It is used to index articles in MEDLINE and other bibliographic databases.

Meta-analysis

A method of statistically combining the results from several studies to estimate the overall effect of a treatment, test or other intervention.

Meta-regression

A structured statistical method for exploring which of a range of factors (for example, gender, age, experience) are most likely to explain the effect of an intervention.

Mixed methods synthesis/review

A literature review that seeks to bring together data from quantitative and qualitative studies integrating them in a way that facilitates subsequent analysis.

MOOC

A Massive Open Online Course (MOOC) is an innovative online educational resource, often free at the point of delivery.

Nanopublication

A community-driven approach to representing structured data along with its provenance into a single publishable and citable entity.

Network meta-analysis

A method of comparing three or more treatments or other interventions using direct evidence (from studies directly comparing the interventions of interest) and indirect evidence (from studies that do not compare the interventions of interest).

Objective search approach

An approach that uses text-analytic procedures to identify free-text terms and subject headings through frequency analysis to develop a search strategy. In this context, relevant articles already known or newly identified through broad searches are systematically analysed. Different software packages are available that differ with regard to costs and functionalities (for example, PubReMiner, Wordstat, AntConc).

Ontology

A representation, formal naming and definition of the categories, properties and relations of concepts, data and entities in order to better understand those things and how they fit together. An example of an ontology for an electronic medical-record system could include a classification of various diseases.

OWL

Web Ontology Language (OWL) is a semantic web language designed to represent rich and complex knowledge about things, groups of things and relations between things.

PICO framework

A structured approach for developing review questions about interventions that is often used as a framework for planning search strategies. The four components are:

- Population: the people, patients, groups or other populations being studied
- Intervention: what is being done
- Comparison: what the main intervention is being compared to
- Outcome(s): the outcome being studied, such as the effectiveness of a treatment.

Precision

In information retrieval, the proportion of results retrieved by the search that are relevant. It is calculated using this formula:

(No. of relevant records retrieved by the search / Total number of records retrieved by the search) x 100 to express as a percentage.

PRESS checklist

Checklist to peer review electronic literature search strategies for systematic reviews, health technology assessments and other evidence syntheses. The goal is to improve the quality and comprehensiveness of the search and reduce errors. The checklist comprises 6 elements:

- Translation of the research question
- Boolean and proximity operators
- Subject headings
- Text word searching
- Spelling, syntax and line numbers
- Limits and filters.

Provenance

The additional information needed to understand the origin of the data or information in question.

Publication bias

The tendency that means reports with statistically significant or clinically favourable results are more likely to be published than studies with non-significant or unfavourable results.

Purposive sampling

A sampling technique in which a researcher relies on their own judgement when choosing members of a population to participate in the study. The sample is chosen non-randomly in order to represent a cross-section of the population of interest.

Qualitative evidence synthesis

An umbrella term popularised by Cochrane and increasingly used to describe a group of review types that attempt to synthesise and analyse findings from primary qualitative research studies.

Randomised controlled trial (RCT)

Trials in which the participants (or clusters) are randomly allocated to receive either an intervention or a control. Random allocation is used to help ensure that the intervention and control groups only differ in terms of their exposure to treatment.

RDF

Resource Description Framework (RDF) is a standard model for data interchange on the web.

Realist synthesis

A method for extending literature review beyond 'what works' questions to examine differences in how people respond to a particular intervention, policy or programme depending on the context. A review team seeks to identify common mechanisms (for example, a sense of belonging) that are triggered by different interventions, to test their effects and then to link them to wider theories or explanations.

Recall

In information retrieval, recall (also known as sensitivity) is a measure of how well a search performs in retrieving relevant references. It is calculated using this formula:

(No. of relevant records retrieved by the search / Total no. of relevant records) x 100 to express as a percentage.

RETREAT

An acronym to describe what to consider when selecting a particular review method: Research question – Epistemology – Time – Resources – Expertise – Audience and purpose – Type of data.

RIS file

A file saved in a format developed by Research Information Systems that is frequently used to download data from bibliographic databases to share that data with reference management software.

Scoping review

A scoping review is used to identify literature relevant to a particular topic for the purpose of identifying key concepts and the main sources and types of evidence available.

Screening

A key step in the systematic review process. The reviewers will adhere to the inclusion and exclusion criteria to screen each record to decide whether or not it is relevant to the review. The screening is often done on the titles and abstracts of records in the first round and those that progress to the second round of screening are assessed on the full text of the publication. It is often done, in whole or part, by more than one person.

Search filter

Search filters are sets of search terms which have been developed using research methods to find a topic with a high degree of consistency.

Selective outcome reporting

This is selecting which outcomes from a clinical trial to report in full, rather than providing data on all outcomes that were measured and analysed in a study. It is a source of bias because it is more likely that the data in favour of a particular conclusion will be selected for dissemination.

Semantic search

A label given to search technologies that seek to bring a better understanding of the information or knowledge being searched, together with a better understanding of the context, and therefore intent, of the searcher.

Sibling studies

Linked publications (published or unpublished) that share a study context, for example, a set of journal articles describing different outcomes from the same clinical trial.

Social media

Any web-based tools used to co-create, share or exchange information, ideas, pictures or videos in virtual communities and networks (such as message boards, social networks, patient forums, Twitter, blogs and Facebook).

SPIDER

An acronym describing an approach to formulating or specifying a review question according to the elements of Sample, Perspective, phenomenon of Interest, Design, Evaluation and Research. It is useful in qualitative evidence syntheses and mixed methods reviews.

Systematic review

A review summarising the evidence on a clearly formulated review question according to a pre-defined protocol, using systematic and explicit methods to identify, select and appraise relevant studies, which are extracted, analysed and collated into a report on the findings.

Systematic review protocol

The protocol to a systematic review defines how it will be conducted. The review protocol will set out the rationale for the review, its aims and objectives, the search, screening criteria and methods of extracting data from the relevant studies. Protocols, where there is a health related outcome, should be made available via PROSPERO to encourage transparency and avoid research waste.

The search protocol is usually part of the review protocol or it may occasionally be a standalone document. The search elements of a protocol should set out the rationale for the approach, the databases, websites or other sources to be searched, other techniques that will be required and the search filters or other limits being applied. It will usually include the strategy for the principal database being searched. Protocols for searches taking an iterative or other approach should indicate how the evidence gathering will develop during its various phases.

The protocol should be available to readers of the completed systematic review so that any deviation from the intended methods can be assessed.

Systematic review question

Review questions define the boundaries of a systematic review and provide a framework for the scope of the search and the other processes required.

Systematic search

A search that uses systematic and explicit methods to identify relevant research. The search is a key component of a systematic review.

Taxonomy

The classification of things or concepts in an ordered arrangement of groups or categories.

Text mining

The UK's National Centre for Text Mining (NaCTeM) defines text mining as 'the process of discovering and extracting knowledge from unstructured data' through identifying relevant texts, identifying and extracting from the texts 'entities, facts and relationships between them' and 'data mining to find associations among the pieces of information extracted from many different texts'.

TF*IDF

TF*IDF (Term Frequency–Inverse Document Frequency) is a statistic which reflects how important a word is to a document in a collection or corpus. The value increases proportionally to the number of times a word appears in the document but is offset by the frequency of the word in the corpus. This helps to control for the fact that some words are generally more used than others.

Unpublished data

Data obtained from unpublished sources may be maintained by regulatory agencies, commercial and non-commercial trial registries or owned by industry (for example, pharmaceutical companies) or individual researchers.

Index